Technology, Work and Globalization

The Technology, Work and Globalization series was developed to provide policy makers, workers, managers, academics and students with a deeper understanding of the complex interlinks and influences between technological developments, including information and communication technologies, work organizations and patterns of globalization. The mission of the series is to disseminate rich knowledge based on deep research about relevant issues surrounding the globalization of work that is spawned by technology.

More information about this series at
http://www.palgrave.com/gp/series/14456

Eleni Lioliou • Leslie P. Willcocks

Global Outsourcing Discourse

Exploring Modes of IT Governance

palgrave
macmillan

Eleni Lioliou
Queen Mary University of London
London, UK

Leslie P. Willcocks
London School of Economics
London, UK

Technology, Work and Globalization
ISBN 978-3-319-74044-7 ISBN 978-3-319-74045-4 (eBook)
https://doi.org/10.1007/978-3-319-74045-4

Library of Congress Control Number: 2018960927

This Palgrave Macmillan imprint is published by the registered company Springer Nature Switzerland AG
The registered company address is: Gewerbestrasse 11, 6330 Cham, Switzerland

Acknowledgements

Foremost we would like to thank the now many hundreds of practitioners who have generously given their time and knowledge in supporting this research stream over many years. Without them, this work just would not have been possible. Special thanks to Albert Plugge, who gave us new contacts for this project and set us on the way to deep access to several major case studies featured in this book. His support had been highly significant for the execution of this project. We are also grateful for the support of Arpan Shah and his generous insights into this work. Eleni would like to thank her institutions and colleagues at London School of Economics and Political Science, Loughborough University, and Queen Mary, for their patience and support over the course of the research. Leslie would like to thank all the doctoral students and colleagues at London School of Economics and Political Science for their wonderful support and engagement over more than 12 years. A special thanks to Mary Lacity, now Walton Professor of Information Systems and Director of the Blockchain Center of Excellence, Sam M. Walton College of Business, University of Arkansas. She is a founder of this area of study, and the research and discussions with her over 25 years have always yielded great ideas and results.

Contents

List of Figures

List of Tables

1

Exploring Outsourcing, Governance, and Discourse

Introduction

The focus of this book is the governance of information technology (IT) outsourcing arrangements. In the next section we look at how modern IT outsourcing and its discourse have developed across the 1989–2019 period. The normative outsourcing discourse that has evolved with outsourcing's rise to prominence and globalism has generated a range of normative concepts, accepted 'best practices', and perennial and changing concerns, for which we provide an introduction here.

We then highlight how this book primarily focuses on governance as part of that discourse. In particular, we investigate formal and relational elements of IT outsourcing governance and how these relate to the conduct of outsourcing and consequent performance. The rationale for this concern relates to the identification in the research literature of governance as a key issue for the outcome of IT outsourcing arrangements—something we look at in the next section. This interest in governance is important because, while the combined IT outsourcing and (IT-enabled) business process outsourcing (BPO) market has grown

E. Lioliou, L. P. Willcocks, *Global Outsourcing Discourse*, Technology, Work and Globalization, https://doi.org/10.1007/978-3-319-74045-4_1

rapidly from 1989 to reach a potential global market revenue of over US $1.5 trillion, outsourcing as a practice has always experienced mixed outcomes.

We then look in more depth at the notion of discourse. A Foucauldian-informed working definition is set out by Lessa (2006). Discourses are "systems of thoughts composed of ideas, attitudes, courses of action, beliefs and practices that systematically construct the subjects and the worlds of which they speak". Here we introduce the theoretical spine of our research, in terms of applying two forms of discourse—transaction cost economics (TCE) and Foucauldian governmentality—to the same case material, the objective being to compare and contrast the insights gained against each other and to the wider global outsourcing discourse. Finally, we introduce the book's rationale, research questions, chapters, and their subject matter.

Global Outsourcing

Outsourcing is "The handing over to a third party of the management of activities, assets and/or people to achieve required outcomes" (Cullen et al. 2014). There are other ways of using external service suppliers, for example, buying in resources and placing them under internal management control; the purchase of software packages; and the rental of applications, infrastructure, people, or automation software through cloud services. In this book we focus entirely on IT services and limit ourselves to outsourcing as the key practice under study.

The last 30 years have seen organizations increasingly move to information technology outsourcing (ITO), that is, choosing to rely on external service providers for IT hardware, software, telecommunications, cloud computing resources, and automation tools. Since 1999 we have also seen outsourcing spread as BPO, to fundamental back office functions like finance and accounting, procurement, legal, real estate, human resources, insurance claims, and general administration. But ITO has remained the dominant outsourced service, though it should be pointed out that BPO has become increasingly IT-enabled and IT-dependent.

These developments are reflected in the market revenue figures. Thus in 1989 ITO was a US $10 billion market. By early 2014, global outsourcing contracts for ITO and BPO services were exceeding US $648 billion (ITO $344 billion; BPO $304 billion). By the end of 2016, according to Snowden and Fersht (2016), the global ITO and BPO services market was estimated to be US $1007 billion (ITO $657 billion; BPO $322 billion). Snowden and Fersht (2016) also suggest a compound annual growth rate of 2.2% ITO and a 4.0% BPO from 2016 to the end of 2020, reflecting more activities being outsourced and new service lines and delivery locations added. Several of our case studies involve offshore outsourcing. Here, 2013 revenues exceeded US $100 billion in revenues, and the market grew by around 12% a year in the 2013–2018 period (Willcocks et al. 2017).

The case studies in this book reflect a period when the use of ITO and of offshoring was accelerating much more than we have seen in the 2016–2018 period or are likely to see over the 2018–2022 period. More recently, we have also seen the development of cloud computing and service automation as more self-serviced-based sourcing options, and these have eaten into the traditional outsourcing markets for both ITO and BPO. In ITO we have seen applications development and managed services increasingly transitioning to digital platforms—not a strong feature of the period we cover in the book case studies. Meanwhile, if the IT infrastructure market was strong and figures highly in our case studies, by 2016–2018 demand was in free fall, with a decline in these traditional services across all regions. Professional services have been seeing a rise, however, especially in the areas of digital transformation, governance, security, and automation. The fundamental moves are caught in the fact that by 2016 traditional ITO was predicted to see a negative 2.4% compound loss over the 2016–2022 period, while digital, cloud, and automated As-A-Service IT services were at some US $100 billion in 2016 and projected to see 21.7% compound annual growth for the same period. Traditional BPO has a similar though less extreme pattern, scheduled to see 2.6% compound annual growth in traditional BPO services and 8.6% compound annual growth in As-A-Service BPO from 2016 to 2022 (Willcocks et al. 2017).

Case Studies and the Developing Discourse

Clearly, our case studies catch organizations, suppliers, and outsourcing as a phenomenon in a specific period of time, in particular from the mid-2000s to around 2012. However, the modern outsourcing discourse we wish to investigate, as it relates to IT decisions and practices, began considerably before that. Our own judgement is that the work of Ronald Coase and Oliver Williamson on why firms exist and on TCE did suffuse into the way in which practitioners talked and acted when it came to outsourcing, even if those practitioners may not have read about TCE or even knew the terms (Willcocks and Lacity 2014). Moreover, TCE did touch directly on the main concerns, with its vocabulary of transactions, types of asset, vendor opportunism, types of uncertainty, modes of governance and contracting, and its focus on cost economizing. Incidentally, cost economizing was always a major objective in outsourcing IT in the early years, and cost savings remain perennially central up to this day. At the same time, as a number of researchers have pointed out over the years, TCE was never developed to predict or explain specifically IT outsourcing decisions and outcomes. This has led to quite a lot of interesting discrepancies between TCE prescriptions—how TCE talks about outsourcing—and actual ITO outcomes and practices, as we shall see in our case studies in this book.

The 1989 Eastman Kodak large-scale outsourcing arrangement with three suppliers probably sees the major start point for the modern IT outsourcing discourse. Then, and thereafter, ITO gained a high profile in the media and in business magazines and newspapers. ITO accelerated, reaching US $50 billion revenues in 1994, US $152 billion in 2000, and over US $344 billion by 2014. An important part of that discourse was the notion of single-supplier 'strategic partnering'. Another was the strong link of outsourcing with the early 1990s debate about the core competence of the corporation. The normative discourse ran that organizations should focus on the relatively few things that they could be world class at and which differentiated them in the marketplace. Important parts of IT, sometimes the whole of IT, could be identified as 'commodity', best outsourced to specialist suppliers, the main objectives being to reduce costs, access expertise, and, if possible, catalyse performance.

If the discourse ran this way from 1989 to 1997, this was not actually a period characterized by large-scale, long-term, single-supplier, IT outsourcing deals. In fact most deals were not like this and few were single supplier. Around 2000 there were, at our count, just over 120 such deals, representing less than 5% of IT outsourcing. However, the notion of 'strategic relationships' with ITO suppliers became popular, and the notion of 'partnering' and the emphasis on the importance of 'relationships', as opposed to just contracts, grew out of this 1989–2000 period. The evidence is, however, that the dominant practice (as it has continued to be) was multiple-supplier selective outsourcing, using midterm length (3–7 years) contracts and focusing on outsourcing stable, discrete activities that were well understood and for which detailed contracts could be written. And indeed a strong discourse developed around these practices (to which the present authors and a range of colleagues contributed over the years). This aspect of the discourse tended to emphasize the importance of detailed contracting, measurement through service level agreements (SLAs) and key performance indicators (KPIs), and monitoring, as well as the importance of retained management capabilities and knowledge. However, while this discourse also became normative over time, and was designed to mitigate risks, there has been a lot of evidence to suggest that clients and suppliers continued to struggle to learn how to manage outsourcing arrangements effectively.

As our case studies in this book reveal, managing outsourcing has remained a problem for many, and this continues to this day, with the difficulties heightened by increasingly volatile business contexts and fast-changing technologies and services. On our own figures, probably only 20% of outsourcing arrangements can be called 'best-in-class' providing cost savings and improved services and delivering business benefits and innovation and high client satisfaction. According to Lacity and Willcocks (2015), up to 15% are poor, and some 40% are probably 'doing OK' (marginal cost savings delivered, acceptable service performance, marginal client satisfaction), while 25% experience 'good' performance (cost savings delivered, SLAs met, good client satisfaction). The case studies in this book fit quite well into these findings on performance. If some of the clients' organizations in this book were doing better than others, one could see that they were all working very hard to find the right recipe for effectiveness while all subscribing, more or less to the prevailing multi-sourcing discourse.

The IT outsourcing market grew apace in the 2000s. As suppliers matured their ability to deliver IT services, more global locations became viable. At the same time clients built their confidence and competence. From around 2005 a more strategic interest in multi-sourcing also developed. Here ABN AMRO set a new landmark. After cancelling prematurely a single-supplier deal with EDS, the bank's deal with four suppliers in 2005 was portrayed as the dominant future pattern for strategic sources to follow. The language thereafter pointed to 'strategic multi-sourcing' as another viable option. At the same time the period 2005–2018 saw more, smaller, shorter-term contracts driving market growth. With the economic downturn from 2008, an interest in consolidating supplier numbers took place. As a result of this, another notion entered the outsourcing discourse, as the touted management and economic advantages of 'bundled' outsourcing—going with one supplier for several different IT and also BPO—gained profile. Another reason for this interest lay in the administrative and management costs of multi-sourcing models and the pressure to develop integrated technology platforms more closely aligned with business needs (Cullen et al. 2014).

From around the mid-2000s, in the face of mixed experiences and often limited outcomes, a much greater focus fell upon governance. Advisory firms and consultants, in particular, suggested that selecting the right mode of 'governance' could lead to significantly better performances. This concern for governance has remained central to the outsourcing discourse ever since, and the case studies in this book reveal five client organizations at various levels of maturity in being able to establish and leverage modes of governance.

One emerging issue in this period was that while outsourcing often produced cost savings, and improved performance, it rarely seemed to create IT, process, or business innovation. A concern for innovation entered the discourse, along with how innovation could be achieved. This does not figure highly in our five case studies, and the years which they cover, but the innovation discourse has subsequently become a significant one (Willcocks et al. 2018). It has led to a renewed emphasis on the need for collaboration, between client and supplier(s), with the notion of coopetition between suppliers also introduced from after 2010 to suggest how multiple suppliers might be induced/managed/governed to collaborate to compete, in the cause of producing superior business value and innovation for a client. Once again, this part of the discourse does not figure highly in our five case studies, though the notions of client-supplier partnering and relationships—precursors to the notion of collaboration—receive a great deal of attention.

So far we have described a largely domestic IT outsourcing trajectory and discourse. In practice BPO probably started in 1991 when the oil company BP Exploration outsourced its European accounting operations to one supplier, Andersen Consulting. Accounting processes were consolidated in a single site at Aberdeen, Scotland. From the late 1990s BPO grew fast, while offshoring/offshore outsourcing also entered the discourse—both driven by a similar logic, concepts, and terms that had developed around IT outsourcing. With offshoring, the 1990s saw several American and West European firms develop 'captive centres', while others outsourced some IT activities offshore to India and elsewhere, while Indian firms began to develop their IT capabilities. The turning point came with the Y2K problem that materialized from 1996 onwards. To prepare for Y2K, companies found themselves short of low-cost, trained resources for its resolution up against a 'drop-dead' deadline. The Indian experience was good, and this really did begin to put offshore models on the map from around 2000, with the phenomenon taking off really from around 2003, with significant cost savings being a main driver.

Of all the outsourcing variants, offshore outsourcing saw much the fastest growth in the 2000–2010 period. India had a head start; it had developed scale and a group of major suppliers and by 2010 dominated the global offshore market. At the same time many other countries have been actively offering services and developing their outsourcing service industries, often most successfully with local government backing. By 2016 one could count viable offshore/nearshore locations in over 120 countries worldwide, with India earning over 65% of the revenues and the Philippines having the second largest industry, with both countries offering multiple ITO and BPO services (Willcocks et al. 2017). Several case studies in this book fit into these offshore developments.

The case studies in this book predate subsequent developments in the outsourcing discourse, which became shaped largely by technological progress. Thus, by 2016, cloud sourcing had become a potentially massive market for As-A-Service external service provision. Potentially cloud sourcing has also been enormously disruptive of more traditional outsourcing models that had developed over outsourcing's brief 26-year history as an industry (Willcocks et al. 2015). A major reason for this is that cloud computing enables and amplifies the effects of other emerging technologies and in particular blockchain, social media, analytics, the internet of things, digital fabrication, robotics, and the automation of knowledge work. Such developments do raise fundamental questions for both researchers and practitioners about the future shape and trajectory of the global sourcing phenomenon and for client and service provider strategies. Some in the discourse have portrayed this as the 'death of outsourcing', but more accurately it changes the nature of outsourcing and its traditional dependence on labour arbitrage models.

The years 2015–2016 also saw the development of service automation. Though a small market by the end of 2018, as Willcocks and Lacity (2016) and Lacity and Willcocks (2018) discuss, robotic process automation and cognitive automation have the potential to be very disruptive of the more conventional people-centric outsourcing model that offshore outsourcing vendors and captive centres were based on. Looking across these technological developments in cloud computing and service automation, it is probable that the speed with which they will eat into traditional ITO and BPO models and markets has been overestimated. As Snowden and Fersht (2016) suggest, it is likely that there will be a huge amount of legacy enterprise ITO and BPO business in play for a decade or more. However, these emerging technologies are undoubtedly changing irreversibly how the outsourcing discourse will be conducted from now on.

Even by 2018 the outsourcing industry was still in the early stages of professionalizing itself. Professionalization brings with it the benefits of such things as codes of conduct, minimum standards of competence, standardized practices, a coherent career structure, and an understanding of key roles required and what it takes to fill them. While client-retained capabilities have become, generally, more mature, and more relevant to the tasks in hand in recent years, the days of global sourcing becoming a profession on both client and service provider sides were not with us yet. This makes the outsourcing discourse we are choosing to study weaker and less discernible and so has required detailed in-depth analysis of players, documents, practices, conversations, texts, and contexts, as detailed in Chaps. 3, 4, and 5 of this book. Discerning the discourse and reading it into these case studies under review has also been helped immensely by the fact that we have been part of the discourse since 1993 and have, indeed, contributed to its development in the period 1993–2018 through many research studies and practical interventions.

Conditioning the Discourse: Client Learning and Evolution

The other dimension worth pointing to in the outsourcing discourse is the slow evolution of client and vendor capabilities and types of objectives and management adopted. Elsewhere we have suggested four phases that a typical organization passes through with its outsourcing experiences. The first—'hype and fear'—sees clients believing too much in suppliers' marketing promises, and the power of outsourcing, or, conversely, are very dubious about what outsourcing can deliver. If the client proceeds to outsource, invariably it is with insufficient managerial competence, not realizing that outsourcing tends to require different management capabilities and ethos from managing in-house resources. Neither approach adds up to a resilient way of trying to leverage outsourcing.

In Phase 2, after some hard learning through their first-generation outsourcing experiences, clients then tend to focus primarily on cost, becoming sceptical about how much can be really achieved, though often still insisting on benefits beyond cost and service improvements. The outsourcing literature sees phrases like 'your mess for less' as clients focus on the cost-service trade-off in their discussions and disputes with their suppliers. As far as their learning went, at least three of our case studies (DUTCH) could be positioned in this phase.

Two others were either at the late stage of Phase 2 or shifting into Phase 3. We have found many clients making it through to Phase 3 usually in their third- or fourth-generation outsourcing deals. These clients tend to look for value-added rather than just cost savings and are searching for multiple business benefits from closer relationships with their service providers. At the same time they frequently look to reduce the number of their suppliers and control them more closely on outcomes. Such clients have learned a great deal from previous outsourcing experiences, have built strong retained management capabilities, and are able to get the balance of contract and relationship management right. They have focused on leveraging the relationship with their suppliers for mutual business benefit. Few organizations—and certainly none included in this book—have reached Phase 4 of their journey. In research into high performance in outsourcing, Lacity and Willcocks found some 20% of outsourcing arrangements putting in 'world-class' performance as at 2015. The management practices adopted included leadership pairings across client and supplier; a primary focus on business and strategic benefits; strong transition change management and transformation capabilities; a partnering approach; the retained organization aligned to business goals and its supplier; issues and conflicts resolved collaboratively with the provider; the use of technology as an enabler, deployment of domain expertise, and business analytics; and prioritization and incentivizing of innovation (Lacity and Willcocks 2015).

Clients and suppliers at different phases tend to focus on different components of the larger outsourcing discourse, seeking answers to the problems immediately to hand, given the agendas they are pursuing. In our cases an early Phase 2 client like DUTCH (see Chap. 5) struggles with moving to more detailed contracting as a solution to naivety over the power of 'partnering'. An early Phase 3 client like BANK (see Chap. 4) has contracting largely sorted and looks to gain further advantage for more partnering and will move on to focus on gaining innovation from its outsourcing suppliers. LION, the insurance company in Chap. 3, reports a lot of value from offshore outsourcing but is searching for ways to gain even more.

These differing emphases in the outsourcing discourse reflect primarily the degree of maturing in service provider learning and capabilities over the years. But we find that while service providers frequently try to institutionalize their learning on managing outsourcing and on sector-specific know-how, clients all too frequently have not. Objectives change quite quickly in modern business environments, and new contract forms, new sourcing arrangements, and new suppliers bring new unknowns into the picture requiring ever new learning, as do new technology innovations like cloud computing, business analytics, and service automation. Global sourcing has become a fast-moving, dynamic high-profile and impactful set of activities that remain difficult to deliver. Enter IT governance.

The Centrality of Governance

IT governance in and between organizations is the way the rules, norms, and actions about IT procurement and use are structured, sustained, regulated, and held accountable. Governance sets up the constitution, the rule of the game, by which IT is managed, setting up decision rights, who is responsible for what actions, budget allocations, and how the governance itself will be run.

Governance of IT has always been both central and problematic in IT outsourcing. Statistics from EquaTerra and Mercer have connected poor outsourcing outcomes to ineffective governance of IT outsourcing arrangements (Equaterra 2010; Mercer 2010). A survey from the International Association of Outsourcing Professionals (IAOP) showed that IT outsourcing governance and control were the top challenges IT outsourcing professionals were facing at the time our case studies were beginning (IAOP 2008). Academic studies have perennially cited the poor governance and management of the ongoing relationship between the outsourcing partners as amongst the primary reasons for failing ventures (e.g. only see Lacity et al. 2010; Kern and Willcocks 2002).

Interestingly, however, the ongoing management and governance of the IT outsourcing relationship has stayed a relatively under-researched area (Oshri et al. 2015; Willcocks et al. 2017). Kern and Willcocks (2002) observed in the early 2000s that while the emerging outsourcing relationship was being widely acknowledged to be the most important determinant of the outcome of any outsourcing venture, only a limited number of studies were concerned with it. The authors characterized our understanding of the operations of IT outsourcing relationships "limited at best" and called for more research in this area. Along the same lines, Dibbern et al. (2004), Gonzalez et al. (2006), Goles and Chin (2005), and Lacity et al. (2010) in their later reviews of the IT outsourcing literature identified the IT outsourcing relationship as a relatively neglected yet critical area for future research.

Drawing from the interorganizational relationship (IOR) literature, most research on the IT outsourcing relationship has treated the formal and the relational sides of the venture as two distinct aspects of governance. As illustrated in later chapters, a major stream of research has focused on the contract as a tool for the ongoing governance of the outsourcing arrangement. Studies from this perspective have tended to use economic theories in order to make prescriptions on the optimization of governance.

Research from a social perspective, however, has argued that while the contract is a very important element in the governance of the venture as a formal control mechanism, there are relational norms such as trust and commitment that may become substitutes of, or augments to, the contract. The argument has been that these relational norms manifest a form of social control that can be at least as, and possibly more, important in directing individual behaviours.

Interestingly, a number of authors argue that the combined use of formal and relational governance is fundamentally problematic. Their reasoning is that formal contracts signal distrust, while relational governance is based on trust. Contrary to this substitution position, Poppo and Zenger (2002) demonstrate in their empirical study that contracts and relational governance functioned as complements. These authors suggest the need to explore further the interplay between contractual and relational forms of governance—an objective we set ourselves in writing this book.

Introducing Discourse

Fairclough (2005) defined discourse as a particular way of representing certain parts or aspects of the world (physical, social, psychological). For instance, there are different political discourses (liberal, conservative, social-democratic) that represent social groups and relations between social groups in a society in different ways. Some forms of discourse analysis carry out various types of detailed linguistic analysis (e.g. analysis of grammar, semantics, vocabulary, metaphor, forms of argumentation or narrative, and so forth) and/or detailed analysis of other semiotic features of texts such as their visual aspects (Mingers and Willcocks 2016). There are analytical advantages in taking discourse analysis further, as we do in this book. According to Foucault (1972), discursive practices are the local sociohistorical material conditions that enable and constrain disciplinary knowledge practices such as speaking, writing, thinking, calculating, measuring, filtering, and concentrating. Discursive practices produce, rather than merely describe, the 'subjects' and 'objects' of knowledge practices. On Foucault's account these 'conditions' are immanent and historical rather than transcendental or phenomenological, that is, they are actual historically situated social conditions.

For our purposes, Foucault is interesting for moving from his earlier view of discourse as a rule-governed, autonomous, and self-referring system to discourse as embodying circuits and relations of power and creating meaning as power/knowledge (Foucault 2003). For Foucault (1977, 1980, 2003), discourse is related to power in operating by rules of exclusion. In his view, discourse is controlled by objects (what can be spoken of), ritual (where and how one may speak), and the privileged (who may speak). This draws upon his earlier work on the regulatory nature of discourse. Foucault (1980a, b) uses the notion of power/knowledge to analyse how knowledge can be both shaped by and shaper of power. Such an approach allows the researcher to connect up the circuit of interactions between social, material, and personal components and to analyse power relations in the production, and use, of knowledge and meaning. In the context of information and communication technologies, rich examples of such studies can be found in Davies and Mitchell (1994), Doolin (1998), and Willcocks (2006). In later work, Foucault also turned to the concept of governmentality. For Foucault (1980a, b) to govern is "to structure the possible field of others". He traces how modern governmentality became based on new knowledge and techniques of normalization, regulation, and control of bodies. In this book we draw selectively upon Foucault's concepts of discourse, power/knowledge, and governmentality to provide a Foucauldian-informed exploration of our five in-depth case studies. In this context we treat the normative outsourcing discussion as detailed above, TCE, and Foucault's concepts as forming parallel discourses that can be contrasted and compared.

Rationale and Structure of This Book

Having outlined the book title's key terms of outsourcing, governance, and discourse, we now look at what we are trying to achieve with this study. The primary objective is to illuminate through empirical study both formal and relational forms of governance, as well as their interplay. In our examination, we focus initially on the characteristics of the exchange as these are instructed by the theory of transaction costs and investigate the predictive power of this theory on the choice of governance structures (i.e. hierarchies, markets, or hybrids). In particular, the analysis will focus on the effectiveness of choices made by organizations, with regard to keeping the IT activities in-house, outsourcing using primarily the contract as a tool of governance, and outsourcing using relationships as a primary tool of governance.

We have said little so far about TCE. The reason a major assessment of the usefulness of transaction costs theory is made is that it is one of the most extensively used theories in the study of governance structures, yet the outcomes are mixed (Wang 2002). In the IT context, Lacity and Willcocks (1995, 2009) provided a particularly influential account of the limited predictive power of the theory of transaction costs. Their findings demonstrated discrepancies in the predictive power of TCE in 87.5% of the cases. In their critique, Aubert and Weber (2001) argued that a significant part of the anomalies that Lacity and Willcocks (1995) identified in their study may be stemming from the problematical measure of asset specificity rather than a flaw in the theory of transaction costs.

Following this debate and more recent studies on the topic (e.g. Karimi-Alaghehband et al. 2011; Lacity et al. 2011), a further problematization occurs regarding the applicability of the theory of transaction costs in the IT sourcing context and its predictive power on the choice of governance structures. In our view this can be pursued most constructively through detailed longitudinal, comparative case study work. Such a problematization is important not only from a theoretical point of view, as TCE is one of the most widely used theories in the study of governance structures, but also from a practical viewpoint, since practitioners should be informed on how insightful the framework of TCE on sourcing decisions can be, both as a guide to decision-making and in terms of predictive power. On this basis, and building on previous studies, this book aims towards extending our understanding of the usefulness of the theory of transaction costs when making choices on governance structures in IT outsourcing contexts.

Secondly, the book takes a more integrating perspective towards the assessment of the formal and relational aspects of governance of outsourcing arrangements. On this basis, the book seeks to demonstrate how the Foucauldian theorizations of power can illuminate our understanding of outsourcing governance. In particular, we will be using the Foucauldian notions on governmentality, discourse, and power relations to illustrate how competing rationalities of governance co-exist and take over one from another. Foucauldian notions are particularly useful because they have been widely used and shown their applicability in a range of empirical organizational studies. Furthermore, these notions provide a different set of assumptions, emphases, and perspectives on organizations and human relations, thus providing a counterpoint of reference for analysis. To this day, Foucault's notions have been rarely used in the domains of IT and outsourcing research. On this basis, the book aims to make a theoretical contribution in encouraging further uses of such work, as well as demonstrating the explanatory value of the technique in providing alternative theoretical perspectives on the same data. In this way, the present study aims to illuminate the social aspects of the outsourcing arrangement that dominant neo-classical economic theories such as the theory of transaction costs tend to neglect. This is also in line with the Foucauldian impulse to question dominant logics in systems of thought (Veyne 2010).

Against this background, the main research questions of this study are:

1. How successful is the theory of TCE in the prescription of governance structures in IT outsourcing arrangements? Here 'success' refers to the predictive power as this relates to outsourcing decisions and outcomes.

2. What issues around IT outsourcing governance are being illuminated by a Foucauldian-informed perspective on governmentality, discourse, and power relations? Here, we use carefully selected Foucauldian concepts, nevertheless loaded with countervailing assumptions and analytical intentions, relevant to the specific study of IT outsourcing, and able to provide an alternative perspective and critique of TCE.

Chapters of the Book

Chapter 2 first provides a detailed review of the IT outsourcing research literature. In particular, the changing focus of the IT outsourcing literature is presented, as well as the literature on the formal and relational aspects of IT outsourcing governance. The development of the contemporary literature on governance of IT outsourcing arrangements with regard to its epistemological roots and theoretical orientations is presented, as well as a critique of this literature.

The chapter then discusses the theoretical ideas used in our analysis. In particular, a detailed review of the theory of transaction costs as well as some key applications of the theory in the IT domain is provided. The chapter proceeds with an illustration of Foucault's concept of governmentality as well as an overview of the major studies utilizing this concept within the domain of accounting. An outline of Foucault's notions of discourse and power relations is described, as well as a presentation of studies that have used these ideas in the IT domain. The chapter finishes with an outline of the rationale for using concepts from TCE and Foucault for our discourse analysis.

Chapters 3, 4, and 5 present the case studies under investigation. These provide the evidence for the discourse (s) that this book seeks to explore. In particular, each of these chapters includes a detailed outline of outsourcing decisions made by the participant firms (i.e. type of activities, scope of outsourcing, supplier selection, and so on) and a presentation of the clients' and suppliers' capabilities. Then details of the contracts as formal tools of governance are discussed, as well as issues around the evolution of the relationships between the outsourcing clients and suppliers. Finally, issues around the performance of the vendors are presented.

Chapter 6 presents the results of the TCE analysis, while Chap. 7 provides the findings analysed from a Foucauldian-informed perspective. Chapter 8 presents a meta-discussion on the findings on discourse. In particular, it includes a representation of the main findings and assesses these against the contributions made by previous empirical and theory-based studies in the literature. It also compares three discourses with one another, the transaction costs, Foucauldian, and outsourcing discourses. The final chapter provides the conclusions of and contributions made by this book.

References

Aubert, B., & Weber, R. (2001). *Transaction Cost Theory, the Resource Based View, and Information Technology Sourcing Decisions: A Re-Examination of Lacity et al.'s Findings*. Working paper, ISSN 0832-7203.

Cullen, S., Lacity, M., & Willcocks, L. (2014). *Outsourcing – All You Need to Know*. Melbourne: White Plume.

Davies, J., & Mitchell, G. (1994). The Dual Nature of the Impact of IT on Organizational Transformations. In R. Baskerville, S. Smithson, O. Ngwenyama, & J. DeGross (Eds.), *Transforming Organizations with Information Technology*. Amsterdam: North Holland.

Dibbern, J., Goles, T., Hirschheim, R., & Jayatilaka, B. (2004). Information Systems Outsourcing: A Survey and Analysis of the Literature. *The Database for Advances in Information Systems, 35*(4), 6–102.

Doolin, B. (1998). Information Technology as a Disciplinary Technology: Being Critical in Interpretive Research in Information Systems. *Journal of Information Technology, 13*, 301–312.

Equaterra. (2010). *Governance Best Practice Masterclass*. Retrieved June 2010, from http://www.equaterra.com/_filelib/filecabinet/newsletters/equaterra_masterclass_-_optimising_outsourcing_governance_-_june_2010.pdf.

Fairclough, N. (2005). Peripheral Vision: Discourse Analysis in Organization Studies: The Case for Critical Realism. *Organization Studies, 26*, 915–939.

Foucault, M. (1972). *Archaeology of Knowledge*. New York: Pantheon.

Foucault, M. (1977). *Discipline and Punish*. New York: Pantheon.

Foucault, M. (1980a). *Power/Knowledge: Selected Interviews and Other Writings, 1972–1977*. New York: Pantheon.

Foucault, M. (1980b). Two Lectures. In C. Gordon (Ed.), *Power/Knowledge: Selected Interviews*. New York: Pantheon.

Foucault, M. (2003). *Society Must Be Defended*. New York: Picador.

Goles, T., & Chin, W. (2005). Information Systems Outsourcing Relationship Factors: Detailed Conceptualization and Initial Evidence. *Database for Advances in Information Systems, 36*(4), 47–67.

Gonzalez, R., Gasco, J., & Llopis, J. (2006). Information Systems Outsourcing: A Literature Analysis. *Information & Management, 43*(7), 821–834.

IAOP. (2008). *The 2008 IAOP Governance Forum*. Retrieved May 2008, from http://www.outsourcingprofessional.org/content/23/154/1607/.

Karimi-Alaghehband, F., Rivard, S., Wu, S., & Goyette, S. (2011). An Assessment of the Use of Transaction Cost Theory in Information Technology Outsourcing. *Journal of Strategic Information Systems, 20*(2), 125–138.

Kern, T., & Willcocks, L. (2002). Exploring Relationships in Information Technology Outsourcing: The Interaction Approach. *European Journal of Information Systems, 11*(1), 3–19.

Lacity, M., & Willcocks, L. (1995). Interpreting Information Technology Sourcing Decisions from a Transaction Cost Perspective: Findings and Critique. *Accounting Management and Information Technologies, 5*, 203–244.

Lacity, M., & Willcocks, L. (2009). *Information Systems and Outsourcing: Studies in Theory and Practice*. London: Palgrave.

Lacity, M., & Willcocks, L. (2015). *Nine Keys to World Class Business Process Outsourcing*. London: Bloomsbury.

Lacity, M., & Willcocks, L. (2018). *Robotic Process and Cognitive Automation: The Next Phase*. Stratford: SB Publishing.

Lacity, M., Khan, S., Yan, A., & Willcocks, L. (2010). A Review of the IT Outsourcing Empirical Literature and Future Research Directions. *Journal of Information Technology, 25*(4), 395–433.

Lacity, M., Willcocks, L., & Khan, S. (2011). Beyond Transaction Cost Economics: Towards an Endogenous Theory of Information Technology Outsourcing. *Journal of Strategic Information Systems, 20*(2), 139–157. ISSN 0963-8687.

Lessa, I. (2006). Discursive Struggles Within Social Welfare: Restaging Teen Motherhood. *The British Journal of Social Work. Oxford Journals, 36*(2), 283–298.

Mercer. (2010). *Global Governance Survey 2009/2010: Highlights*. Retrieved June 2013, from http://uk.mercer.com/summary.htm?siteLanguage=1008&idContent=1378055.

Mingers, J., & Willcocks, L. (2016). An Integrative Semiotic Methodology for IS Research. *Information and Organization, 27*(1), 17–36.
Oshri, I., Kotlarsky, J., & Willcocks, L. (2015). *The Handbook of Global Outsourcing and Offshoring*. London: Palgrave.
Poppo, L., & Zenger, T. R. (2002). Do Formal Contracts and Relational Governance Function as Substitutes or Complements. *Strategic Management Journal, 23*, 707–725.
Snowden, J., & Fersht, P. (2016). *The HFS Market Index IT Services and BPO Market Size and Forecast, 2016–2020*. Boston: HFS Research.
Veyne, P. (2010). *Foucault – His Thought, His Character*. Cambridge: Polity.
Wang, E. (2002). Transaction Attributes and Software Outsourcing Success: An Empirical Investigation of Transaction Cost Theory. *Information Systems Journal, 12*(2), 153–181.
Willcocks, L. (2006). Michel Foucault in the Social Study of ICTs: Critique and Reappraisal. *Social Science Computer Review, 24*(3), 274–295.
Willcocks, L., & Lacity, M. (Eds.). (2014). *The Economics of Outsourcing*. London: Edward Elgar.
Willcocks, L., & Lacity, M. (2016). *Service Automation, Robots and the Future of Work*. Stratford: SB Publishing.
Willcocks, L., Venters, W., & Whitley, E. (2015). *Moving to the Cloud Corporation*. London: Palgrave.
Willcocks, L., Lacity, M., & Sauer, C. (Eds.). (2017). *Outsourcing and Offshoring Business Services*. Basingstoke: Palgrave Macmillan.
Willcocks, L., Oshri, I., & Kotlarsky, J. (Eds.). (2018). *Dynamic Innovation in Outsourcing*. London: Palgrave Macmillan.

2

The Study of Information Technology Outsourcing

Introduction

As the practice of information technology (IT) outsourcing has been evolving, the research issues concerned with it, and the theories used to explain it, have shifted accordingly (Dibbern et al. 2004; Lacity et al. 2009; Willcocks et al. 2018). In the early stages, research on IT outsourcing was centred on the 'make-or-buy' decision. Researchers from economic perspectives supported that outsourcing is a reasonable option when contracting out the IT function is cheaper than developing it in-house (e.g. Williamson 1975; McFarlan and Nolan 1995; Ang and Straub 1998). On the other hand, scholars adopting a strategic perspective argued that "core activities should stay in-house, whilst non-core activities can be outsourced" (e.g. Jauch and Wilson 1979; Prahalad and Hamel 1990; Hamel 1991; Quinn and Hilmer 1994; Lacity and Willcocks 1995; Cox 1996). In this chapter we explore how the study of information technology outsourcing (ITO) and business process outsourcing (BPO) developed from these beginnings, and the themes and problems dealt with in the literature, with a particular focus on contracts, relationships, and governance—the main concerns of this book.

E. Lioliou, L. P. Willcocks, *Global Outsourcing Discourse*, Technology, Work and Globalization, https://doi.org/10.1007/978-3-319-74045-4_2

ITO: Research Developments

In the 1990s, given ITO was a relatively new phenomenon to major companies, many studies focused on outsourcing advantages and disadvantages. Thus, from an economic perspective, outsourcing may lead to important cost savings through the creation of economies of scale, the reduction or stabilization of overhead costs, and the freeing up of internal resources (Altinkemer et al. 1994; Grover et al. 1996; Lacity et al. 1996; Smith et al. 1998). In addition to the economic benefits, outsourcing may entail several strategic benefits. Concentration on a company's core business may allow it to leverage its internal innovation capabilities (Quinn and Hilmer 1994) and exploit distinctive competencies which will provide formidable barriers against present and future competitors. Furthermore, outsourcing can lead to greater capacity for flexibility, especially in the purchase of rapidly developing new technologies (Altinkemer et al. 1994). Crucially, outsourcing can provide companies with the possibility "of the full utilization of external suppliers' investments, innovations, and specialized professional capabilities which would be prohibitively expensive to replicate" (Quinn and Hilmer 1994). However, IT outsourcing is a managerial decision that entails various risks and problems, so much so that numerous authors have identified an associated drawback for each advantage suggested. A lot of studies have shown that outsourcing, particularly IT outsourcing, not only does not bring the promised cost savings but also generates increased costs (Currie 1996; Domberger 1998). The strategic dangers associated with outsourcing have been also identified to be numerous. Overdependency on outside vendors and the danger of decreased flexibility and control are constituting important risks when making outsourcing decisions (Quinn and Hilmer 1994; Domberger 1998). Outsourcing may also lead to the loss of distinctive capabilities or critical skills of an organization, which can have detrimental effects (Claver et al. 2002).

Towards Multi-sourcing

However, as most research studies considered outsourcing as a significant method for managing information systems, the key issue on IT outsourcing shifted from whether or not to outsource IT to the following: to what extent, and how, should IT be outsourced. The decisions on these questions raise management issues such as total or selective outsourcing (Willcocks and Choi 1995; Lacity et al. 1996; Currie and Willcocks 1998; Dibbern et al. 2004), long- or short-term contractual relationships (Quinn and Hilmer 1994; Lacity et al. 1996; Bensaou 1999), the co-operation with single or multiple vendors (Michell and Fitzgerald 1997; Lacity et al. 1996; Saunders 2002), and the criteria for selecting vendors (McFarlan and Nolan 1995; Lacity and Willcocks 2009). Prior studies suggest that selective outsourcing with multiple vendors and short-term contracts is more likely to achieve a positive outcome (Lacity et al. 1996; Saunders et al. 1997). Selective outsourcing eschews the problem inherent in total outsourcing and demonstrates a way of more flexible and modular outsourcing (Lacity et al. 1996). On the same grounds, short-term contracts and the co-operation with multiple suppliers provide flexibility and reduce dependency (Lacity et al. 1996, 2009). On the other hand, in respect to the selection of the vendor, McFarlan and Nolan, drawing on case research, addressed several topics associated with this issue. The authors highlight the importance for a vendor to be in a financially stable position and to be keeping pace with technological advances. They further point out that vendor selection should be evaluated in light of mutual interests, shared approaches to problem-solving, and a compatible management culture and style (McFarlan and Nolan 1995).

Multi-sourcing, that is, using multiple sources, to deliver service requirements has been a major trend in ITO and BPO for over 25 years (Cullen et al. 2014). But ITO/BPO models have evolved even further in the past decade, and large outsourcing deals with a single supplier have been increasingly replaced by several selective contracts with a set of suppliers (Lioliou et al. 2018; Bapna et al. 2010). Multi-sourcing arrangements have become the dominant trend in the contemporary outsourcing landscape and their growth is increasing (Krancher et al. 2018; Lacity et al. 2017; Plugge and Bouwman 2015; Plugge and Janssen 2014).

Relationships as a Major Study Area

A further focus of the IT outsourcing literature has been on the relationship between the client and the vendor and its key aspects. Fundamentally, outsourcing is a legal agreement in which a client relies on a supplier for a given service. This legal agreement is administered by a contract. While contracts outline the roles to be played by each party and set a framework to the relationship, they are limited by virtue of uncertainty about the future. Thus, there are other factors based on awareness and mutual understanding that become relevant to the governance of the ongoing IT outsourcing relationship (Oshri et al. 2015a, b; Krancher et al. 2015; Lioliou and Zimmermann 2015; Lioliou et al. 2014; Lacity and Willcocks 2009; Kern and Willcocks 2002). The next sections provide us with an examination of the governance of IT outsourcing relationship and its key determinants.

In the most recent review of all relevant studies, Lacity et al. (2017) found that relationship and contractual governance and the length of relationships were important determinants of outsourcing outcomes. Particularly important for relational governance were communication, effective knowledge sharing, trust, formal governance commitment, co-operation, and client provider alignment. For contractual governance, particularly important were detailed contracts, control mechanisms, and key performance indicators. We investigate these findings in our case studies in the next three chapters.

Governance of the Relationship

With the gathering focus on relationships, by the early 2000s, a more developed debate developed around the governance of those relationships. In particular: could good governance be achieved formally or informally? Was the contract the major determinant of outcomes, or were there other relationship-based mechanisms that were equally or more effective? Were contracts and relationship-based mechanisms substitutive or complementary?

Formal Aspect of Governance

The formal aspect of governance refers to the development of a good contract. The outsourcing contract provides a detailed specification of "the exchanges of services and/or products, financial matters, assets and/or staff transfers, communication and information exchanges, service enforcements and monitoring methods, key personnel, dispute resolution procedures and other formal issues" (Kern and Willcocks 2000).

Several authors have pointed out certain attributes to a good contract. For example, according to Parkhe (1993), the more complete the contract, the smaller the exposure to the potential opportunism of the vendor and the smaller the probability that costly renegotiations will be needed. Aubert et al. (2003), on the other hand, argued that in cases of activities that are not easy to predict or difficult to measure, more incomplete forms of contracts are required.

Gietzmann (1996) as well as Beulen and Ribbers (2003) appeared to be more concerned with the importance of flexibility at the contractual level and argued that adjustments and changes may be needed at any point of the outsourcing relationship, especially in its early stages. Andersen and Christensen (2002) further underlined the value of flexibility by pointing out that "when making adjustments is costless the problem is trivial, but if adjustment entails costs in an uncertain environment, then the problem becomes much bigger".

Saunders et al. (1997), on the other hand, highlighted precision as an important attribute of a good contract. The authors explained that ill-defined contracts generally result in high IT costs and poor IT service levels. Allery (2004) further asserted that without clarity there is an element of uncertainty that, apart from legal problems, can also cause operational problems and result in the creation of "hidden costs". Bennedsen and Schultz (2005) went a step further and indicated that an adaptive, "trial-and-error" approach when preparing the contract may be a good way to prevent errors.

Still, a significant number of authors have argued that there are no "one-size-fits-all" clauses and thus that partnership quality goes to a large extent beyond the contents in the contracts (Barthelemy 2003; Lacity et al. 2017). Therefore, some researchers started to investigate other determinants of successful IT outsourcing partnerships and shed light upon the other, "soft" and "more human", side of the relationship (i.e. Kern and Willcocks 2002; Barthelemy 2003; Lee and Kim 2003; Tompkins et al. 2006).

Relational Aspects of Governance

The relational aspect of governance refers to the more human aspects that characterize the relationship between the client and the vendor. The importance of trust was widely acknowledged as a key indicator of the quality of the outsourcing relationship (i.e. Sabherwal 1999; Barthelemy 2001, 2003; Oshri et al. 2015b). Pruitt (1981) emphasized that trust is highly related to firms' desire to collaborate, while Zand (1972) highlighted the fact that its absence diminishes the effectiveness of problem-solving. Anderson and Narus (1990) went a step further and noted that once trust is established, "firms learn that joint efforts will lead to outcomes that exceed what the firm would achieve if it acted solely in its own best interests". Sahay et al. (2003) emphasized the dialectical relationship between trust and control and supported that the need for control can be minimized in a trusting environment.

Relationships based on mutual trust provide grounds for the development of stronger bonds between the two parties (Lee and Kim 2003). Barthelemy (2001) highlighted even more the importance of trust in outsourcing relationships by suggesting that in essence, it constitutes the antidote to opportunism. Once a party develops trust in the other, a pattern of commonality arises and both parties become increasingly ready to work cooperatively towards established goals and objectives (Brunard and Kleiner 1994).

Trust is also of fundamental importance to an outsourcing relationship because it is interdependent with commitment. Greater commitment leads to greater trust and vice versa. Either party's commitment to the outsourcing relationship is a clear indication that the party is willing to exert effort on behalf of the relationship and is motivated to make it a success.

Several authors have also highlighted the importance of communication in breeding relationships based on trust and commitment (Kern and Willcocks 2002; Sahay et al. 2003; Lacity et al. 2017). Only through honest and ongoing exchanges of information, the outsourcing relationship can be effectively monitored (Tompkins et al. 2006). Furthermore, communication was recognized to be key for the settlement of conflicts and misconceptions, facilitation of solutions, reduction of uncertainty, and generation of flexibility (Kern and Willcocks 2002). The quality of communication, information sharing, and interfirm adaptation were found to be important generators of trust (Mao et al. 2008). In a similar vein, Kotlarsky et al. (2008) conducted a study on global sourcing ventures and emphasized on the importance of social mechanisms of coordination in the generation of social capital. Knowledge sharing has also been found to be important in breeding relationships of trust (Ghosh and Scott 2009; Kotlarsky et al. 2008; Kotlarsky and Oshri 2005). These results, in composite, are summarized in the comprehensive review by Lacity et al. (2017).

Another stream of researchers, though, have considered the power play between the client and the vendor to be more important in determining the outsourcing relationship. The power play in outsourcing ventures is mainly a result of dependency and tends to cause a power-control dilemma (Easton 1992). According to Fitzgerald and Willcocks (1994), it is difficult to maintain partnerships in the field of outsourcing due to an asymmetry of resources and in the power relationship that tends to favour the service provider once the contract is signed (see also Cullen et al. 2014). Service receivers initially have greater influence than service providers in their relationships. As the nature of the relationship between the service receiver and the provider changes from one that is relatively independent to one that is tightly coupled, service providers are likely to gain more power since service receivers will be facing important switching costs (Lacity and Hirschheim 1993; Fitzgerald and Willcocks 1994; Lacity and Willcocks 2009). Kern and Willcocks (2002) also pointed out that in total outsourcing deals, the supplier will dominate the relationship from the start, as the client is totally dependent on the vendor's services, whereas in selective outsourcing the situation may be more balanced.

Other authors, on the other hand, have stressed the pursuit of mutual benefits as a factor that can generate mutual dependency. When the interests of the client and the vendor are tightly coupled, the bonds in the outsourcing relationship are enhanced. The notion is that the closeness and achievement of mutual goals, the allocation of risks and the shared responsibility, generate a strong feeling of "chemistry" that strengthens the relationship between the client and the vendor (Mohr and Spekman 1994; Kumar and Van Dissel 1996; Kern and Blois 2017).

Towards an Integrated Perspective

This review suggests that earlier research tended to treat the contractual and the relational aspects of outsourcing governance as distinct dimensions in the execution of the venture. Later, there has been an effort towards developing a more thorough understanding of the interrelationship and interaction between the contract and the relational aspects in outsourcing.

Interrelations Between Formal and Relational Governance

More recently, there has been an effort towards developing a more thorough understanding of the interrelationship between the formal and the relational elements of outsourcing governance (Chen and Bharadwaj 2009; Goo et al. 2009; Srivastava and Thompson 2012; Lioliou et al. 2014; Huber et al. 2013). In this stream of research, a major focus has been on the 'substitution' versus 'complementary' nature of the relationship between contractual and relational governance (Gulati and Nickerson 2008; Poppo and Zenger 2002; Vlaar et al. 2007). As recognized by Huber et al. (2013), the substitution stream of research views formal and relational governance as functional equivalents, and since both formal and relational governance are doing the same thing, one can *replace* the other (Huber et al. 2013; Malhotra and Murnighan 2002). Furthermore, the workings of formal governance can *dampen* the levels of relational governance. For instance, the existence of rigid contractual processes can be perceived as a signal of distrust. Conversely, the workings of relational governance can dampen the functioning of formal governance (Huber et al. 2013). Organizations may for instance downplay and by-pass formal governance processes because they are over-depending on their prior good relationship. The complementarity stream of research, on the other hand, argues that formal and relational governance have unique strengths and that one *compensates* for the weaknesses of the other (Carson et al. 2006; Huber et al. 2013; Poppo and Zenger 2002). According to this view, formal and relational governance reinforce and *enable*, rather than negate, each other (Goo et al. 2009; Huber et al. 2013). On this basis, a good contract can actually set the grounds for trustful relationships to develop, and conversely, trustful relationships can facilitate the crafting and design of appropriate contracts (Goo et al. 2009).

Further Developments and Critique

It is useful at this point to look at epistemological standpoints in the literature. Positivist studies are premised on the existence of a priori, relatively fixed relationships within phenomena. These relationships are typically investigated with structured instrumentation. Such studies serve primarily to test theory, in an attempt to identify universal laws and increase predictive understanding of the phenomena (Orlikowski and Baroudi 1991). Interpretive studies, on the other hand, assume that "people create and associate their own subjective meanings as they interact with the world around them" (Orlikowski and Baroudi 1991). Interpretive researchers thus attempt to understand phenomena through accessing the meanings assigned to them.

In the literature reviewed, the majority of the studies on IT outsourcing have adopted a positivist epistemology. All these studies were searching for cause-and-effect relationships and examined the partnership through hypothesis testing, correlation analysis among partnership-related variables, or correlation analysis between partnership success and related variables. Studies which were more interpretive in their nature were by Lacity and Hirschheim (1993), Fitzgerald and Willcocks (1994), Sabherwal (1999), Kern and Willcocks (2002), Kotlarsky et al. (2008), Kotlarsky and Oshri (2005), and Sahay et al. (2003). A comprehensive review of these studies appears in Lacity et al. (2017).

Economic and Social Perspectives

The dominant approaches underlying the investigation of the governance of the IT outsourcing relationship are from the economic and the social viewpoints. From an economic perspective, the vast majority of the studies utilized transaction cost theory (e.g. Gietzmann 1996; Andersen and Christensen 2002; Aubert et al. 2003; Bennedsen and Schultz 2005). Transaction cost theory focuses on the advantages and disadvantages of different types of governance structures for achieving effective and efficient service delivery under uncertainty. Studies from the economic viewpoint are mainly concerned with the contractual relationship between the client and the vendor. These studies primarily highlight the importance of the structure of the contract and appear to downplay other factors that may influence the partnership.

On the other hand, researchers from the social viewpoint used various interorganizational relationship frameworks that incorporate social exchange theory and power-political theory (i.e. Anderson and Narus 1990; Mohr and Spekman 1994; Kumar and Van Dissel 1996; Kern and Willcocks 2002; Lee and Kim 2003). While social exchange theory is based on the concept of trust to interpret interactions between parties, power-political theory is concerned with the power derived from offering valuable resources that few other sources can provide (Lee and Kim 1999). These studies concentrate on more "human factors" such as trust, the balance of power between the two parties, and the pursuit of mutual benefits, as factors that generate a great impact upon the partnership.

Critique

The vast majority of prior studies concentrate only on the perspective of the client or the supplier in isolation when examining the IT outsourcing relationship. Studies that incorporated client and supplier perspectives remain comparatively rare (Koh et al. 2004). This is rather paradoxical as, for a more profound understanding of IT outsourcing and the ongoing relationship between the two partners, the attitude of both outsourcing partners needs to be examined (Willcocks et al. 2017).

Epistemologically, the majority of the studies adopted a positivist stance of research. These have generally ignored the deeper structure of the phenomena. In this book we seek to demonstrate that, in order to reach a more profound conceptualization of the evolution of IT outsourcing relationships and their underlying dynamics, more interpretive research is needed.

The limited scope of the economic viewpoint for studying the IT outsourcing relationship has been highly criticized. For example, Zajac and Olsen (1993) maintained that although transaction cost theory has been taken as an appropriate approach to research on decision-making about governance forms in outsourcing areas, when adopting it to studying interorganizational relationships, at least two important limitations arise. A focus on cost minimization in the focal company neglects the interdependent relationship between exchange partners in their efforts to maximize value; and a focus on the structural features of the exchange neglects significant process issues. Lee and Kim (1999) also asserted that "economic theories treat each sourcing decision as an independent event regardless of prior relationships that affect the ongoing sourcing decision". The authors further attacked economic theories by highlighting that "researching into the relationship between organizations from a purely economic point of view is unjustifiable because interorganizational relationships form from the social learning experiences based on specific sequential interactions" (Lee and Kim 1999).

The social perspective, on the other hand, while it has addressed processes and episodes of exchanges as these are enmeshed in the social context, can be criticized for underplaying the role of perceptions, discourses, and beliefs that result from the respective processes and episodes of exchange. More specifically, the impact of certain discourses or beliefs in the creation of knowledge and the role of specific bodies of knowledge as cognitive tools in the development and governance of IT outsourcing relationships have been rarely if ever addressed (e.g. Yakhlef 1998).

The dominant theories utilized within the social perspective appear to be of limited use for our investigation. For example, social exchange theory relates more to behavioural aspects (Blau 1964) and underplays the role of the individual's perceptions and beliefs with regard to the exchange. Along the same lines, power-political theory provides an instrumental view on power and ignores the fact that power shapes and is constituted through alternative discourses, beliefs, and domains of knowledge. In addition, the role of power in producing discourses and beliefs which in turn influence the episodes of exchange is also neglected (Willcocks 2006).

Theory and IT Outsourcing: Transaction Cost Economics

Let us turn to the theoretical lenses available for studying IT outsourcing. Creon et al. (2017) suggested that resource-based, resource-dependent, transaction costs, and agency are the main usable theories but also develop a contingency model for IT outsourcing. Meanwhile Lacity et al. (2011) argued for an endogenous theory, arising from the empirical evidence of actual case experiences. In practice, transaction cost economics (TCE) constitutes one of the most widely used theoretical lenses in the study of governance structures, yet empirical support in respect to its applicability appears to be mixed (Wang 2002). The theory of TCE forms a good initial theoretical foundation but tends to focus on the formal aspects of the exchange and the structural characteristics of the contract. For this reason, we attempt a more integrated level of analysis of the formal and relational aspects of IT outsourcing governance, utilizing ideas stemming from Foucault's theorization on 'governmentality' and 'power relations'. Let us look at these two theorizations in more detail.

Transaction Cost Economics

TCE belong to the paradigm of new institutional economics. This paradigm has supplemented the traditional stream of neo-classical economics which has been viewing the firm solely as a production function. Contrary to this position, new institutional economics in general and TCE specifically view the firm as a governance structure.

TCE is founded on Coases's (1937) proposition that firms and markets constitute alternative governance structures that differ in their transaction costs. Transaction costs can be described as coordination costs and include ex ante costs of drafting, negotiating and safeguarding an agreement. The essence of TCE is related to the question whether a specific transaction should take place within the firm (hierarchy), take the form of a hybrid (alliance), or should be performed outside (market). The following section will provide a more in-depth presentation of the transaction cost theorization, based on the work of its major proponent Oliver Williamson.

The Transaction and Its Attributes

TCE suggests that the basic unit of analysis is the transaction. Governance is regarded as "the means by which order is accomplished in a relation in which potential conflict threatens to undo or upset opportunities to realized mutual gains" (Williamson 1998). The problem of conflict that the theory of transaction costs is primarily concerned with is that of bilateral dependency (Williamson 1985). While the organization of transactions that include generic investments is easy, potential problems may occur when non-redeployable investments need to be made. As Williamson (1998) put it: "parties that are joined in a condition of bilateral dependency … and are confronted with contractual incompleteness … must confront strains … when faced with the need to adapt cooperatively".

Transaction cost theory suggests that every transaction is characterized by three dimensions: asset specificity, uncertainty, and frequency. Asset specificity refers to "the degree to which an asset can be redeployable to alternative uses and by alternative users without sacrifice of productive value" (Williamson 1991). Uncertainty is generated by phenomena that are hard to anticipate and consequently hard to be specified in the contract, while frequency is related to how often a transaction occurs.

Human Behaviour and Its Attributes

The theory of transaction costs is based on two assumptions regarding human behaviour—bounded rationality and opportunism. Bounded rationality refers to the idea that the human mind has cognitive limitations that put severe constrains on the ability of human beings to fully understand complex situations and address them in a completely rational way. On this basis, although decision-makers intend to act in a rational manner, their ability to do so is constrained because "the capacity of the human mind for formulating and solving complex problems is very small compared to the size of the problems whose solution is required" (Simon 1957). The concept of bounded rationality implies that, unavoidably, all complex forms of contracting are incomplete.

Opportunism is related to the assumption that decision-makers are acting out of self-interest. Williamson (1985, p. 47) defined opportunism as "a lack of honesty or candor in transaction, to include self-interest seeking with guile. This includes but is scarcely limited to more blatant forms, such as lying, stealing and cheating. … More generally, opportunism refers to the incomplete or distorted disclosure of information, especially to calculated efforts to mislead, distort, disguise, obfuscate, or otherwise confuse." This concept assumes not only the capability but also the willingness of organizations to act solely on the basis of their own interests.

For TCE the hazards of contracting emerge from these two characteristics of human behaviour. In other words, a contract can never be complete but will contain errors, omissions, and misspecifications due to bounded rationality; and contractual obligations are not self-enforcing because of opportunism. The next section will provide us with a review of studies that have utilized the theory of transaction costs in the information systems (IS) field.

The Theory of Transaction Costs and IS Research

Studies from this stream of research have focused primarily on the effects of the characteristics of the exchange on the choice of governance, (that is, keep the activities in-house, and thus maintain high levels of control over the IT function or outsourcing), as well as on firm performance. As examples only, Aubert et al. (2004) used the theory of transaction costs to study which types of IT activities constitute good candidates for outsourcing and which should be kept in-house. Interestingly, they found inconsistent results on the effect that asset specificity can have in the evaluation of candidate IT activities for outsourcing and suggested that more research should be carried out in the examination of the asset specificity of a particular IT activity and the decision to outsource. Thouin et al. (2009) conducted a survey to analyse the effect of low asset specificity outsourcing on firm-level financial performance and demonstrated that outsourcing such IT activities considered of low asset specificity is associated with increased financial performance.

Other studies utilized the theory in the offshore context and tried to examine how transaction costs are generated and managed. Ellram et al. (2008) investigated how firms manage costs and risks of offshore outsourcing of IT professional services. Fixed costs of establishing the arrangement dominate the variable day-to-day transaction costs in the offshore context, and thus low transaction volumes become unattractive because the per-unit cost allocation would go up. They also found that organizations will not offshore outsource areas where there is a high degree of perceived risk. Nicholson et al. (2006) adopted a TCE and management control theoretical framework to examine case studies of offshore outsourcing. They identified potential transaction costs and control problems that were occurring during different stages of the outsourcing relationship and tried to identify practices that could mitigate the transaction costs that were the result of high uncertainty and opportunism.

Another stream of research utilized the theory of transaction costs in conjunction with other theories widely used in the management field. This stream of research tried to complement the theory of transaction costs and other more socially based theories, aiming to account for societal influences and norms upon the exchanges under investigation. Ang and Cummings (1997) combined the theory of TCE to concepts from the theory of institutions to empirically investigate the effect of institutional influences on IT outsourcing in the banking sector. They found that where institutional pressures were regulatory in nature and involved the potential for sanctions, banks adhered to these pressures and responded less to strategic economic contingencies in their decision to outsource. When institutional pressures were related to mimetic behaviour, banks tended to respond more on strategic economic contingencies and less to institutional pressures from their peers in their outsourcing decisions.

Similar to Ang and Cummings (1997), Miranda and Kim (2006) combined the theory of transaction costs to concepts from the institutional theory to study the effects of institutions in the IT outsourcing decision. In particular, the authors tried to examine how different institutional contexts affect the way that decision-makers utilize the logic of the theory of transaction costs in IT outsourcing decisions. Goo et al. (2007) developed a multi-theoretic perspective aiming to explore the factors that influence the duration of IT outsourcing relationships. In their model they incorporated constructs from the organizational learning theory (i.e. knowledge acquisition), resource dependence theory (i.e. strategic importance of the IT activity), and social exchange theory (i.e. levels of satisfaction) in conjunction to constructs utilized in the transaction cost literature (i.e. relationship-specific investment, requirement uncertainty, and extent of substitution). Griffith et al. (2009) utilized the theory of transaction costs in conjunction to the resource dependence theory and examined the effects of new product development offshoring factors (namely modularity, strategic importance of the project, specificity of project technology, cultural distance, and technological discontinuity) on the choice of governance structures. While this stream of research has yielded results that make some reference to the context within which the transactions take place, David and Han (2004), in their extensive review of the transaction costs literature, suggested that more research is needed regarding the circumstances within which the theory has significant explanatory power.

Problematizing the Explanatory Power of Transaction Cost Theory

If TCE has been extensively used, it has also been heavily critiqued. As already indicated, Lacity and Willcocks (1995) provided a particularly influential account of the explanatory power of the theory of transaction costs in the IT outsourcing context. Their results demonstrated anomalies in the explanatory power of TCE in 87.5% of the cases under investigation. In their discussion Lacity and Willcocks (1995) suggested that part of these anomalies might be explained by the exclusion of uncertainty in their analysis or some re-interpretation around the construct of 'asset specificity'. However, they emphasized that they primarily sought to engage a fruitful discussion around the applicability of theories from other disciplines within the IS context.

Aubert and Weber (2001) got triggered by the results of Lacity and Willcocks (1995) and examined to what extent these could be re-interpreted. In their critique, Aubert and Weber (2001) primarily focused on how Lacity and Willcocks (1995) had used the notion of asset specificity. More specifically, the authors argued that Lacity and Willcocks (1995) did not have a valid measure of asset specificity by not having made a clear distinction between specialized and specific assets. Aubert and Weber (2001) critiqued that specialized assets are not necessarily specific and thus high (or low) specialization should not be necessarily associated with high (or low) asset specificity. On this basis Aubert and Weber (2001) argued that a significant part of the anomalies that Lacity and Willcocks (1995) identified in their study may be stemming from the problematical measure of asset specificity rather than a flaw in the theory of transaction costs. The critique by Aubert and Weber (2001) was particularly useful in putting emphasis on the fact that some assets can be neither specialized nor specific, specialized but not specific, specific but not specialized, and both specific and specialized (see Fig. 2.1).

However, Aubert and Weber (2001) suggested that in the context of TCE, only the latter two types of assets have an impact upon the sourcing decision, a claim that appears to depart from Williamson's theorization. More specifically, Williamson (1979) appeared to be putting emphasis on the specialization of assets, regardless if they are specific or not, taking into account however the number of alternatives that existed in the market: "The crucial investment distinction is this: to what degree are transaction-specific (nonmarketable) expenses incurred. Items that are **unspecialized** among users pose few hazards, since buyers in these circumstances can easily turn to alternative sources, and suppliers can sell output intended

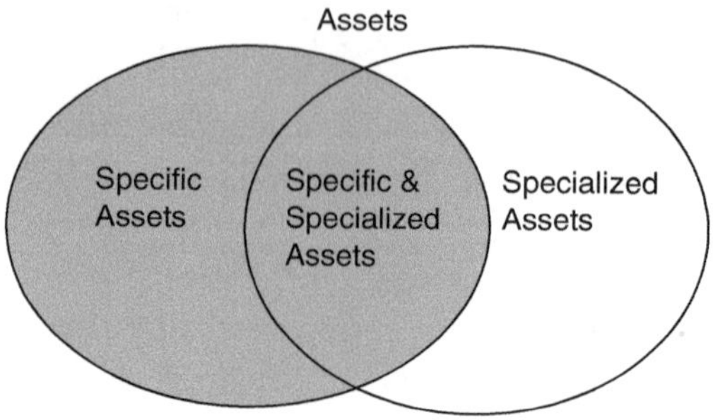

Fig. 2.1 Classification of assets (Aubert and Weber 2001)

for one order to other buyers without difficulty." From this statement, it appears that Williamson did place some emphasis on the degree of specialization of the assets (regardless of how much specific they are) and suggested that for unspecialized items there is a small danger for high switching cost because of the existence of alternatives. In contrast, in case of specialized assets, there is a greater hazard for high switching costs as buyers might not be able to turn easily to alternative sources. Consequently, when there are only a small number of alternative sources of supply within TCE theory, the so-called problem of small numbers arises.

In particular, Aubert and Weber (2001) suggested that "the essence of specialization is that the functions performed by an asset (person, machine, work team, firm, etc.) can be performed by **only a subset** of all assets". Since certain functions can be performed by only a subset of all assets, the 'small numbers' problem is being introduced. More specifically, Williamson (1975) suggested that "opportunistic inclinations pose little risk to trading partners as long as competitive (large numbers) exchange relations obtain". Thus Williamson (1975) linked situations of small numbers to the possibility of high opportunistic behaviour, thus higher transaction costs. An organization considering outsourcing is in a poor position to bargain with its supplier(s) if there are only few alternatives in the market (Lacity and Hirschheim 1993). Consequently, contrary to the claim of Aubert and Weber (2001), the degree of asset specialization does matter in the TCE theorization, in conjunction with the number of alternatives or substitutes. It thus might be more accurate to say that asset specificity is related to specific but not specialized or both

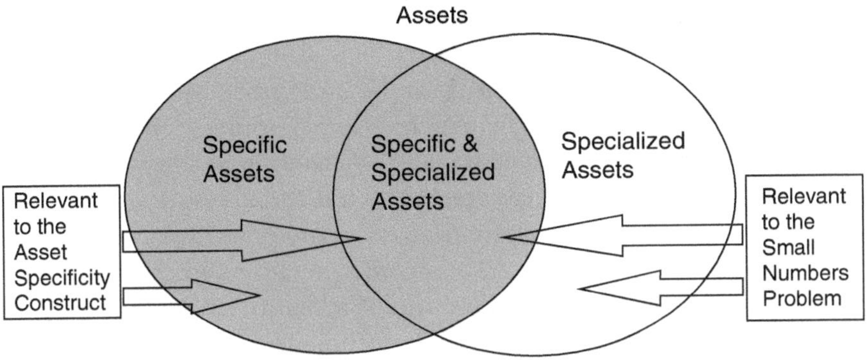

Fig. 2.2 Classification of assets relevant to the asset specificity construct

specific and specialized assets, while specialization itself is an element that is highly linked to the existence of a small number of alternatives (see Fig. 2.2).

Following Lacity and Willcocks (1995) as well as Aubert and Weber (2001), and particularly the later debate between Karimi-Alaghehband et al. (2011) and Lacity et al. (2011), we suggest that further problematization is needed regarding the predictive power of the theory of transaction costs in the IT sourcing context. Such a problematization—informed by further case study evidence—is a feature of this present study, and important theoretically, but also from a practical view point, since practitioners should be informed on how insightful the framework of TCE can be on the choice of governance.

Having reviewed transaction costs, the next section will explain the usefulness, for analytical purposes, of the Foucauldian notions of 'governmentality' and 'power relations'. These theoretical lenses can provide a more integrated, richer perspective in the study of the formal and relational aspect of governance.

The Foucauldian Concept of Governmentality

Foucault defined governmentality as "the conduct of our conduct" (Foucault 1980a, b). With the first 'conduct' in this phrase, Foucault wanted to imply that government is about leading, directing, and guiding.

But he also gave the verb 'to conduct' a reflexive meaning, in that government is not only about leading others, it is also about leading oneself. From this perspective, government can be understood as a "reflexive self control, creating situations in which external sources of surveillance become unnecessary" (Clegg et al. 2002). According to this theorization, practices governing individuals operate in and through various State and non-State institutions, organizations, tactics, and procedures.

Various theorists assigned different interpretations to the term 'governmentality'. For example, Hunt and Wickham (1994) conceived of the term as consisting of two parts—'governmental', meaning pertaining to the government of a country, and the suffix '-ity', meaning the study of. Kerr (1999), on the other hand, conceived of the term as an abbreviation of 'governmental rationality' and defined it as a way of thinking about the government and its practices. Both Hunt and Wickham, as well as Kerr, defined governmentality only in terms of the State. Dean, however, criticized this approach and suggested that a complete definition of the term governmentality must include not only government in terms of the State but government in terms of any "conduct of conduct" (Dean 1999).

Irrespective of these distinctions, however, governmentality studies share a common objective of capturing the "changing logic or rationality of government" (Sending and Neumann 2006). Even more important in this analysis is the redirection of attention away "from the actions of representatives of capital and State who are commonly held to exercise power towards the local settings in which power actually makes itself visible and sensible" (Uitermark 2004).

The notion of governmentality has been applied in a range of domains including psychology (Rose 1996), education (Hunter 1994), political theory (Hindess 1996), environmental sciences (Bulkeley et al. 2007), criminology (Carrabine 2000), law (Hunt and Wickham 1994), and economics and accounting (Miller and Rose 1990; Miller and O'Leary 1993; Preston et al. 1997; Miller 2001). The following section presents the major studies within the domain of accounting as contributions in this area appear to be providing more relevant insights to organizational analysis.

Governmentality Studies in Accounting

Miller and Rose's (1990) is one of the most influential studies in the governmentality literature. The authors highlighted how governmentality focuses the researcher's attention on the diverse mechanisms through which actions and judgements of different entities are linked to political objectives. On this basis they saw the governmentality concept supporting investigation of the indirect mechanisms for aligning economic, social, and personal conduct with socio-political goals.

Along this influential line of enquiry, a number of governmentality studies within the accounting research emphasized that power does not reside solely within the State but disperses via different disciplinary technologies to diverse sites and that bodies of knowledge such as accounting enable government or action from a distance. More specifically, accounting and other numerical techniques were recognized as playing a very significant role for governing—in the sense that they become carriers of knowledge from distant sites to local centres of calculation (Miller and Rose 1990). Furthermore, budgets, cost allocation mechanisms, auditing, and other accounting inscriptions not only facilitate the coordination of action in distant locales (Miller and O'Leary 1993; O'Leary and Miller 2007) but also regulate these distant locales through the introduction of new practices and vocabularies and by encouraging self-disciplining activities on the part of the field's participants (Hoskin and Macve 1986). Neu and Graham (2006) pointed out that this distance can be not only geographical but also conceptual and cultural, in that it can be referring to different spaces, vocabularies, habits, customs, worldviews, and so forth between those who are attempting to govern and the governed population. In their study they showed how political relations are enacted and extended through administrative accounting procedures "not just radiating outwards to 'cover' an existing political territory, but in fact to acquire new geographical territory and convert it into politically governable space by eliminating the effective distances involved". In effect, accounting techniques not only "convey" information between different sites but also serve to standardize practices across these sites. Such standardization involves both the standardization of certain practices and the standardization of common vocabularies and common behaviours.

Rose and Miller (1992) recognized this 'decentring' of the State as a key feature of governmentality studies. However, their position was criticized by a number of scholars within the accounting literature who demonstrated how State and law have played a significant role in certain modes of governmentality. For example, Bush and Maltby (2004) showed the influential role of colonial administrations in West Africa with regard to shaping the proliferation of taxation.

Governmentality studies from the field of accounting also demonstrated the central role of experts in the production of knowledge (Rose and Miller 1992; Dean 1999; Miller 2001). Rose and Miller (1992) argued that experts exert a high influence in establishing both the possibility and the legitimacy of government: "By means of expertise, self regulatory techniques can be installed in citizens that will align their personal choices with the ends of government." In contrast, Chan (2000) argued that there is a tendency towards non-experts becoming co-producers of knowledge. Consequently, he suggested that it is important that governmentality studies do not focus solely on experts as producers of knowledge but also examine and contrast the influence and the role of non-experts in such processes.

However, governing a sphere requires that it can be represented and depicted in a way which both grasps its truth and represents it in a calculable form. On this basis, Miller and Rose argued (1990) "for the importance of an analysis of language in understanding the constitutions of the objects of politics, not simply in terms of meaning or rhetoric, but as 'intellectual technologies' that render aspects of existence amenable to inscription and calculation". In a later study the authors emphasized the importance of the theories of the social sciences, economics, sociology, and psychology in providing "a kind of intellectual machinery for government, in the form of procedures for rendering the world thinkable, taming its intractable reality by subjecting it to the disciplined analysis of thought" (Rose and Miller 1992).

Miller and Rose (1990) also emphasized the discursive character of 'governmentality' and supported a view of 'discourse' as a technology of thought. On this basis they underlined that 'knowing' an object in a certain way entails procedures of 'inscriptions' and that, through such procedures, the diverse domains of 'governmentality' are made amenable to intervention, calculation, and regulation. Along these lines, a number of studies indicated that accounting and financial relations not only make a domain visible and amenable to intervention but also shape the grounds upon which subsequent interventions can be based upon. For example, Preston et al. (1997) showed in their study of the diagnosis-related group costing in the US healthcare system that the reimbursement rates attached to specific medical procedures influenced if and how medical providers treat certain medical conditions. Following Preston et al. (1997), Neu and Heincke (2004) suggested that such techniques as accounting serve to structure the conditions of possibility within a particular institutional field. In this sense, such techniques not only frame potential problems but also shape possible solutions. The accounting literature provides us many promising leads on how the concept of governmentality can be utilized in our study of IT outsourcing relationships.

Foucault and Power Relations

Foucault is also useful for understanding power relations. He was one of the first theorists not to view power as a resource but as something embedded in all social relations. His writings extended the discussion of the concept of power from the field of sociology to all the fields of the social sciences. For Foucault, power is not a group of institutions and mechanisms which ensures the obedience of the population of a given State. It is not a general system of domination exerted by one group over another. It is rather a dynamic set of relationships that is constantly changing from one point in time to the next.

According to him, power passes through people, and people constitute the relays of power. Foucault also suggested that such power relations do not need to be experienced negatively and highlighted that apart from its constraining character, power can have productive, disciplining and normalizing results. In his view, there is no single source of power but an infinite series of practices that shape 'discourses'. Power works through discourse to shape popular attitudes towards phenomena. Expert discourses established by those with power or authority can often be countered only by competing expert discourses. In such a way, discourses can be used as a powerful tool to restrict alternative ways of behaviour. "Discourse can be both an instrument and an effect of power, but also a hindrance, a block, a point of resistance and a starting point for an opposing strategy. Discourse transmits and produces power; it reinforces it, but also undermines and exposes it, renders it fragile and makes it possible to thwart it" (Foucault 1980a, b). Consequently, discourse produces its own 'truth effects'. For Foucault, 'truth production' and the dynamic of knowledge are situated in a theory of power. He argued that "truth is linked in a circular relation with systems of power which produce and sustain it, and to the effects of power that induce and extend it" (Foucault 1977). Moreover, in the dynamics of forming regimes of truth, certain 'knowledges' are disqualified. These are called *subjugated knowledges* and they may co-exist with the prevailing body of knowledge. On this basis, it is power that enables, drives, and shapes the production of new 'truths' and constitutes new knowledge. This means that the production of truth and hence knowledge is inseparable from power. Furthermore, it is implied that the production of 'truth' and knowledge in any cultural formation is the consequence of a struggle for power.

Foucault and IS Research

Foucault's work has also been applied in several studies of IS management, development, and organization as well as in surveillance studies. His concepts of disciplinary power and the intertwined nature of power and knowledge have influenced a number of IS researchers as well as organizational analysts studying information and communication technologies (e.g. Morgan and Willmott 1993; Knights and Murray 1994; Knights et al. 1997; Introna 1997; Willcocks 2006).

An early stream of IS research was concerned mainly with the disciplinary effects of IT. The work developed by Zuboff (1988), Poster

(1990), and Lyon (1994) had been particularly influential in this area of research. The authors translated Foucault's image of the Panopticon directly into studies of surveillance technologies of the use of information and databases and of discipline, information use, and technologies at work. Zuboff described the use of IT as leading to an "Information Panopticon" where all areas of organizational life become transparent. Poster (1990) raised the idea of the "SuperPanopticon", where all aspects of life are subject to surveillance, though he did not suggest that our society has reached that stage yet. Lyon (1994) examined the use of CCTV, the linking of government databases, and electronic tagging and suggested that the Panopticon is no longer limited by the walls of institutions but has been extended in both space and time.

On the same basis, Doolin (1998) outlined IT as a disciplinary technology through a hospital case-mix information system. The author showed how disciplinary technologies of surveillance enhanced the calculability of individuals through the comparative application of measures that represented the norm. Another study that demonstrated the disciplinary effects of IT was carried out by Humphreys (2006). The author used Foucault's theory to examine 'Amazon.com' as a site for the construction of the consumer as an object of knowledge through the use of technologies of surveillance. Using examples of marketing practices and internet technologies employed by 'Amazon.com', the author explored how site-based technologies of power shaped consumer agency.

However, Munro (2000) suggested that Foucault's concept of disciplinary power is not adequate to describe the power relations that emerge through the latest developments in IT. In his study he used Foucault's notion of a 'diagram of power' and demonstrated that power derived from networks transformed many areas of modern society and provided the grounds for other forms of power to be brought to life.

Another stream of IS research using Foucauldian ideas concerned itself with the power/knowledge relationship and its agency. In this category,

Introna (1997) applied Foucault's theorization of power/knowledge in harness with Clegg's (1989) conceptualization of circuits of power to explain the legitimization of rationalities generated by IS experts in the National Health Service (NHS). Furthermore, a study by Coombs et al. (1992) adopted a power/knowledge perspective to demonstrate how development of an internal market in the UK stimulated tensions between doctors and hospital administrators during the development of an information system to support these reforms. The authors emphasized that the information dimension of ICTs gave them a distinctive character and argued that information is intimately linked with power/knowledge relations and the forms of subjectivity that reside in them.

Knights and Murray (1994) applied Foucault's concept of power/knowledge relations to investigate the constraining and productive effects of power relations on the development of an IS project in a UK life insurance company. In a later study, Knights et al. (1997) integrated Foucault's concept of power/knowledge with actor-network theory to investigate the activities of a company which was set up to promote and develop an interorganizational network for electronic trading in the UK life insurance industry. The authors argued that critical organizational analysis should focus on how networks, both as practices and discourses, are sustained by power relations that are themselves supported by particular regimes of truth.

Davies and Mitchell (1994) adopted a research perspective that sought to understand technology formation as a power/knowledge object used within the Australian socio-political context. The researchers showed how applying Foucauldian principles to analysing the discursive context of IT use in an organization can provide in-depth insight into the role of power and politics. Cordoba and Robson (2003) developed a critical view of the process of information systems evaluation based on Foucault's ideas on power/knowledge and ethics. The authors demonstrated that Foucault's theorization provides an alternative understanding of information systems evaluation as a process of continuous tension between discourses and ethics. Finally, more recently, Avgerou and McGrath (2007) in their study of a social security organization in Greece drew on Foucault's work on power/knowledge and the aesthetics of existence to challenge the technical rationality underpinning IS innovation. The authors further argued that the rational techniques of IS practice and the dynamics of power between an organization and its social context are closely intertwined.

In reviewing the concepts of power relations, power/knowledge and discourse, and how these have already been used productively in previous IS research studies, we see Foucault's work, used selectively, as a very promising avenue for developing explanatory theories with which to conduct our analysis.

Conclusion

From reviewing the evolution of the ITO literature, it turns out that, historically, there has been a lack of studies that treat the IT outsourcing venture as an emerging relationship, where the contractual and the relational elements interact and influence one another. Disregarding the impact that is generated by the interplay of these elements constrains current studies into providing a somewhat sealed understanding of the IT outsourcing relationship. For this reason, studies, like the present one, that take a longitudinal perspective are important for their ability to generate a more profound understanding of evolving relationships between outsourcing partners.

This chapter also provided a presentation of the concepts that will be deployed in the next three chapters for purposes of analysis. These are based on Williamson's TCE and the work of Foucault on governmentality, power relations, and discourse. Having presented the major theoretical lenses, we would also refer readers to Appendix A which provides a note on the research methodology employed across the cases represented in the next three chapters.

References

Allery, P. (2004). *Effective Outsourcing: Practice and Procedures*. London: LexisNexis.

Altinkemer, K., Chaturvedi, A., & Gulati, R. (1994). Information Systems Outsourcing: Issues and Evidence. *International Journal of Information Management, 14*(4), 252–268.

Andersen, T., & Christensen, M. (2002). Contract Renewal Under Uncertainty. *Journal of Economic Dynamics and Control, 26*(4), 637–652.

Anderson, J. C., & Narus, J. A. (1990). A Model of Distributor Firm and Manufacturer Firm Working Partnerships. *The Journal of Marketing, 54*(1), 42–58.

Ang, S., & Cummings, L. (1997). Strategic Response to Institutional Influences on Information Systems Outsourcing. *Organization Science, 8*(3), 235–256.

Ang, S., & Straub, D. W. (1998). Production and Transaction Economies and IS Outsourcing: A Study of the US Banking Industry. *MIS Quarterly, 22*(4), 535–552.

Aubert, B., & Weber, R. (2001). *Transaction Cost Theory, the Resource Based View, and Information Technology Sourcing Decisions: A Re-Examination of Lacity et al.'s Findings*. Working paper, ISSN 0832-7203.

Aubert, B., Houde, J. F., Patry, M., & Rivard, S. (2003). *Characteristics of IT Outsourcing Contracts* (p. 269b). IEEE.

Aubert, B. A., Rivard, S., & Patry, M. (2004). A Transaction Cost Model of IT Outsourcing. *Information and Management, 41*, 921–932.

Avgerou, C., & McGrath, K. (2007). Power, Rationality, and the Art of Living Through Socio-Technical Change. *MIS Quarterly, 31*(2), 295–315.

Bapna, R., Barua, A., Mani, D., & Mehra, A. (2010). Research Commentary—Cooperation, Coordination, and Governance in Multisourcing: An Agenda for Analytical and Empirical Research. *Information Systems Research, 21*(4), 785–795.

Barthelemy, J. (2001). The Hidden Costs of IT Outsourcing. *Sloan Management Review, 42*(3), 60–69.

Barthelemy, J. (2003). The Hard and Soft Sides of IT Outsourcing Management. *European Management Journal, 21*(5), 539–548.

Bennedsen, M., & Schultz, C. (2005). Adaptive Contracting: The Trial and Error Approach to Outsourcing. *Economic Theory, 25*(1), 35–50.

Bensaou, M. (1999). Portfolios of Buyer-Supplier Relationships. *Sloan Management Review, 40*(4), 35–43.

Beulen, E., & Ribbers, P. (2003). *IT Outsourcing Contracts: Practical Implications of the Incomplete Contract Theory*. Proceedings of the 36th Hawaii International Conference on Systems Sciences.

Blau, M. (1964). *Exchange and Power in Social Life*. New York: John Wiley & Sons.

Brunard, V., & Kleiner, B. H. (1994). Developing Trustful and Co-operative Relationships. *Leadership and Organization Development Journal, 15*(2), 16–19.

Bulkeley, H., Watson, M., & Hudson, R. (2007). Modes of Governing Municipal Waste. *Environment and Planning, 39*, 2733–2753.

Bush, B., & Maltby, J. (2004). Taxation in West Africa: Transforming the Colonial Subject into the "Governable Person". *Critical Perspectives on Accounting, 15*(1), 5–34.

Carrabine, E. (2000). Discourse, Governmentality and Translation: Towards a Social Theory of Imprisonment. *Theoretical Criminology, 4*(3), 309–331.

Chan, J. (2000). Globalization, Reflexivity and the Practice of Criminology. *Australian and New Zealand Journal of Criminology, 33*(2), 118–135.

Chen, A., & Bharadwaj, A. (2009). An Empirical Analysis of Contract Structures in IT Outsourcing. *Information Systems Research, 20*(4), 484–506.

Claver, E., Gonzalez, R., Gasco, J., & Llopis, J. (2002). Information Systems Outsourcing: Reasons, Reservations and Success Factors. *Logistics Information Management, 15*(4), 294–308.

Clegg, S. R. (1989). *Frameworks of Power*. London: Sage Publications.

Clegg, S., Pitsis, T., Rura-Polley, T., & Marosszeky, M. (2002). Governmentality Matters: Designing an Alliance Culture of Inter-Organizational Collaboration for Managing Projects. *Organization Studies, 23*(3), 317–337.

Coase, R. H. (1937). The Nature of the Firm. *Economica, 4*, 386–405.

Coombs, R., Knights, D., & Willmott, H. (1992). Culture, Control and Competition: Towards a Conceptual Framework for the Study of Information Technology in Organizations. *Organization Studies, 13*(1), 51–72.

Cordoba, J., & Robson, W. (2003). Making the Evaluation of Information Systems Insightful: Understanding the Role of Power-Ethics Strategies. *Electronic Journal of Information Systems Evaluation, 6*(2), 55–64.

Cox, A. (1996). Relational Competence and Strategic Procurement Management. *European Journal of Purchasing and Supply Chain Management, 2*(1), 57–70.

Creon, M. J., Grover, V., & Teng, J. T. (2017). Theoretical Perspectives on the Outsourcing of Information Systems. In *Outsourcing and Offshoring Business Services* (pp. 25–52). Cham: Palgrave Macmillan.

Cullen, S., Lacity, M., & Willcocks, L. (2014). *Outsourcing – All You Need to Know*. Melbourne: White Plume.

Currie, W. L. (1996). Outsourcing in the Private and Public Sectors: An Unpredictable IT Strategy. *European Journal of Information Systems, 4*, 226–236.

Currie, W. L., & Willcocks, L. P. (1998). Analyzing Four Types of IT Sourcing Decisions in the Context of Scale, Client/Supplier Interdependency and Risk Mitigation. *Information Systems Journal, 8*(2), 119–143.

David, R. J., & Han, S. K. (2004). A Systematic Assessment of the Empirical Support for Transaction Cost Economics. *Strategic Management Journal, 25*(1), 39–58.

Davies, J., & Mitchell, G. (1994). The Dual Nature of the Impact of IT on Organizational Transformations. In R. Baskerville, S. Smithson, O. Ngwenyama, & J. DeGross (Eds.), *Transforming Organizations with Information Technology*. Amsterdam: North Holland.

Dean, M. (1999). *Governmentality*. London: Sage.

Dibbern, J., Goles, T., Hirschheim, R., & Jayatilaka, B. (2004). Information Systems Outsourcing: A Survey and Analysis of the Literature. *The Database for Advances in Information Systems, 35*(4), 6–102.

Doolin, B. (1998). Information Technology as a Disciplinary Technology: Being Critical in Interpretive Research in Information Systems. *Journal of Information Technology, 13*, 301–312.

Domberger, S. (1998). *The Contracting Organization: A Strategic Guide to Outsourcing*. Oxford: Oxford University Press.

Easton, G. (1992). Industrial Networks: A Review. In B. Axelson & G. Easton (Eds.), *Industrial Networks: A New View of Reality*. London: Routledge.

Ellram, L., Tate, W., & Billington, C. (2008). Offshore Outsourcing of Professional Services: A Transaction Cost Economics Perspective. *Journal of Operations Management, 26*(2), 148–163.

Fitzgerald, G., & Willcocks, L. (1994). *Contract and Partnerships in the Outsourcing of IT*. Proceedings of the Fifteenth International Conference on Information Systems, Vancouver, British Columbia.

Foucault, M. (1977). *Discipline and Punish*. New York: Pantheon.

Foucault, M. (1980a). *Power/Knowledge: Selected Interviews and Other Writings, 1972–1977*. New York: Pantheon.

Foucault, M. (1980b). Two Lectures. In C. Gordon (Ed.), *Power/Knowledge: Selected Interviews*. New York: Pantheon.

Ghosh, B., & Scott, J. (2009). Relational Alignment in Offshore IS Outsourcing. *MIS Quarterly Executive, 8*(1), 19–29.

Gietzmann, M. B. (1996). Incomplete Contracts and the Make or Buy Decision: Governance Design and Attainable Flexibility. *Accounting, Organizations and Society, 21*(6), 611–626.

Goo, J., Kishore, R., Nam, K., Rao, H. R., & Song, Y. (2007). An Investigation of Factors That Influence the Duration of IT Outsourcing Relationships. *Decision Support Systems, 42*(4), 2107–2125.

Goo, J., Nam, K., & Kishore, R. (2009). The Role of Service Level Agreements in Relational Management of Information Technology Outsourcing: An Empirical Study. *MIS Quarterly, 33*, 119–145.

Griffith, D. A., Harmancioglu, N., & Droge, C. (2009). Governance Decisions for the Offshore Outsourcing of New Product Development in Technology Intensive Markets. *Journal of World Business, 44*(3), 217–224.

Grover, V., Cheon, M. J., & Teng, J. T. C. (1996). The Effect of Service Quality and Partnership on the Outsourcing of Information Systems Functions. *Journal of Management Information Systems, 12*(4), 89–116.

Gulati, R., & Nickerson, J. A. (2008). Interorganizational Trust, Governance Choice, and Exchange Performance. *Organization Science, 19*, 688–708.

Hamel, G. (1991). Competition for Competence and Interpartner Learning Within International Strategic Alliances. *Strategic Management Journal, 12*(1), 83–103.

Hindess, B. (1996). Liberalism, Socialism and Democracy: Variations on a Governmental Theme. In *Foucault and Political Reason: Liberalism, Neo-Liberalism and Rationalities of Government* (pp. 65–80). Chicago, IL: University of Chicago Press.

Hoskin, K., & Macve, R. (1986). Accounting and the Examination: A Genealogy of Disciplinary Power. *Accounting, Organizations and Society, 11*(2), 105–137.

Huber, T., Fischer, T., Dibbern, J., & Hirschheim, R. (2013). A Process Model of Complementarity and Substitution of Contractual and Relational Governance in IS Outsourcing. *Journal of Management Information Systems, 30*(3), 81–114.

Humphreys, A. (2006). The Consumer as Foucauldian Object of Knowledge. *Social Science Computer Review, 24*(3), 296–309.

Hunt, J., & Wickham, G. (1994). *Foucault and Law*. London: Pluto Press.

Hunter, I. (1994). *Rethinking the School: Subjectivity, Bureaucracy, Criticism*. Sydney: Allen and Unwin.

Introna, L. (1997). *Management, Information and Power*. London: Palgrave.

Jauch, L. R., & Wilson, H. K. (1979). A Strategic Perspective for Make or Buy Decisions. *Long Range Planning, 12*(6), 56.

Karimi-Alaghehband, F., Rivard, S., Wu, S., & Goyette, S. (2011). An Assessment of the Use of Transaction Cost Theory in Information Technology Outsourcing. *Journal of Strategic Information Systems, 20*(2), 125–138.

Kern, T., & Blois, K. (2017). Norm Development in IT Outsourcing Relationships. In L. Willcocks, M. Lacity, & C. Sauer (Eds.), *Outsourcing and Offshoring Business Services*. Basingstoke: Palgrave Macmillan.

Kern, T., & Willcocks, L. (2000). *The Relationship Advantage*. Oxford: Oxford University Press.

Kern, T., & Willcocks, L. (2002). Exploring Relationships in Information Technology Outsourcing: The Interaction Approach. *European Journal of Information Systems, 11*(1), 3–19.

Kerr, D. (1999). Beheading the King the Enthroning the Market: A Critique of Foucauldian Governmentality. *Science & Society, 63*(2), 173–203.

Knights, D., & Murray, F. (1994). *Managers Divided: Organizational Politics and Information Technology Management*. Chichester: Wiley.

Knights, D., Murray, F., & Willmott, H. (1997). Networking as Knowledge Work. In B. Bloomfield, R. Coombs, D. Knights, & D. Littler (Eds.), *Information Technology and Organizations*. Oxford: Oxford University Press.

Koh, C., Ang, S., & Straub, D. (2004). IT Outsourcing Success: A Psychological Contract Perspective. *Information Systems Research, 15*(4), 356–373.

Kotlarsky, J., & Oshri, I. (2005). Social Ties, Knowledge Sharing and Successful Collaboration in Globally Distributed System Development Projects. *European Journal of Information Systems, 14*(1), 37–48.

Kotlarsky, J., Van Fenema, P., & Willcocks, L. (2008). Developing a Knowledge-Based Perspective on Coordination: The Case of Global Software Projects. *Information & Management, 45*, 96–108.

Krancher, O., Huber, T., & Dibbern, J. (2015). *Explaining Endogenous Control Change in Outsourced Software Projects*. The 9th Global Sourcing Workshop, La Thuile, Italy.

Krancher, O., Kotlarsky, J., Oshri, I., & Dibbern, J. (2018). *Bilateral Versus Collective Governance: How Clients Promote Relational Norms in Multisourcing* (Online). The 12th Global Sourcing Workshop, La Thuile, Italy.

Kumar, K., & Van Dissel, H. G. (1996). Sustainable Collaboration: Managing Conflict and Cooperation in Interorganizational Systems. *MIS Quarterly, 20*(3), 279–300.

Lacity, M., & Hirschheim, R. (1993). *Information Systems Outsourcing*. Chichester: John Wiley and Sons.

Lacity, M., & Willcocks, L. (1995). Interpreting Information Technology Sourcing Decisions from a Transaction Cost Perspective: Findings and Critique. *Accounting Management and Information Technologies, 5*, 203–244.

Lacity, M., Willcocks, L., & Feeny, D. (1996). IT Outsourcing Maximizes Flexibility and Control. *Harvard Business Review, 73*(3), 84–93.

Lacity, M., & Willcocks, L. (2009). *Information Systems and Outsourcing: Studies in Theory and Practice*. London: Palgrave.

Lacity, M., Khan, S., & Willcocks, L. (2009). A Review of the IT Outsourcing Literature: Insights For Practice. *Journal of Strategic Information Systems, 18*(3), 130–146.

Lacity, M., Willcocks, L., & Khan, S. (2011). Beyond Transaction Cost Economics: Towards an Endogenous Theory of Information Technology Outsourcing. *Journal of Strategic Information Systems, 20*(2), 139–157. ISSN 0963-8687.

Lacity, M., Khan, S., & Yan, A. (2017). Review of the Empirical Business Services Sourcing Literature: An Update and Future Directions. In L. Willcocks, M. Lacity, & C. Sauer (Eds.), *Outsourcing and Offshoring Business Services*. London: Palgrave Macmillan.

Lee, J. N., & Kim, Y. G. (1999). Effect of Partnership Quality on IS Outsourcing Success: Conceptual Framework and Empirical Validation. *Journal of Management Information Systems, 15*(4), 29–61.

Lee, J. N., & Kim, Y. G. (2003). *Exploring a Causal Model for the Understanding of Outsourcing Partnership*. Proceedings of the 36th Hawaii International Conference on System Sciences.

Lioliou, E., & Zimmermann, A. (2015). Vendor Opportunism in IT Outsourcing: A TCE and Social Capital Perspective. *Journal of Information Technology, 30*(4), 307–324.

Lioliou, E., Zimmermann, A., Willcocks, L., & Gao, L. (2014). Formal and Relational Governance in IT Outsourcing: Substitution, Complementarity and the Role of the Psychological Contract. *Information Systems Journal, 24*(6), 503–535.

Lioliou, E., Willcocks, L., & Liu, X. (2018). Researching IT Multi-Sourcing and Opportunistic Behavior in Conditions of Uncertainty: A Case Approach. *Journal of Business Research*, forthcoming.

Lyon, D. (1994). *The Rise of Surveillance Society*. Cambridge: Polity.

Malhotra, D., & Murnighan, J. K. (2002). The Effects of Contracts on Interpersonal Trust. *Administrative Science Quarterly, 47*, 534–559.

Mao, J. Y., Lee, J. M., & Deng, C. P. (2008). Vendors' Perspectives on Trust and Control in Offshore Information Systems Outsourcing. *Information & Management, 45*(7), 482–492.

McFarlan, W., & Nolan, R. (1995). How to Manage an IT Outsourcing Alliance. *Sloan Management Review, 36*(2), 9–23.

Michell, V., & Fitzgerald, G. (1997). The IT Outsourcing Market-Place: Vendors and Their Selection. *Journal of Information Technology, 12*, 223–237.

Miller, P. (2001). Governing by Numbers: Why Calculative Practices Matter. *Social Research, 68*(2), 379–396.

Miller, P., & O-Leary, T. (1993). Accounting Expertise and the Politics of the Product: Economic Citizenship and Modes of Corporate Governance. *Accounting Organizations and Society, 18*, 187–206.

Miller, P., & Rose, N. (1990). Governing Economic Life. *Economy and Society, 19*(1), 1–31.

Miranda, S. M., & Kim, Y. (2006). Professionalism Versus Political Contexts: Institutional Mitigation and the Transaction Cost Heuristic in Information Systems Outsourcing. *MIS Quarterly, 30*(3), 725–753.

Mohr, J. J., & And Spekman, R. E. (1994). Characteristics of Partnership Success: Partnership Attributes, Communication Behavior, and Conflict Resolution Techniques. *Strategic Management Journal, 15*(2), 135–152.

Morgan, G., & Willmott, H. (1993). The "New" Accounting Research: On Making Accounting More Visible. *Accounting, Audibility and Accountability Journal, 6*(4), 3–36.

Munro, I. (2000). Non-Disciplinary Power and the Network Society. *Organization, 7*, 679–695.

Neu, D., & Graham, C. (2006). The Birth of a Nation: Accounting and Canada's First Nations, 1860–1900. *Accounting, Organizations and Society, 31*(1), 47–76.

Neu, D., & Heincke, M. (2004). The Subaltern Speaks: Financial Relations and the Limits of Governmentality. *Critical Perspectives on Accounting, 15*(1), 179–206.

Nicholson, B., Jones, J., & Espenlaub, S. (2006). Transaction Costs and Control of Outsourced Accounting: Case Evidence from India. *Management Accounting Research, 17*(3), 238–258.

O'Leary, T., & Miller, P. (2007). Mediating Instruments and Making Markets: Capital Budgeting, Science and the Economy. *Accounting, Organizations and Society, 32*, 701–734.

Orlikowski, W. J., & Baroudi, J. J. (1991). Studying Information Technology in Organizations: Research Approaches and Assumptions. *Information Systems Research, 2*(1), 1–28.

Oshri, I., Kotlarsky, J., & Gerbasi, A. (2015a). Strategic Innovation Through Outsourcing: The Role of Relational and Contractual Governance. *The Journal of Strategic Information Systems, 24*(3), 203–216.

Oshri, I., Kotlarsky, J., & Willcocks, L. (2015b). *The Handbook of Global Outsourcing and Offshoring*. London: Palgrave.

Parkhe, A. (1993). Strategic Alliances Structuring: A Game-Theoretic and Transaction Cost Examination of Interfirm Cooperation. *Academy of Management Journal, 36*(4), 794–829.

Plugge, A., & Bouwman, H. (2015). Understanding Collaboration in Multisourcing Arrangements: A Social Exchange Theory Perspective. In *International Workshop on Global Sourcing of Information Technology and Business Processes* (pp. 171–186). Cham: Springer.

Plugge, A., & Janssen, M. (2014, March). Governance of Multivendor Outsourcing Arrangements: A Coordination and Resource Dependency View. In *International Workshop on Global Sourcing of Information Technology and Business Processes* (pp. 78–97). Cham: Springer.

Poppo, L., & Zenger, T. R. (2002). Do Formal Contracts and Relational Governance Function as Substitutes or Complements. *Strategic Management Journal, 23*, 707–725.

Poster, M. (1990). *The Mode of Information: Poststructuralism and Social Context.* Cambridge: Polity.

Prahalad, C., & Hamel, G. (1990). The Core Competence of the Corporation. *Harvard Business Review, 68*(3), 79–91.

Preston, A., Chua, W. F., & Neu, D. (1997). The Diagnosis-Related Group-Prospective Payment System and the Problem of the Government of Rationing Health Care to the Elderly. *Accounting, Organizations and Society, 22*(2), 147–164.

Pruitt, D. (1981). *Negotiation Behavior*. New York: Academic Press.

Quinn, J. B., & Hilmer, F. G. (1994). Strategic Outsourcing. *Sloan Management Review, 35*(4), 43–55.

Rose, N. (1996). *Inventing Our Selves: Psychology, Power and Personhood.* Cambridge: Cambridge University Press.

Rose, N., & Miller, P. (1992). Political Power Beyond the State: Problematics of Government. *British Journal of Sociology, 43*(2), 173–205.

Sabherwal, R. (1999). The Role of Trust in Outsourced IS Development Projects. *Communications of the ACM, 42*(2), 80–86.

Sahay, S., Nicholson, B., & Krishna, S. (2003). *Global IT Outsourcing – Software Development Across Borders*. Cambridge: Cambridge University Press.

Saunders, C. (2002). Outsourcing: A View from Those Doing the Work. In R. Hirschheim, A. Heinzl, & J. Dibbern (Eds.), *Information Systems Outsourcing: Enduring Themes, Emergent Patters, and Future Directions.* New York: Springer-Verlag.

Saunders, C., Gebelt, M., & Hu, Q. (1997). Achieving Success in Information Systems Outsourcing. *California Management Review, 39*(2), 63–79.

Sending, J. O., & Neumann, B. I. (2006). Governance to Governmentality: Analyzing NGOs, States, and Power. *International Studies Quarterly, 50*, 651–672.

Simon, H. (1957). *Models of Man*. New York: Wiley.

Smith, M., Mitra, S., & Narasihman, S. (1998). Information Systems Outsourcing: A Study of Pre-Event Firm Characteristics. *Journal of Management Information Systems, 15*(2), 61–93.

Srivastava, S., & Thompson, S. H. (2012). Contract Performance in Offshore Systems Development: Role of Control Mechanisms. *Journal of Management Information Systems, 29*, 115–158.

Thouin, M., Hoffman, J., & Ford, E. (2009). IT Outsourcing and Firm-Level Performance: A Transaction Cost Perspective. *Information & Management, 46*, 463–469.

Tompkins, J., Simonson, S., Tompkins, W., & Upchurch, B. (2006). Creating and Outsourcing Relationship. *Supply Chain Management Review, 10*(2), 52–58.

Uitermark, J. (2004). The Genesis and Evolution of Urban Policy: A Confrontation of Regulationist and Governmentality Approaches. *Political Geography, 24*(2), 137–163.

Vlaar, P., Van den Bosch, F., & Volberda, H. (2007). On the Evolution of Trust, Distrust, and Formal Coordination and Control in International Relationships: Toward an Integrative Framework. *Group & Organization Management, 32*, 407–429.

Wang, E. (2002). Transaction Attributes and Software Outsourcing Success: An Empirical Investigation of Transaction Cost Theory. *Information Systems Journal, 12*(2), 153–181.

Willcocks, L. (2006). Michel Foucault in the Social Study of ICTs: Critique and Reappraisal. *Social Science Computer Review, 24*(3), 274–295.

Willcocks, L., & Choi, C. J. (1995). Co-operative Partnership and Total IT Outsourcing: From Contractual Obligation to Strategic Alliance? *European Management Journal, 13*(1), 67–78.

Willcocks, L., Lacity, M., & Sauer, C. (Eds.). (2017). *Outsourcing and Offshoring Business Services*. Basingstoke: Palgrave Macmillan.

Willcocks, L., Oshri, I., & Kotlarsky, J. (Eds.). (2018). *Dynamic Innovation in Outsourcing*. London: Palgrave Macmillan.

Williamson, O. E. (1975). *Markets and Hierarchies Analysis and Antitrust Implications: A Study in the Economics of Internal Organization*. London: Collier-Macmillan.

Williamson, O. E. (1979). Transaction-Cost Economics: The Governance of Contractual Relations. *Journal of Law and Economics, 22*(2), 233–261.

Williamson, O. E. (1985). *The Economic Institutions of Capitalism*. New York: Free Press.

Williamson, O. (1991). Strategizing, Economizing, and Economic Organization. *Strategic Management Journal, 12*, 75–94.

Williamson, O. E. (1998). Transaction Cost Economics: How It Works; Where It Is Headed. *De Economist, 146*, 23–58.

Yakhlef, A. (1998). IT Outsourcing and the Construction of Accountable Worlds. *Organization, 5*(3), 425–446.

Zajac, E. J., & Olsen, C. P. (1993). From Transactional Cost to Transactional Value Analysis: Implications for the Study of Interorganizational Strategies. *Journal of Management Studies, 30*(1), 131–145.

Zand, D. (1972). Trust and Managerial Problem Solving. *Administrative Science Quarterly, 17*(2), 229–239.

Zuboff, S. (1988). *In the Age of the Smart Machine: The Future of Work and Power*. New York: Basic Books.

3

Inside Global Offshore Outsourcing in Insurance

Introduction

LION is a global financial institution offering a variety of products and services ranging from banking and insurance to asset management. It employs about 115,000 people and serves private, corporate, and institutional clients in more than 50 countries.[1] In the mid-2000s offshore outsourcing really took off, and this case study provides one example of a successful experience. In 2006 the savings and loan division of LION Netherlands initiated a major outsourcing agreement. The agreement was signed with FDL,[2] an organization that LION had already been co-operating with. At the time FDL was a leading outsourcing provider specializing in the financial industry. The company had a global presence and served more than 60 countries. The contract was on application development, support, and maintenance. The cost model appeared to be very efficient, as 70% of the labour was offshored to India, namely, in Bangalore and Chennai, and 30% was based in Amsterdam. The offshored service was delivered by an Indian supplier which was an FDL company.

[1] All figures relate to 2012.

[2] FDL is a made up acronym for the supplier company.

E. Lioliou, L. P. Willcocks, *Global Outsourcing Discourse*, Technology, Work and Globalization, https://doi.org/10.1007/978-3-319-74045-4_3

In their co-operation, the two organizations went through a 'get-to-know' period, where they faced various challenges that will be illustrated further on. Their venture, overall, progressed in a satisfactory manner for both sides. LION seemed to have chosen the right supplier for the services it was seeking to outsource. However, tensions appeared to arise as the period for contract renewal approached. We examine this period.

Outsourcing Decisions

A major outsourcing objective for LION was to achieve higher service quality for its savings and loan products. As will be illustrated, service quality played a major role during the supplier selection process and it constituted the primary reason for awarding the deal to FDL. In the contract with FDL, service quality was mentioned first among other objectives that LION wanted to achieve:

> *Following a strategic review of its savings products information technology requirements, LION has decided to outsource various functions to achieve improved service quality, scalability, value for money and cost reduction.*

This constituted a further indicator of the importance that LION placed on service quality.

In addition to service quality, Bamse (LION business manager) commented on scalability as an important outsourcing driver for LION:

> *The main drivers for outsourcing were quality and scalability. … In an organization like ours, if you only develop for your own organization you need people to do that of course and you have them on your payroll. And there are times when they do not have anything to do and there are times when they have too much to do. There is never a smooth line in the work. An outsourcing vendor has more flexibility in putting the right people, at the right time, in the right company.*

The contract with FDL was on application development, support, and maintenance services for savings and loan products. The contract started in 2006 and would run for five years.

For the selection of the outsourcing supplier, a formal RFP (request for proposal) procedure was followed. At the beginning there were five suppliers and three of them got short-listed: a Dutch, an Indian, and FDL which was an American company. In line with its outsourcing objectives, LION did not choose its outsourcing supplier based strictly on cost but placed more emphasis on the potential for the delivery of service quality. FDL was already doing a big part of the work that would be outsourced and had demonstrated a satisfactory competence in that work. A number of interviewees within LION commented that the prior good relationship between the two organizations, together with the satisfactory performance that FDL has been demonstrating, constituted the major reasons why FDL won the contract. This rationale was also reflected in the contract. As one client executive commented:

> *LION selected FDL to offer services based on responses provided by FDL to an RFP for the outsourcing of the applications for savings and based on past experiences in working with FDL.*

From the vendor's side, Haresh (account manager from FDL) recognized that LION chose to work with a low-risk rather than a low-cost outsourcing partner:

> *We made it very clear to LION that we are very trustworthy … the other suppliers were by far the cheapest in terms of cost savings, but we were by far the lowest risk because we had the skill set and we had a track record with LION. … This is what convinced LION to work with us.*

Client and Supplier Capabilities

In this section the capabilities of the client and the supplier are going to be illustrated. Client capabilities will be discussed based on the 'nine core IS capabilities' framework, by Willcocks and Craig (2008). Supplier capabilities will be outlined based on the 'twelve key supplier capabilities' framework, developed by Willcocks et al. (2011). For a more detailed illustration of these frameworks, please see the Appendices. From our interviews it appears that LION valued the technical capabilities of FDL. Ron (LION director) suggested that he regarded FDL as a trustworthy and dependable vendor. Marjike (LION senior manager) noted that in her view FDL is a technically superior organization. It is worth mentioning that a major reason why FDL won the LION contract in the first place was the fact that it had demonstrated significant technical expertise and knowledge.

FDL appeared to have a good understanding of the LION business processes and Jeremy (contract manager from FDL) seemed to play a key role in the management of the venture. Martin (LION service manager) elaborated on the role of Jeremy:

> *Jeremy came from LION and thus he knows very well our business and processes. He is also very good in giving announcements for new projects and rough estimations. He is able to do this because he knows our processes and he knows what is possible in the FDL architecture. … It is really positive that FDL knows and understands our business processes … they know for sure how our business is designed and what our needs are. … So in a case of escalation when we call Jeremy, he understands the priority of it and he will try to do everything he can to deal with it. … The knowledge he has is particularly significant for our venture.*

Furthermore, FDL appeared to have a very flexible operating model and particularly clear working practices. FDL appeared to have demonstrated a great competency in accommodating to requirement changes by LION. Jeremy (contract manager from FDL) elaborated on this issue:

> *The difficulty starts when LION as a client is changing the requirements and that is the most difficult situation in our offshore outsourcing model. Sending the plan, sending the requirements … and then it starts. … Because from the moment you have the signatures on paper, they start changing the rules (laughter). … And we have shown that we are flexible and we can handle a lot but at a certain point it becomes impossible.*

Jeremy further explained that in the past, FDL had faced some issues when LION was changing its requirements, especially in relation to the involvement of the Indian supplier, but now they have set down a very clear procedure:

> *What happens is that LION changes its requirements and the people in India say "yes, yes, yes" because that is their culture. But in essence they cannot address the problems. So for that, the change in requirements needs to go via our FDL office to make sure that everybody understands and you are changing the requirements because the Indian side says "yes" but then you cannot make it. So that is described very clearly in the working practices document.*

Regarding LION's capabilities, while LION had some knowledge of the systems that FDL would be handling, it does not appear that it had enough retained management capability. It actually seems that the outsourcing venture has been successful managerially because there was expert knowledge and familiarity with the business on the part of FDL. Marjike (LION senior manager) noted that in her view the contract management capability of LION should be improved:

> *On the level of contract management we need to professionalize still. We are a very big organization and we have a number of different disciplines. Sometimes it is difficult to really get close to each other within LION. Going outside is even more difficult. So the co-operation with our vendor management organizations has to grow. The contract management is still an issue.*

Rajesh (consultant from FDL) highlighted that in LION there were severe issues in identifying their business requirements. This in effect made the job of FDL very challenging:

> *Proper requirements management was not done properly. Even project management may not have a clue about what they really want. … It is difficult for them to collect their system requirements and turn it into a business requirement and send it to us actually.*

Thus it appears that LION was getting away with not having a properly set-up retained capability and they were helped by the competencies of the supplier and the prior knowledge that the supplier had of the LION organization.

Contract (Master Services Agreement and Project Descriptions)

LION and FDL signed a Master Services Agreement (MSA) which constituted an umbrella contract framing individual project descriptions. The MSA mentioned that LION considered FDL as a company with excellent skills and major outsourcing expertise, including in offshore ventures. The structure of the MSA was as follows:

1. Agreement structure
    (a) Definitions
    (b) Contract structure
    (c) Interpretations
2. Service provision
    (a) Service scope: LION is expected to perform its respective obligations in relation to the specific project description but also in accordance with the rules set out in the MSA.
    (b) Service performance: LION is expected to provide the service in relation to each project in accordance with the service definition, time frames, and any other obligations that may be set out for individual projects. Furthermore, a review of the FDL's performance will take place in accordance with the time frames that each project entails and in any case once every calendar month during the transition period for a project and once every six months (at the request of LION). This review will include an examination of FDL's performance of the services, including performance against relevant project exhibits, as well as an assessment of procedures and processes to improve and/maintain performance.
    (c) Changes to services
    (d) Allocation of resources: in the case that LION does not use the entire contracted volume of services for a particular project, it maintains the right to allocate the unused volume of services to any other project.
3. Further obligations
    (a) Supplier obligations
    (b) LION obligations
4. Intellectual property rights
    (a) LION materials and LION data
    (b) Supplier materials
    (c) Deliverables

Table 3.1 LION and FDL engagement model

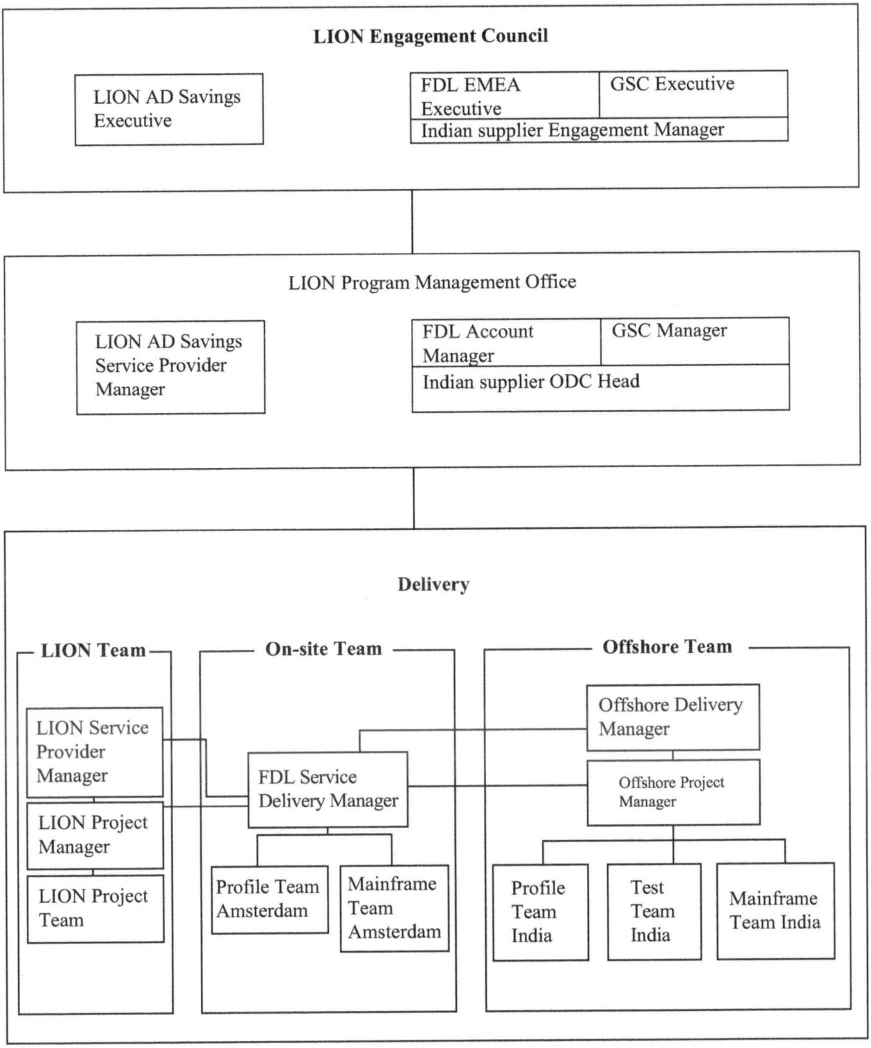

5. Governance

   (a) Engagement model (Table 3.1)
   (b) Dispute escalation: any dispute will be settled according to the dispute escalation procedures set out in the particular project. Meanwhile, LION and FDL will continue to carry out their

respective obligations, in relation to the provision of services under all other projects not related to the dispute.

6. Charges and VAT
7. Pricing
8. Taxes
9. Term
10. Initial term
11. Renewal and extension
12. Project term
13. Termination
    (a) Termination for cause: any of the two parties can terminate the MSA in the case that (a) the other party has committed a material breach of the MSA that is irremediable; (b) the other party has committed a material breach of the MSA which is remediable and has failed to remedy the breach within twenty (20) business days of receiving notice of the breach; (c) any of the parties commits a series of breaches and in each case the other party fails to remedy the breach within twenty (20) business days of receiving notice, and collectively the unremedied breaches constitute a material breach of the MSA; and (d) if the performance by one of the parties in relation to one or more of its obligations becomes permanently impossible and affects the provisions of services.
    (b) Step-in rights
    (c) Termination for convenience
    (d) Termination for insolvency
    (e) Termination for regulatory change
    (f) Post-termination
14. Warranties
    (a) Mutual warranties
    (b) Supplier warranties
15. Indemnities
    (a) LION's intellectual property rights (IPR) infringement indemnity
    (b) Supplier's IPR infringement indemnity

16. Liability
    (a) Exclusions
    (b) Liability cap
    (c) Invalidity
    (d) Claim expiration
    (e) Duty to mitigate
17. Compliance
18. Confidentiality and data protection
19. Benchmarking: LION may initiate a benchmarking process to compare (a) the charges payable for all the services against the prices achieved by the industry for equivalent service provision and (b) the service levels against those offered within the industry for equivalent services to those received by LION, including FDL's performance against those service levels.
20. Escrow agreement
21. Parent company guarantee

Regarding individual project descriptions, there was a specific template needed to be filled in. The template of the project description may be followed by project exhibits, which may address issues such as:

- Definition of scope of initial services relevant to the project
- Service levels and credits to be applied when particular levels of performance are not met
- Transition timetable and process
- Human resource information—setting out names of required 'key personnel' and other personnel or staffing requirements that are agreed by the two organizations for a project
- Charges
- Details of communication lines between the LION, FDL, and potentially other sub-contractors, including committees, monitoring, and reviews
- Escalation process for conflicts
- Exit obligations and assistance to be provided by FDL following expiry or termination of a particular project
- Form of change request
- Regulatory requirements

Haresh (account manager from FDL) underlined the importance of the contract in keeping the outsourcing venture by emphasizing that people may change roles and/or organizations, but the contract is there for steering the agreement:

> *Whatever the contract, it stays longer than individuals who run the business … either within LION or within the vendors. … The contract is thus very important and I think we worked quite a lot, about four to five months, purely on making the contract sufficiently equipped for LION and also for FDL.*

The MSA itself appeared to have a clearly defined scope of application development, maintenance, and support set of services. The service levels in relation to these services, as well as a methodology against which the supplier's performance is going to be assessed, were also thoroughly described. However, as happens with most contracts in the outsourcing industry, setting out a fixed set of requirements was hardly feasible. On this issues Boris (LION lawyer) noticed:

> *After the assessment of services you are supposed to have an idea of the scope … but this is never the case within LION, because scope can change until you have signed the contract and after. … So one of the big issues with any contract is that you need fixed requirements. If you know that they are hard to fix, like the LION case, you need a very firm change process and you have to stick to that.*

Boris (LION lawyer) also noted the importance of documentation in keeping track of the outsourcing venture, especially during any changes in processes:

> *All these changes may have a significant overrun both in time and money … then the outsourcing parties come to legal and say that the other party did not stick to these requirements. … Well yes, but what did you as a client do in between? Did you record all your communication with the supplier? Do you have minutes of meetings? Do you have call sheets? What do you have in order to substantiate your position?*

Regarding the role of penalties in the outsourcing venture, Bamse (LION business manager) appeared rather against the practice of imposing penalties in order to discipline the supplier:

If you have to go to the contract and look at the penalty part, you do not have a good relationship. In this case there is certainly something wrong and probably you can go with your legal team and you might be right but you will not benefit your long-term goals as an organization. That is a very confronting thing because a lot of people work very hard to think of good penalty clauses but I personally do not believe in them. It will not work in the long-term. Probably you need to them when there is a divorce coming basically … but you do not need them for a good relationship and to work together.

Martin (LION service manager) highlighted that a major problem that came out of the contractual agreement with FDL was the fact that the volume of services that LION needs had changed because of the economic climate affecting the financial industry. LION had contracted more hours to FDL than it needed and this was going to be a major sticking point to be raised during the renegotiation of the contract:

In the contract it was agreed that we could get a fixed amount of hours per year from FDL. And we had the strange situation that we needed to take hours from FDL and we have no projects where they can be delivered. So we paid more than we received from FDL. It is thus a challenge to look forward and to make an agreement that can sustain also these kind of economic situations, where we have a lower load of projects … currently we need to ask FDL to do projects and there are no projects.

Ron (LION director) as well as Sandro and Daniel (LION contract managers) emphasized that the changing volume of services that LION requires because of the recession constituted a major issue to be discussed in the negotiations of the renewal of the contract with FDL.

Relationship Between LION and FDL

LION started its outsourcing venture with FDL in 2006. Each organization valued the reputation and prestige of the other. Our interviewees in FDL characterized LION as high-profile customer and Ron (LION director) suggested that this is for two reasons: firstly, LION was one of the top three financial institutions and thus it adds to a vendor's credibility to have LION as a client. Secondly, LION was a big user of the Profile software. Thus, in addition to LION Netherlands, all LION Direct companies were basically using Profile.

While LION and FDL had a supplier-client relationship before signing their outsourcing arrangement, there was still a period during which the two organizations were getting familiarized with each other's operations, processes, and objectives. Bamse (LION business manager) illustrated:

> *At the beginning you start off by looking at each other, searching for ways to work together, challenging each other, questioning why the supplier can not be cheaper or can not work faster and so on. … I have been in a few meetings between LION and FDL back then which where tough meetings, because we did not know how the other person or the other company worked and we had different expectations and different visions which had not been communicated in the right way.*

Bamse (LION business manager) brought an example where LION realized that FDL did not have a good understanding of its needs and objectives:

> *We had a program integrating Postbank and LION Bank and at a certain time, while we thought that FDL knew why we were doing the project, what our goals where, what our timelines where, what we expected from them, we realized that this was not the case. While we thought we had communicated that in a very good way, mainly through the IT department, we recognized that we needed to go and tell them what the program was about. Someone from the business, who had nothing to do with IT, explained to them our commercial idea and the reasons we wanted to do the merger. We did spend some time telling our story, answering questions, explaining why were doing this program.*

In discussing how LION was exercising control over FDL, Martin (LION service manager) highlighted the role of retained knowledge. He emphasized that an outsourcing client should not be using its retained knowledge in order to find solutions on behalf of the supplier but merely for controlling purposes:

You need to have some basic understanding of what your suppliers are delivering ... you need to check them and to control them. It is a challenge not to use the knowledge of the things that we outsource to FDL. ... The purpose is to use that knowledge to challenge FDL and not to find solutions ourselves.

Regarding the development of the relationship between LION and FDL, Bamse (LION business manager) mentioned that there had been some difficult points. He gave an example where they had run into serious cost and time overruns and emphasized on how the two organizations work together and smoothed their operation:

As an example, before we outsourced we would develop a new product and it would cost us 800,000 Euros and it would take a throughput time of nine months. And the claim from FDL when we were negotiating the contract was "we can do it in a short period of time for you, we can do it cheaper". So the first time we developed a product, they came back and it cost 1.2 million and it took them twelve months. Anyone can imagine what kind of clash happened with LION at that moment. This was not what LION anticipated. ... LION was very much in the offensive mode and they reacted very defensively.

Bamse (LION business manager) noted that this was a case where the two organizations had to go back to their contract and LION actually considered exercising penalty clauses:

At that time we went back to the contract to find out what we had agreed in terms of penalties when FDL does not deliver on time. So it started to become a clash and we did not trust each other. ... Certainly there was no partnership.

On the other hand, Martin (LION service manager) highlighted that FDL was very transparent and very open in its communications with LION and this was a very significant factor in the development of their relationship:

FDL had an open calculation model with us where they were fully transparent in terms of what is the cost of their front office in the Netherlands and what is the cost of the offshored part of the deal in India. ... In every decision we take and every forecast we do for what is the amount that we need for system maintenance or system development, they are always very transparent and they give us the opportunity to co-decide with them. … We know what we pay for, and we openly discuss the economics behind about it.

Ron (LION director) gave an example where the two companies worked very transparently on their agreement and demonstrated a partnership-style behaviour. He explained that LION was facing a big pressure to reduce its costs and thus it was forced to cut down on systems development and subsequently on the hours they would need from FDL. He suggested that the two companies had a very honest discussion on the salaries of the Indian and Dutch employees (including the cost of lay-offs) and they changed the cost-structure of the contract accordingly:

Last year in 2008 until the middle of this year, like all banks, we had a huge cost reduction … one of the decisions we took was to seriously cut back on systems development, which of course reduced the number of hours we would need from FDL. They came back to us and said "The India part is not a problem. In India you simply say to your people going to the office that you do not need them any more and that you will give them a.call whenever you need them again. So there is an immediate ability to reduce labour costs." … In the Netherlands the story is different because you first have to pay them to leave and then again if you would like to hire them again … so it is an expensive process. So they said "Isn't it a good idea if you think that this cost pressure is a temporary thing to do the cost reduction in India? Of course the mix of employees based offshore versus the ones based onshore will be different, resulting in an increase on the average price per hour … but in total, the business case is better. … That is under the condition, you as a customer, think this is a temporary thing." We discussed this together and decided to keep the people in the Netherlands. … And this is a very transparent way—and I think an example of partnership-where they said "lets openly discuss the choices we have".

Manoj (programme manager from FDL) demonstrated that there has been a significant level of co-operation in the outsourcing venture between the Indian team, the onshore team, and LION:

In each project, we have learned lessons. We see the improvement opportunities and we keep all these lessons learned as part of our project repository. We look back, we evaluate the project and we write down all those things as part of the project evaluation report. Every fortnight we have a working practices improvement meeting with LION. Maybe for their part they have some new things which could have been done in a better way. We are constantly looking for improvement opportunities.

Bamse (LION business manager) noted, however, that it was a constant challenge for the two outsourcing partners to have a good relationship:

FDL wants to make money, we want to make money so we want our costs as low as possible and they want to earn as much as possible. So there is always a difference in the way you think and this is normal. You have to work together with that and see where you are, the good places where you are both happy but that is a continuing challenge.

In FDL they seemed to understand that their familiarity with the Dutch regulatory environment worked on their behalf. Jeremy (contract manager form FDL) mentioned that this was a major reason why, in his view, LION considered FDL a dependable outsourcing partner. Jeremy noted:

We have a lot of experience and we know the regulations. … This is very important to LION. … They are also happy because they know the application is selected by other big banks as well. Consequently FDL is a trustful company and this is a bigger advantage than the competitor aspect of sharing the information.

As an example of the influence of regulatory issues on the outsourcing of LION in the Netherlands, Ron (LION director) commented:

Back in 2006, we tried to outsource our securities business as well but it failed because it was so much driven by local legislation that we hardly could find any partner who had experience in the Dutch fiscal area that we felt safe enough to outsource that to. So otherwise that would have gone well.

However, the familiarity of FDL with the Dutch regulatory environment was not the only factor that creates dependency on FDL. Sandro (LION contract manager) noted that the more FDL tried to penetrate LION, the more that important lock-in issues were created for LION:

> *FDL is broadening its scope so they can have a sort of global banking platform which they can offer to the market. … Regarding LION, the more FDL penetrates LION, the higher the chance that LION cannot get rid of FDL. They are trying to create a lock-in situation … from a supplier point of view that is a good tactic.*

A number of interviewees commented on the cultural issues between the on-site and the offshore team. Language barriers were reported as a major cultural problem that posed great challenges. As indicative example, Rajesh (consultant from FDL) noted that understanding the LION requirements was in some instances particularly difficult:

> *The thing is that Dutch people, while they are nice and helpful, they have a tendency to translate the Dutch language to English and they always have their own Dutch words in their text. Understanding the requirements has been a big challenge for us in many instances.*

Similarly, Marjike (LION senior manager) noted:

> *There is a significant language barrier because we are not native English and the people in India are not native English speakers either, so sometimes you really have to search for what both parties mean when they say something.*

On the positive side, Marjike (LION senior manager) noted that the offshore team in India is very approachable and willing to provide their assistance:

> *What is very good is that they are on the floor. They are very reachable. They are also there when you need them … even at night time, there are often times that we need them at three o'clock in the morning and they are willing to be here for us. They are very willing, I must say.*

A major cultural difference appears to be that the Indian team was not as proactive as LION wanted them to be. A number of interviewees within LION commented on this issue. Martin (LION service manager) noted that, to his frustration, although the Indian people had good technical competencies, they did not exploit them in order to come back with a new proposal for LION:

> *The Indian people are really on the working floor, so they can hear what the dynamic is ... they could use that more to enlarge their own contracts. They are not very good at seeing opportunities and work these opportunities out for themselves to come back with a concrete proposal to us. ... There has never been an instance that they will say "Hey, I think this is going wrong in your organization and we could offer this kind of service to you". ... This kind of participation is not there. ... They are only good in just doing what we ask them.*

Marjike (LION senior manager) also noted this issue:

> *The Indian team does what we wrote down in our agreement. ... It is not that they will do less, but they are not proactive ... they are more reactive than the people that were within LION and this is a major difference.*

Liam (LION demand manager) highlighted that while the performance of FDL was good, this was not enough, since LION was looking for a proactive attitude from its outsourcing supplier:

> *I think they are confident that they will close another agreement because they do the work ... and the work they do it perfectly, no issues about that. But this is really not enough, they need to be much more proactive.*

On a similar vein, Martin (LION service manager) noted that FDL was fulfilling its obligations towards LION to a very good extent, but he did not appear to think that FDL was a partner to LION:

> *FDL is very good in doing what they need to do. ... They have a very good contract management organization, knowing the contract by heart. ... They will do perfectly what we agreed and will not do what we have not agreed. The issue is that colleagues do not just do what was agreed. ... If FDL was a partner they should also do what they think is necessary for LION. ... Our people who are managing the contract of FDL, maybe sometimes think that FDL will think for us and do more than just the asked things ... for this reason there might be gaps for these points in the relationship.*

Likewise, Daniel (LION contract manager) pointed out that FDL was not putting any emphasis on developing the LION business:

I think that FDL sees LION as an organization where they could get more turnover from … but I do not think they consider LION to be a partner because the external market has changed … and they are not thinking how they can make their contract suited to the changed environment.

Sandro (LION contract manager) further noted that in his view strategic partnerships required for some kind of mutuality in running a venture, and this did not exist between LION and any of its vendors including FDL:

We do not have strategic vendors within LION because when you have a real strategic vendor this means that you are actually running along (together) in business.

Liam (LION demand manager) very vividly explained how he expected the relationship between the two organizations to grow. He indicated that in the first year of the venture the two organizations learned how each other worked and they basically set out the processes. In the second year, the two organizations worked in order to improve these processes. Up to that point, he felt that the venture was progressing alright, but to his frustration, FDL did not take the opportunity to further grow into the business of LION and demonstrate a more proactive behaviour:

At the start we defined a lot of procedures, we had to learn how all these procedures worked. For instance, if we ask for a change from FDL, it has to go through a specific procedure here within LION. … It has to go through the procurement department, it has to go through the finance department … another guy has to give approval on that … etc etc … and then it goes to FDL. And FDL gives us a proposal on our request for change and this is how it goes … we all had to learn how these procedures work. … That was the first year, we were learning. … The second year was to grow into a more mature level and to improve these procedures because what we saw is that some of these procedures did not work or could be more efficient. … In the third year the plan was to let FDL grow more into our organization and to see by themselves what kind of work will come and give us proactive advice on what we should do. … But the situation today is still that FDL is in a reactive mode. … That means … "we ask, they run … we ask, they run".

LION entered a renegotiating period towards the end of 2010. There were significant issues for renegotiation. According to Bamse (LION business manager), the situation of LION had changed a lot since the time that the contract with FDL was signed. LION had run into a difficult financial situation potentially affecting its very existence. Bamse (LION business manager) explained he hoped that FDL would demonstrate an understanding of the situation of LION and help them improve their cost-structure:

> *Our world changed substantially, so we have to do something. We need you guys to help us otherwise we are just going to be broke and there is no deal anymore … then there is no work for you to do. … We need to go on as a company, we need to lower our costs, please help us.*

While FDL was doing a good job, there were some questions about whether they could continue in this, because LION was the only real (European) customer they had and FDL was a US operation. Ron (LION director) said that in the past, the outsourcing of securities at LION failed because the previous supplier could not maintain its operations in the Dutch market:

> *They were too optimistic about acquiring new customers and they underestimated the investments needed. We did not bring them the latest up to date infrastructure because we knew two years in advance we would outsource it. So that is not in particular the area where you start investing a lot. So they underestimated the money needed for keeping that infrastructure up to date and make it into a market standard to acquire new customers. So all in all, they were too optimistic about their business and their ability to acquire new customers and like Americans do, if the water gets too cold, they said "we pull out".*

Ron further emphasized his concern about the American way of doing business:

> *That's the difference between a European way of doing business and Americans. They put a toe into the water and when it is cold, they pull back and they simply go off to home again. And Europeans tend to remain longer.*

FDL Performance

A number of interviewees within LION noted that their company was satisfied with the performance by FDL. More specifically, Ron (LION director) mentioned that, in a multi-supplier set-up, this was the outsourcing venture that he felt most happy with. He further explained:

> *There has never occurred any major escalation as far as I am aware of, which is quite unique in outsourcing, because most of the time you have all kinds of stuff you have to discuss. But in this case, it is running very smoothly … there were hardly any escalations or disagreements on major things … they certainly seem to be in control starting at the front end to the back end and back again. … No big things in terms of time to market, no big things in terms of how do we prioritize all the projects, no big things in terms of double cost of ownership.*

On a similar basis, Marjike (LION senior manager) noted:

> *I asked my people if we could choose again, would we go with FDL again? Their answer was yes … although we have had some problems in the operation, they said yes.*

Marjike (LION senior manager) further suggested that her company outsourced one more system to FDL the previous month, which was a major indication that LION was satisfied with the performance of FDL.

LION managed to get the return on its investment earlier than it had expected. Liam (LION demand manager) suggested that the estimated cost of the outsourcing project was about €4.5 million and the expectation of LION was to start making profit on this project within two years and a half. In less than two years, however, LION made its return on investment. More specifically Liam (LION demand manager) commented:

> *The investment we had to do in order to outsource the equivalent of 40 FTEs (Full time employees) was about 4.5 million Euros. That was the total cost of this outsourcing project. The knowledge transfer, the reorganization of the department, getting rid of the existing staff, all those costs together was about 4.5 million. In the business case, based on the yearly workload, we calculated that this investment should be in two years and a half. This is what we thought*

when we were trying to decide if we should go ahead with this project or not. Afterwards we concluded that in less than two years we had already made this outsourcing deal into a profit.

Ron (LION director) identified three reasons why in his view the outsourcing venture progressed successfully: firstly, the time that LION outsourced to FDL coincided with a renewal of the system itself and thus LION did not outsource something messy. Secondly, FDL had already had knowledge of the Profile system. Thirdly, FDL has a practice of being transparent in their way of communication, even regarding calculations of cost.

However, while the performance of FDL had been satisfactory, within LION some managers questioned what was going to happen when they came up to contract renewal. As above, both Liam (LION demand manager) and Martin (LION services manager) expressed some doubt whether the renewal of the contract with FDL would be the right option. Nevertheless, it also appeared that the LION internal managers were trying to create a question mark around the suitability of FDL so that the renewal of their contract would not be seen as a non-competitive inevitability.

Ron (LION director) highlighted that a new supplier selection would be initiated where FDL would have to compete with other vendors in order to be awarded the contract:

We will do a new partner selection process, where of course FDL does have the big advantage of a three year period where they have done business with us, but having said that, they are just one of the vendors that we will look at … because maybe there are other companies in the world that have developed even better skills over the period we were with FDL.

It appeared that LION was trying to create some competition between FDL and other vendors, in order to keep pricing as low as possible. While this was a very good tactic to put pressure on the vendor, in this case it appeared that FDL was aware of its very strong advantages over any competition, including the demonstration of familiarity with the Dutch regulatory environment and the knowledge of the business and processes of LION.

4

Inside Global Outsourcing in Banking and Finance

Introduction

GIB[1] is a major European bank with operations in more than 75 countries spread across Europe, the USA, and the Asia-Pacific.[2] In 2012 it had more than 80,000 employees and provided a range of investment and financial services to individuals, corporations, and institutional clients. PV is a major IT company that provides a variety of products and services including software, BPO, and infrastructure management services and it is one of the primary vendors of GIB. PV is based in India; it employs about 55,000 people and is one of the country's largest IT service exporters. GIB and PV have a long-standing outsourcing relationship. The project under examination was called X-RAY and had three objectives:

1. Supporting a set of non-strategic applications under one managed service

[1] GIB and PV are made up acronyms to anonymize the bank and the service provider.

[2] Figures all relate to 2012.

E. Lioliou, L. P. Willcocks, *Global Outsourcing Discourse*, Technology, Work and Globalization, https://doi.org/10.1007/978-3-319-74045-4_4

2. Having a fixed cost for maintaining and running these applications
3. Decommissioning any of these non-strategic applications where appropriate

The project started officially on August 1, 2008, and ran under a three-year contract. The formal governance between GIB and PV was run by their Master Services Agreement (MSA) which was an umbrella contract that encompassed individual project descriptions, which were essentially individual contractual agreements. The outsourcing venture between the two organizations was to a major extent managed on the basis of the contractual obligations of each party, but the relational element had been particularly strong as well.

Outsourcing Decisions

The following sections provide a detailed overview of GIB's objectives when entering into the outsourcing arrangement and the scope of the outsourcing project, as well as issues around the selection of the supplier.

Outsourcing Objectives

Regarding the drivers of GIB to outsource, our interviews indicated that these could be grouped into the following categories:

- Cost
- The focus on core competencies
- Scalability
- Access to talent and expertise

Although within GIB the focus on core competencies, scalability, and access to talent and expertise was acknowledged as important drivers for outsourcing, the vast majority of interviewees recognized cost as the primary driver. On this issue Mark (GIB lawyer) noted: "We would always argue that cost should not be the primary driver, but there is no doubt that it is, particularly in the current climate."

Outsourcing Scope

Initially X-RAY would host 150 from around 1000 applications that the bank had within its IT operations. These applications were servicing a group of users that did all the back office and some middle office activities within investment banking. Typically these applications were at the lower end of the investment scale. The idea was that by establishing a managed service on these non-strategic applications, more GIB management time could go on the more strategic applications. Later on, after transitioning these 150 applications—which was achieved around January 2009—the project entered a second phase where 150 more applications would be transferred to X-RAY.

Supplier Selection

The process of supplier selection went through a number of stages. Originally, there were 12 vendors on the list. Over a three-month period, these were reduced to five. Those five vendors were asked to present their approach to running a managed service based on 140 applications. Based on these presentations, the candidate vendors were reduced to three. The bank created an invitation to tender for a fixed price deal for three years.

GIB set some clear requirements that the suppliers were expected to meet. One of these requirements was a very flexible charging structure. Andrea (GIB Vendor decisions/Relationship management) noted:

> *The difficulty with many contracts is change and the cost of change. So, you may go into a contract thinking that you are going to put in 140 applications and you agree on a certain price with the vendor … but then what happens if these applications become 130 or 150? How do you actually cost that? And do you actually get a reduction if it goes down to 100? You need to have a financial structure in terms of the commercial model to allow for that.*

Each application was priced individually within a cost matrix. In this matrix there was a set of 27 prices for the different applications. Each application was rated according to various criteria. If an application did not go into or got out of X-RAY, GIB would not pay for it. The cost was also fixed for three years. Additionally, when additional applications got into X-RAY, these would be priced on the same basis.

Andrea (GIB Vendor decisions/Relationship management) noted:

> *With this pricing structure we are not exploited by the vendor because they have got no ability to exploit it. So that was one of the fundamental corner stones of the contract.*

IBM and PV had accepted the flexible cost-structure that GIB was proposing. Infosys did not and this was the primary reason why it was put out of the contest. However, there was another important requirement by GIB that Infosys did not accept. GIB wanted a programme-wide service level agreement (SLA) on things like response times to incidents. Infosys did not accept this condition. Andrea (GIB Vendor decisions/Relationship management) noted that the Infosys' statement on this issue was "We will tell you after six months of running the contract what your SLA is".

Thus, while Infosys bid the lowest price, they did not manage to get the business. Andrea (GIB Vendor decisions/Relationship management) added:

> *They left themselves a lot of room for manoeuvre to increase the price later … the concern was that the price they bid was not the price it would be because within months you would have other things being brought back in. I'd made it clear to them, and all the vendors during the bid process that they had to come, I didn't want them to come to the final bid, in terms of their submittal with any exceptions. If they were uncertain about anything they had to come to me and say "Right, you know, we're concerned about how much support we need to provide on a particular application because we haven't got enough detail therefore we are going to cost it higher". I would want them to tell me that so we can have further discussions with the people that had run that application and try and eliminate that risk. So that was the emphasis.*

GIB also placed a big emphasis on people. In other words, it did matter to GIB that the people who were included in the bids from each vendor are the same people who would be included in the management of the service later on. This was the issue that ruled IBM out. The IBM bid team did not include people who would run the project afterwards. Andrea (GIB Vendor decisions/Relationship management) noted:

> *Whereas with PV and with Infosys, the people who were running the bid were probably at least 80% of the people who would actually run the project afterwards. With IBM it was probably 40% that were involved and I'm talking about the top management positions. If you're establishing a managed service you have to have confidence in the managers that the vendor's putting there because they're the people you're going to deal with.*

Andrea (GIB Vendor decisions/Relationship management) further added:

> *So for the final presentation of the bid by each vendor had to send in the bid in advance and then they had to present to myself and the management team within this part of the bank, on the IT side. We asked that it was only people who were going to run the project from the vendor that could present. So you can see the problem probably already. … So Infosys and PV could put forward a very knowledgeable team to present to us because they had been involved all the way round. IBM started having to juggle people around so they had to get guys in from India, as did the other vendors, but people who'd never taken part in the two months previous work on putting the bid together. So in terms of their alignment with the project that we wanted, you know, they didn't give you confidence that they knew how they were going to do things and what we wanted because they hadn't been sufficiently involved. So that was an important mistake by IBM.*

However, this was not the only reason why IBM was ruled out. It appeared that IBM did not have expertise in this sort of projects. Andrea (GIB Vendor decisions/Relationship management) noted on this issue:

> *It would be their first major managed service contract within investment banking, so there was some apprehension that we would be the guinea pigs of that and therefore that would be risky.*

It also appeared that IBM tried to make promises the fulfilment of which would be highly improbable according to Andrea (GIB Vendor decisions/Relationship management):

IBM had too adventurous a transition timescale. So obviously you have to have, all of the three vendors bid a structured process in how they would take applications over, but the timescales varied. IBM was the fastest, they said they could transition 140 applications in four months. PV said it would be around about eight months and I think Infosys were around six months or so. Now four months for 140 applications just did not give us confidence that they would do it properly. It is not that you cannot transition it in that time because clearly you can, but how good will the support be after that period, I mean that is the thing. Because from the bank's point of view it is great to have a quick transition because we get the financial benefit sooner, but if the support we get at the end of that short transition period is poor you could lose far more money through errors.

Andrea (GIB Vendor decisions/Relationship management) emphasized that the project would be very complex. For this reason, GIB was alert to not falling for exaggerated promises like those by IBM. The supplier would have to undertake a number of applications of varying complexity from ten different countries, currently supported by three different vendors:

There were really practical sides to that, so you have a whole range of applications in terms of complexity and to take on a big complex application takes time, you know, typically it would take four or five months to take on a big application. To try and take on 140 in parallel, which is really what they were saying, just didn't sound credible because you've got to scale up the team immensely, you've got to go from zero to 100 people to take on 140 applications, as I say, spread around the world. It just didn't sound a practical proposition.

Andrea (GIB Vendor decisions/Relationship management) further underlined the knowledge that the bank had around these applications and how this enabled it not to fall for 'big promises':

We were also conscious that our users had been the victims of fast transitions before, you know, we worked with some vendors, because this is not the first change of vendor that many of these applications have gone through, this might be the second or third time that an application has changed hands. So we have a lot of longstanding staff on the business side who've seen it all before and seen it go wrong through hurried transitions.

Andrea (GIB Vendor decisions/Relationship management) also noted that some of the applications that PV was currently supporting took a two-month period of transition, while the previous vendor had taken only two weeks. However, this relatively long period gave the bank a solid basis for running the application:

> *Two weeks we know had caused so much pain for the end users that they said it was a two week transition but it was six months before they actually got a quality service from the previous vendor. We were conscious that we had to set ourselves up for success and success was not achieved through fast transitions that deliver poor service.*

Regarding the cost, Infosys was the cheapest. IBM was close to the price of Infosys, something that according to Andrea (GIB Vendor decisions/Relationship management) was a sign that IBM was trying very hard to get the business:

> *Even with an outsourced model, you would not feel that IBM would be as cheap as they came in. So you definitely knew they were hungry for the business.*

PV was the most expensive by far, yet GIB managed to bring it down to the IBM price. According to Bart (GIB director of risk), the negotiation period and the competition among the three vendors empowered GIB to close a good deal. Andrea (GIB Vendor decisions/Relationship management) made a similar comment: "We got the benefits for a good price with what we regarded as a safe vendor."

There were several reasons why PV was regarded as a safe vendor within GIB. Apart from the sensible transition plan that PV was suggesting, they already ran one third of the applications, including quite a complex set in New York. Andrea (GIB Vendor decisions/Relationship management) noted:

> *Risk-wise, going to PV was the lowest because we had got a price that was fixed at a good level, they did not have excuses about how they would raise it, they already had 50 of the 140 applications, and some of the more difficult ones, so*

> *that was quite safe. They had a sensible transition plan in terms of the duration and the people involved had lived and breathed the X-RAY initiative for a long time so they were totally in tune with what we wanted to do.*

Bart (GIB director of risk) added:

> *GIB maintained a long relationship with PV. ... We know PV very well ... the people, the management. .... We knew that support and maintenance of applications was something that they are good at.*

Client and Supplier Capabilities

In this section the capabilities of the client and the supplier are identified. In parallel to the LION-FDL case, client capabilities will be outlined based on the 'nine core IS capabilities' framework, by Willcocks and Craig (2008) and supplier capabilities will be illustrated based on the 'twelve key supplier capabilities' framework, developed by Willcocks et al. (2011).

GIB Capabilities

Leadership: GIB had a strong IT governance framework. Governance itself was facilitated by the organizational structure of IT. On this basis, all of the IT functions were linked to each of the businesses (e.g. there is front office IT which is aligned to the front office, there was market risk IT aligned to the market risk division, and so on). The role of IT was absolutely critical for the business at GIB. This was why there are a lot of business stakeholders responsible for the delivery of IT projects. The involvement of business stakeholders actually empowered the IT people and contributed to more efficient IT governance.

GIB had three very distinctive IT segments. These included front office (IT trading systems), middle office/support services IT (IT that supports the non-generating revenue systems of the bank, e.g. HR IT, audit, compliance, legal IT, risk IT), and infrastructure/hardware services (infrastructure enterprise services). Governance was heavily dependent on the type of the IT service. Front office IT was much more critical for the bank compared to middle office/support services and the infrastructure or hardware services. On this basis, front office systems required a governance that was flexible and enabled quick decision-making (and not, e.g. comprehensive analysis). But in HR IT, compliance IT, and so on, the governance structure was more rigid because there was a lot more time to make decisions.

It is worth noting that for banks, IT is of vital importance for their very own survival. Regarding GIB, if its IT systems failed and if there was no disaster recovery site to host its operations, GIB would survive only for two days. As Mark Millward (GIB lawyer) emphasized:

> *If we lost any of the actual management departments, we wouldn't make as much profit but the bank would continue. But if the IT systems fail and do not come back up online again it can have a catastrophic effect on the business.*

In addition to its major role for the maintenance of the very own operation of banks, IT constituted a basis for competitive edge in the banking industry. On this issue Mark (GIB lawyer) suggested:

> *Banks are financial institutions ... but actually we are IT houses, we are software houses. So the way we make our money is by sort of having better quality software which can maybe settle things more quickly and more cheaply than our competitors so we can underbid them on price for a particular service. IT is really important to us.*

Business systems thinking: GIB was thinking a lot of years ahead regarding where it wanted its business systems and corresponding IT architecture to be. More specifically, it had developed a 2012 programme, basically aimed at trying to map out the IT systems architecture two years in advance. In this way GIB sought to establish a clear vision of where its IT systems needed to be. However, envisioning where IT should be in the future is very challenging, because business requirements are changing continuously and IT has to be flexible enough in order to accommodate changing business requirements. Furthermore, within GIB there was the philosophy that IT had to align itself with where the money was being made. As an example, a lot of money in the financial sector was being made out of a lot of complex structured products (securitization). In the 18 months previous to our interviews, much more money was made from simple vanilla securities (foreign exchange, interest rate flow products).

Relationship building: According to a senior GIB manager, this was a key challenge for every bank. He suggested that a bank needed to have a strong project management team because they acted as a link between the business users and the IT teams. He also emphasized that GIB was doing well in terms of relationship building.

Architectural planning and design: Until recently, project managers and developers within GIB were taking care of duties related to the role of the architect. However, the company more recently began recruiting individuals specifically for the role of the architect. The aim was to be able to deliver increased scale and capability in order to meet the continually changing business challenges.

Making technology work: GIB had been effective in connecting business with IT. The IT people were facing a lot of challenges (e.g. the fact that the business people very often require a particular IT service very fast and it became hard for the IT people to communicate to them why certain IT issues could not be solved immediately). The company, however, was overall quite successful in connecting technology to business needs. According to Bart (GIB director of risk), in order to make technology work it was very critical that an organization maintained the right resource mix (i.e. obtains the right expertise) and it also followed what peer bank organizations were doing. He emphasized that especially in the financial sector it was very common among banks to follow what each one was doing. Bart (GIB director of risk) highlighted that achieving technological progress was important as long as particular advancements were being tailored to the business requirements. He vividly noted: "Making technological progress is great if it helps your business … otherwise it is useless".

Informed buying: The role of the MSAs was fundamental in making sure that GIB had a holistic view of what the overall relationship with each of its suppliers was. As will be further discussed, a challenge that GIB had been facing was to prevent suppliers from charging different prices to different business units of the bank across the globe. The implementation of MSAs was forcing suppliers into a very standardized, bank-wide, uniform set of rules and regulations. In other words, they enabled the relationship between different silos within a bank and a supplier to be standard. This standardization facilitated informed buying.

Contract facilitation: IT and the business were involved in contract facilitation by determining whether or not a vendor performed well. This assessment was being made on a quarterly basis. In essence, this assessment aimed to address not necessarily what was written in the contract but how much value each vendor was delivering to the business. Contract facilitation was a function that complemented contract monitoring within GIB.

Contract monitoring: GIB had a very integrated approach to contract monitoring and was trying to make sure that this function was taking place on a cross-division basis. The areas within the bank that were monitoring how well the vendor was able to meet its contractual obligations included the legal, the smart sourcing, and the global sourcing divisions. The legal division was trying to make sure that each of the vendors was meeting its contractual obligations from a purely legal perspective. Their assessment was completely independent of the vendor's performance or how the vendor was perceived to be performing. The smart sourcing division was aiming to focus less attention on the contract and put more emphasis on performance and the perception of how the vendor is performing. Again, this assessment had to be on the basis of the contract itself. The global sourcing division was working closely with the legal department to make sure that any demand revisions (or other amendments needed) were within the terms of the contract. The legal division tended to play a strong role in the drafting of the contract and then a periodic role in its monitoring. The smart and global sourcing divisions were more closely involved in the ongoing contract maintenance and monitoring functions.

Vendor development: A number of MSAs within GIB required from the vendor to develop in areas like performance, quality, speed, and so on. This requirement was built into these contracts. Furthermore, the process of vendor certification aimed to ensure that the vendor had the minimum level of capability in certain areas that have more to do with the vendor's infrastructure (such as security, business continuity, etc.). If the vendor did not reach these minimum levels of capability, it had to redevelop itself. The process of vendor certification was not related to the ability of a vendor to deliver its service.

In the case of PV, vendor development changed from developing in-house capability (DSL)[3] to forcing vendor development through contractual and relationship interactions. According to a number of interviewees within GIB, it appeared that PV had not developed itself fast enough.

PV Capabilities

Delivery and transformation capabilities: PV had a very strong capability in application support and maintenance. The organization had a smaller competence in application development. It appeared that at PV they were good at maintaining systems and not at building systems or fundamentally changing the architecture of a financial institution such as GIB. Carsten (GIB IBIT Sourcing and Vendor Management of IT portfolio): "PV does not have much thinking power … it tends to be a follower. … It does not look for innovative solutions."

Relationship competency: PV had been putting significant effort into the relationship with GIB because it was its major customer. More specifically, it tried to gear its business model towards serving GIB better. It appeared, however, at the time of interviews that GIB was looking at other vendors as well. In the past few years PV had lost a significant stake to Indian as well as Russian vendors within GIB. GIB had been very honest about moving to other vendors.

Formal Governance

Intra-group Sourcing Versus Outsourcing: Implications for Governance

There were two types of sourcing within the bank. One option was sourcing from another business unit within the bank's group of companies.

[3] DSL is an acronym for the internal IT department.

This was referred to as intra-group sourcing. Another option was to source from an external organization that did not belong to the bank's group of companies and thus performed outsourcing in its classic sense.

With intra-group sourcing, problems would be managed by corporate governance. The idea was that if there was some sort of conflict between the two parties and this was not covered by the contract as you go up the management chain of both parties trying to resolve that dispute, you would eventually get to the same person. Thus from a corporate governance perspective, that person was able to—in effect—make the decision as to how that dispute down the chain should be resolved. This was a major difference in the relationship management of intra-group and outsourcing arrangements. On this issue Mark (GIB lawyer) noted:

> *In an intra-group arrangement, if things go bad, one company is never going to sue another company, it is always going to be resolved by the Chief Executive or his delegates at the top. Whereas if an outsourcing does go truly wrong, there is no relationship, you have a bad contract, you may end up having to resort to the courts as a way of resolving your dispute, which is a very, very messy process.*

Mark (GIB lawyer) added:

> *The only thing I've seen which was a kind of hybrid is, it's taking a small stake in the supplier so as a shareholder it might secure you a Board seat which at least might give you some influence over the management of the company.*

As illustrated in Table 4.1, GIB follows the same procedures for intra-group sourcing and outsourcing supplier issues:

Outsourcing Policy

The standards of the outsourcing policy had to be adhered during all phases of the outsourcing life cycle: from the concept and deal phases to the implementation, as well as monitoring and governance phases.

The outsourcing policy insisted on extensive documentation requirements for all outsourcing projects. The idea was that to enable the control, quality management, and risk management of outsourcing projects,

Table 4.1 The intra-group outsourcing model of GIB

Governance Control

Outsourcing Phases	**Initiation**	**Service Provision**	**Expiration**
	Outsourcing Policy Agreement + Project Descriptions	Outsourcing Policy + Master Services	
	Major stakeholders (departments): - Operational risk - Compliance - Legal - Controlling/Finance - Tax - Insurance - IT security - Data protection/ Privacy - Regulatory reporting - Human Resources	(Vendor Governance and Annual Review)	

written documentation of all key deliverables and decisions was of fundamental importance during the entire outsourcing life cycle.

All outsourcing projects were entered into a global database. The information on this database had to remain up to date during the entire outsourcing life cycle for all projects. The documentation file for an outsourcing project had to include the general information of the outsourcing project, as well as a description of the business case, contractual documentation, risk estimation, risk assessment, and all significant changes. The documentation was essential for both internal and external auditors and thus its importance was fundamental for all outsourcing arrangements.

The purpose of the outsourcing policy was to ensure that an appropriate review and control were put in place in relation to the actual outsourcing of the IT function. The processes of review and control were set by the outsourcing policy in such a way that the interested internal departments were given the opportunity to review the transaction before the contract is signed.

A number of departments were involved in this process. These included:

- Compliance
- Legal
- Controlling/finance
- Tax
- Insurance
- IT security
- Data protection/privacy
- Regulatory reporting
- Human resources

Each of these departments had its own policies and requirements. The project manager in charge of the outsourcing venture had to make sure that each of these departments did not have issues with the way that the project was being approached. For example, the Data Protection department would ensure that the Data Protection Directive and the Data Protection Act were not being violated, the human resource department would have to make sure that the outsourcing took place in accordance with the TUPE regulation, and so on. The stakes of each department were incorporated in the schedules of the contract.

Master Services Agreement and Project Description(s)

The service provision until the expiration of the venture was managed by the MSA with the relevant project description(s). The MSA set out the fundamental terms and conditions governing the relationship between GIB and its respective supplier. Its principal aim was to provide the backbone of the governance of GIB's outsourcing relationships. The MSA in essence constituted an umbrella contract, framing different project descriptions which constituted individual contracts themselves. In other words, each project description formed a distinct contract containing details of specific services and/or deliverables to be provided but also incorporated the terms and conditions of the MSA.

More specifically, the project manager would liaise with the GIB global sourcing department and they would work out the project description. After examining the project, determining the commercial implications of the outsourcing venture, and obtaining approval from the relevant stakeholders during the initiation phase, GIB would send to the supplier a project request. The project request was expected to include sufficient details of the requirements and specifications of the proposed services. Project requests could also include additional requirements regarding, for example, the personnel involved, personnel requirements, and project timelines.

After the receipt of the project request, the supplier had, within a certain time frame, to provide a project response. In the case that GIB notified the supplier that it intended to proceed with the outsourcing, the two parties would negotiate and mutually agree upon the more detailed description of the project arising from the project request. If the two parties did not reach an agreement within 20 business days from the day that GIB informed the supplier of its intention to proceed with the outsourcing (or for the period of time specified in each individual case—if different), the co-operation would not be pursued further. In the case that the two parties agreed on the terms and conditions of the project descriptions, they signed it and regarded it as a distinct contract which, however, operated in conjunction with the MSA.

Against the background set by the MSA and the subsequent project descriptions, governance took place along three layers of governance:

- The 'execution layer': This layer of governance was executed through weekly meetings mainly associated with issues at the operational level. It was responsible for making sure that the required service is delivered to GIB.
- The 'direction layer': This layer of governance was executed through monthly meetings. It was concerned with issues regarding where the

programme was at present and where it should be at the future. The direction layer was mainly steering in its nature. Issues discussed included what happened in the past month, what lessons have been learnt, and what improvements need to be made.

- The 'strategic layer': This layer of governance was executed through quarterly meetings and was concerned with decisions of strategic nature. An important issue of discussion in the 'strategic layer' was which other parts of GIB could benefit from a particular outsourced programme. Another issue was the impact of financial markets on a particular programme. For example, the trade volumes go up or down, depending on the conditions of the market. How does that affect the programme? Are the systems capable of handling and supporting this kind of volumes? If the answer was no, was there a real need to make additional investment?

The following sections present the major provisions of the MSA.

Obligations of the Supplier

As already discussed, project descriptions contained mostly technical specifications of the services and deliverables required from the supplier. In the MSA, however, GIB set out explicitly a number of obligations to the supplier pertaining to the ongoing outsourcing relationship. These included:

1. The provision of services and/or deliverables to GIB in accordance with (1) the specified service levels, (2) the relevant project description, (3) the MSA, (4) the direction and control of GIB in ensuring that the delivery of service is in compliance with the legal regulatory and compliance obligations, (5) good industry practice, (6) the policies of GIB that are notified to the supplier from time to time, and (7) reasonable skills, competence, and care.
2. The skills and care necessary for the proper execution of each project description.

3. The provision of services and/or deliverables in a timely manner.
4. The provision of services and/or deliverables in a manner that meets the requirements that are specified in the project description.
5. The accurate and complete release of services and deliverables required.
6. Co-operation with the relevant GIB directors, officers, employees, sub-contractors, and agents for the proper execution of the service.
7. Assurance that their personnel pays attention and care in the service provision.
8. Assertion that the personnel involved in each project is sufficiently competent and that they comply with GIB's security requirements.
9. Use of a 'clean desk' policy by all supplier's personnel.
10. Execution of an un-amended GIB confidentiality undertaking by all supplier's personnel.
11. No breach of any express or implied obligation to GIB during their outsourcing co-operation.

In addition to these general obligations, the supplier also had to undertake a number of various other obligations relating to reporting, communication, operational, infrastructural, regulatory, and disaster recovery.

Reporting Obligations

The supplier (unless different reporting requirements are specified in a project description) will, every six months or at any time within two business days of GIB's request, deliver a progress report. This progress report will include (1) a summary of services performed until that date, (2) a summary of overall progress achieved in relation to the entire project, (3) problems encountered or anticipated and their impact, and (4) an update on general market developments in the context of the relevant services provided.

Furthermore, unless otherwise specified in the specific project description, within one month of the beginning of the co-operation, GIB may require from its supplier to produce a document which will include more procedural information. Such information includes (1) the processes that the supplier will follow in order to reach its target performance, (2) sources from which the supplier will gather information that may be relevant to the provision of services, (3) details of the 'skills' that personnel need to have in the specific project, and (4) any other matters that GIB may reasonably want to have information on. Each of these documents will be updated by the supplier on a regular basis and at least on a quarterly basis to include performance, quality, or any other requirements requested.

With regard to its ongoing performance, the supplier will have to provide to GIB on a monthly basis (unless otherwise specified in the project description) a service level report and other metrics on performance that might have been agreed.

The SLAs establish the minimum standard of performance that the supplier has to achieve. The service levels may need to be amended from time to time in light of any changing regulatory practices or any new industry-wide procedures. The supplier is expected to have the appropriate resources available to manage volumes of services and work which are predictable or that constitute a reasonable variation of any reasonable predictions actually made. In cases where GIB becomes aware of unusually large volumes of work, it has to give prior notification to the supplier. If GIB does not manage to give a reasonable prior notification to the supplier for large volumes of work, the supplier is not relieved from the obligation to use all reasonable efforts to perform the relevant services in accordance with GIB's needs.

The supplier will not be liable to any service credits if its failure to meet SLAs stems from one of the following reasons: (1) GIB's actions, mistakes, or breaches of the MSA; (2) violation of law by GIB; (3) service reductions requested by GIB and agreed by both parties through the change control procedure, provided that the supplier has previously notified GIB in writing that the implementation of a change control procedure would result in a failure to meet the service levels; (4) failure to conduct repair on equipment that has been identified and agreed in writing by GIB to be unserviceable equipment; and (5) services performed during the execution of the disaster recovery plan, the execution of which is in support of a GIB declared disaster.

Communication Obligations

After signing this MSA, GIB and its supplier would each appoint an account manager to manage it. GIB had the opportunity to consider and approve the relevant individual nominated by the supplier and/or its replacements from time to time. The account managers from each of the two parties would participate in a conference call held at least on a quarterly basis (or more frequently if required by GIB) to discuss any issues relating to the operation of the MSA, the provision of services, the deliverables, and other agenda items raised.

The supplier would have to ensure that each of its account managers and other personnel communicated on a regular basis with the relevant GIB people in relation to the provision of the services and other relevant matters and that they put their best effort in order to respond to GIB's enquiries as soon as possible.

The supplier had also to inform GIB of any changing circumstances that may affect the delivery of its service, including (1) change in the role or status of any personnel involved in a specific project, (2) change of its organizational structure, (3) change in its physical security arrangements, (4) change in its IT security policies and procedures, (5) delay or failure of performance of the services, (6) threat of planned industrial action such as strikes or lock-outs, (7) unavailability of power supplies or telecommunication networks, (8) failure of any of its systems or equipment, and (9) loss or corruption of any GIB data.

Operational Obligations

The supplier was responsible, at its own cost, for updating its methods of delivering its services to GIB. The supplier also recognized that GIB operated in an unstable and constantly changing environment and thus its requirements could be changing from time to time. The supplier was obliged to perform the services as necessary to meet GIB's needs using generally accepted 'good industry practice' processes and/or technological improvements at its cost in the methods of delivering services.

Infrastructural Obligations

The supplier was also obliged to maintain its facilities in a standard that is in accordance with GIB policies. More specifically, the supplier had to handle and oversee all of maintenance, testing and monitoring of facility systems, air handlers, and uninterruptible power supply systems at supplier-owned facilities and GIB facilities operated by the supplier and inform GIB of the results. Furthermore, the supplier had to make sure that there is adequate physical security and telecommunication connectivity and capability and that the whole of its facilities were being overseen by properly trained staff.

Regulatory Obligations

The supplier was obliged to comply with all laws, regulations, and rules in place at each point in time relating to the provision of services. If there was any regulatory change affecting the provision of services, both parties would co-operate in good faith to amend the MSA and any relevant project description and to effect changes to any services in order to comply with regulatory requirements.

GIB may decide at its discretion to carry out compliance-related training of provider's personnel, and in such a case the supplier is expected to assist GIB to facilitate the implementation of training.

However, GIB had to undertake all necessary steps to notify the supplier in writing of specific internal regulatory and compliance policies and procedures at times. The supplier would keep itself reasonably informed of the regulations applying to the financial service industry and the outsourcing sector and keep up with changes and developments.

The supplier was obliged to deliver services in a manner consistent with the regulatory and compliance policies and procedures that underpin GIB's operations.

Disaster Recovery Obligations

The supplier was obliged to comply with the disaster recovery terms predicated to each project description. It was the supplier's responsibility to maintain the disaster recovery plan throughout the term of the relevant project description and take appropriate action where necessary in order to minimize the effect of any unpredictable incident affecting the provision of services to GIB.

Each disaster recovery plan would provide for fast and efficient management of incidents affecting the provision of services to GIB and facilitate for the sourcing of alternative promises and facilities for the continuation of the provision of services. After a disaster, GIB could request temporarily supplier's personnel to be relocated to GIB facilities. In such a case the supplier would have to co-operate and provide for a smooth transition of personnel.

Finally, each disaster recovery plan had to comply with the relevant policies of GIB.

Process Improvement Obligations

The supplier was also obliged to periodically identify technology improvements and to give improvement reports to GIB on an ongoing basis to ensure that the services they provide were in line with good industry practice. Every 12 months the supplier had to deliver a process improvement report containing a material reduction in cost and material increase in quality.

GIB's Obligations

GIB had to provide all relevant information and co-operation reasonably required by the supplier to provide the services required. Furthermore, where it was agreed, GIB was obliged to provide office and other relevant facilities reasonably required for the provision of all or any part of the services to supplier personnel.

GIB's Rights

The MSA sets some specific rights for GIB. These related to:

Acceptance of Service

If the supplier did not manage to provide the service and deliverables as outlined in the project description, then GIB maintained the right to reject these. In its absolute discretion, GIB could request from the supplier to remedy the services at its own cost and in that case the supplier was obliged to comply with such a request. GIB may also decide to revoke all or part of the relevant project description to which the services relate. In this case the supplier would have to repay GIB any sums paid by it in respect of the defective services.

If the services and/or deliverables failed to conform to any of the requirements set out, GIB had the right to require from the supplier to reperform or fix defective services and/or deliverables at its own expense.

Service Augmentation

If the supplier failed to meet the service levels as agreed in the project description, GIB had the right to require from the supplier to augment the service by dedicating additional personnel to the provision of the service—up to the extent that the supplier could meet the service levels.

If GIB requested 'service augmentation', the supplier would, for a maximum of six months, provide additional staff to make sure that the service levels were reached. After three months during this service augmentation period, the supplier would determine the cost of the additional resources and notify GIB. If GIB wished to continue with the service augmentation, the relevant changes would be made to the relevant project description through the change control procedure.

Benchmarking

GIB had the right to engage a benchmarking exercise, by giving not less than 30 days' prior notice to the supplier. The aim of this procedure was to measure the supplier's performance and to determine if service performance matched and the charges were in line with best practice. Both parties agreed to assist the benchmarker in this process with the facilitation of any relevant information and assistance needed. For each category of the services to be subject to benchmarking, the benchmarker would have to:

1. Compare the price the services received to the price of similar services
2. Determine if the supplier follows best practice (and/or any technological improvements) with regard to the method that he is delivering the service
3. Recommend appropriate/corrective practices
4. Present a full report of the findings to both parties

Benchmarking would take place in terms of price and performance.

The benchmarker would be paid by GIB. Both parties would accept the benchmarker's findings. If the benchmarking showed that the charges for services were higher than what prevailed in the market, the supplier would have either to fully justify the price difference or reduce charges. In the case that the benchmarking showed that the charges for the services were higher relatively to comparable services and the supplier failed to demonstrate the reasons why its charges were higher, GIB could terminate the relevant project description.

If the benchmarking showed that supplier's performance of the services was at a level below best practice, GIB would reasonably assist the supplier in determining the reasons of this variance and decide where necessary the two parties would implement an action plan and decide upon the terms associated with this plans to mitigate variance. Examples of actions that might be deemed necessary included additional equipment, software, additional staffing, training, technological improvements, and so forth.

Monitoring Procedures

Governance reports included information on adherence to SLAs and controls, significant changes to costs, regular risk reports, risk indicators that were relevant to the type of activities outsourced, and financials and key performance indicator (KPI) review.

The annual review template had to be completed annually within two months after the annual date of the contract. The basic rationale behind these annual checks was to ensure the alignment of outsourcing outcomes with GIB strategy, objectives, and risk management requirements.

All outsourcing arrangements with risk grades 1, 2, or 3 (where grade 1 is the category with the higher risk and grade 4 with the lowest risk) and outsourcing arrangements that were either regulated or with a contract value of more than €1 million were subject to an extensive review. On the other hand, outsourcing arrangements with risk grade 4 and the outsourcing arrangements that were non-regulated or of contract value less than €1 million were subject to a limited review. Furthermore, contracts affecting SOX-relevant activities or functions were subject to an annual SAS 70 (level 2) or equivalent review, independent of any given thresholds.

Both extensive and limited reviews included information on financial performance (changes of pricing, savings realized, price benchmarking, actual vs. planned spent, etc.); operational performance (SLAs, non-compliance, sub-contractor review, quality improvements, service provider's performance, governance scope changes); risk rating; contract breaches; and service provider reports of independent network penetration and vulnerability assessments.

The extensive review additionally covered operational performance (customer satisfaction, on-site visits, analytical description of processes, and documentation); scope review (amendments to the original contract, business objectives, and so forth); legal (confirm contract changes, amendments, and contractual updates); SOX/audit (review of internal/external audit results); business continuity management/disaster recovery reviews and on-site visits; crisis management procedures tested; and security standards reviewed.

Service Levels and Service Level Principles and Reporting

The service levels established a minimum standard and the supplier would aim to outperform the standards and provide increased flexibility and response times for the services. These may be required to be changed in the light of any applicable regulations from time to time.

The supplier was expected to have the appropriate resources available to handle the predictable levels of work or reasonable variations from the predictable levels. In the case of predicted unusually large volumes of work, GIB was obliged to give prior notification to the supplier.

Even if GIB failed to meet this obligation, the supplier was still responsible to perform the relevant services in accordance with the service levels in respect of those parts of the service unaffected by GIB's failure to perform its obligations. The supplier also was obliged to use all reasonable endeavours to perform the relevant services in accordance with the service levels in respect of those parts of the service affected by GIB's failure to perform its obligations.

With regard to the modifications on service levels, GIB would have to send written notice to the supplier at least 90 days prior to the date that additions, deletions, or modifications to the service levels were required.

The supplier's obligations with regard to the new service levels would begin on the date set forth. In addition to the effective date, the supplier and GIB would agree on an elapsed number of months (after the effective date) that the supplier would be responsible to provide measurement data in support of the service levels and the supplier would be responsible for service level credits (if applicable) for any failures to attain the service level.

Change Control Procedures

Changes may be classified as 'procedural changes' or 'significant changes'. Procedural changes were changes in the manner in which the services were performed or provided, which, when implemented, did not modify, add to, or reduce the scope of the services and which did not fall within any of the categories of significant change. Significant changes included the following cases:

1. Changes that modify, add to, or reduce the scope of the services or any service

2. Changes to the terms of the MSA, including changes to service levels, to charges, or to any schedule
3. Changes that affect the function or performance of, or decrease the resource efficiency of, the services or the way in which GIB (or any of its group members) conducts its business or operations or increase any GIB group member's costs
4. Changes that are explicitly stated in this MSA to be significant
5. Any other changes which the parties agree from time to time are significant changes

Term and Termination

Unless stated otherwise, a project description would take effect from its commencement date and continue for an initial fixed term of one year, unless terminated in accordance with the terms of the MSA. Termination could become for reasons of cause or convenience.

Termination for cause included cases that:

1. The supplier has breached some of its material obligations under the MSA or a project description or a number of non-material breaches of its obligations under the MSA or a project description which in aggregate are material and, if these breaches are remediable, fails to remedy that breach within 30 business days.
2. If the supplier breached any of its material and non-material obligations to GIB and the nature of the breach is such that it can be remedied within 30 business days.
3. In case there are serious and reasonable concerns over the financial stability of the vendor, as well as its ability to perform its obligations under the project description both in a consistent and in a sustained manner.
4. If the supplier breaches any confidentiality requirement.
5. An insolvency event occurs in relation to supplier.
6. There is a change of business.
7. There is a change of control of supplier.
8. There is a service disruption which continues for a period of 30 business days or more.

Furthermore, GIB could terminate the MSA without cause but for reasons of convenience, by giving six months prior written notice to the supplier. Notwithstanding any provision to the contrary contained in this agreement or a project description, GIB could decide to terminate any project description to which it was a party or any part thereof without cause and without payment of any termination fees or other compensation giving the following prior written notice to the relevant supplier: For project descriptions, which have a project description term of up to 3 calendar months, 3 business days' notice; for project descriptions that have a project description term of between 3 and 6 calendar months, a 10 business days' notice; for project descriptions which have a project description term of more than 6 calendar months and up to and including 12 calendar months, 15 business days' notice; and for project descriptions that have a project description term of 12 calendar months or more, 20 business days' notice.

Reflections on Formal Governance

Clearly, we, as researchers here, had in-depth access to the governance and contractual arrangements pertaining to this outsourcing arrangement. For this reason, and because such access is normally difficult to achieve (there was less access to the relevant documents in the other two cases studied), we have made available these details to provide additional relevant evidence that can be later analysed in terms of our theoretical (TCE and Foucauldian) frameworks.

According to the comments of the GIB lawyers that participated in our research, having an MSA in place to steer the relationship and individual project descriptions that will administer particular projects carries important benefits:

1. No need to renegotiate terms: The MSA contains all the provisions expected in a one-off contract (i.e. obligations for duty of care, obligations to comply with the bank's standards and regulation, indemnities, liability clauses, etc.). However, after signing the MSA GIB does not have to renegotiate all of the terms every time it makes arrangements

for a new deal with a particular supplier. Mark (GIB lawyer) highlighted: "You don't have the supplier negotiating different terms in different places, you don't have to renegotiate every time, so you're not investing lawyers time in doing multiple deals over and over again, liability clauses, indemnity clauses blah, blah." The same GIB lawyer noted that the MSA "does streamline the contractual process I think a lot more and it means that there's less legal effort and business effort expended on putting a contract in place".

2. Flexibility: A number of interviewees characterized the MSA as a relatively rigid document. However, the GIB lawyers recognized that it does allow for some flexibility. They noted that they have dealt with cases where suppliers want to be able to contract at the local level. The supplier might want this for different reasons, including commission and local revenue recognition issues. The GIB MSA is completely flexible on that. Mark (GIB lawyer) more specifically commented

   > *the MSA is a very effective way of commencing the legal relationship that also provides enough flexibility to be manipulated for different projects … you can deal with just one supplier globally but have local GIB entities at the project description level, or you can have local supplier and local GIB entities at the project description level and then the two main companies, let's say Dell Ireland and GIB Germany can sign at the MSA level and that's like signing in spirit to the framework. There is no services under that until you sign a project description.*

3. Efficient track of the outsourcing relationship: The efficient tracking of the outsourcing relationship can take two forms:

   (a) First of all, by 'locking' the supplier into working under the MSA, GIB gets the supplier to work under a document which is in compliance with the policies and requirements of its stakeholders (i.e. departments of insurance, tax, human resources, and so on). Along these lines, there is less legal risk involved and the outsourcing takes place in conjunction with the requirements of the different stakeholders of the bank. On this issue Mark (GIB lawyer) noted:

   > *It is a kind of pillar of stability for the bank to know that we've contracted on terms which have been approved by most of the stakeholders … a lot of the clauses in the contract have been provided by not legal,*

> *but they've been provided by the compliance department or they've been provided by Tax or Insurance or Corporate Security … IT Security, which is very, very important etc. … So they* (meaning the stakeholders) *know that when the MSA has been used, if they have to approve the deal in our Smart Sourcing database, which is our database of all our outsourcing projects, when a new deal comes up for approval it's easier for them to go 'Yes okay, provided it's being carried out on the standard terms'.*

(b) Second, the bank is enabled to maintain a closer monitoring of its outsourcing relationship and prohibit the existence of agreements at the local level which could be at the expense of the bank. To illustrate this issue, Mark (GIB lawyer) explained:

> *You know that the supplier at the local level isn't going to be able to go off and do a local deal and get better terms for the supplier on liability on indemnities, on all manner of legal obligations or restrictions, because it's already been nails down between the two main organizations. … They* (meaning suppliers) *can do a lot of mini deals all over the place and, you know, the right hand doesn't know what the left hand is doing.*

Mark (GIB lawyer) further underlined his experience on such local arrangements that suppliers get into:

> *I mean we used to find, because suppliers are, they're not stupid, they know how to make money and they go around an organization the size of GIB and they make friends with all people, all over the place, all over the world and they do mini deals with all of them. There's different pricing and there's different liability regimes and there's different commissions and different service levels and different service credits. In some cases they may introduce service debits which is effectively a payment for over performance. We might not want over performance we might just want them to perform to the standard we asked for in the first place, so why pay them more for over performing?.*

On the same issue, Mark (GIB lawyer) added:

> *I think at least the MSA structure, if it is properly managed, you know that you have got key suppliers to sign up to a key set of terms that they should not be going off and negotiating different contracts … you have*

> *pricing knocked down at a global level that you're happy with and you're involving your procurement department so that they can police the relationship as well.*

According to Daryn (GIB lawyer), following the very detailed apparatus of governance created in the MSA was not very straightforward in practice. He pointed out that the documentation of this apparatus of governance was very long and formalistic, and because it included various different groups within the bank, it became complicated to follow. For these reasons he suggested that although

> *a lot of time and effort is put in to agreeing these schedules … on the ground level, when this actual service delivery is happening people get so wrapped up in the ongoing mechanism of the services that I think the governance structure sort of gets put to one side.*

Daryn (GIB lawyer) characterized the apparatus of governance set by the MSA as 'ideal'—by which he meant idealistic. He specifically mentioned:

> *This is exactly what a governance schedule should look like and it's got the various steering committees and where they need to meet and what meetings will be.*

However, he recognized that in practice, project managers find it very difficult to follow:

> *The project managers … I think they would find it extremely difficult to adhere to something as strict as this. … You know, they have so many other things going on about the services and the service delivery and that kind of stuff it's quite tough for them to follow something as formalistic as this.*

He further highlighted that

> *most project managers they're just interested in the delivery of the service no matter how it happens. So it's quite tough to see that this is actually put in place.*

Regarding the use and value of the apparatus of governance set by the MSA, Daryn (GIB lawyer) suggested that it became more useful and important during turbulent times:

> *I think the intentions are very good, I think when the service is going really well you don't really need the governance schedule because the services are good and everybody is happy. But a governance schedule or provisions come into play when things are going badly, because that's important. Then you need to know who are the right people, where do we need to go to discuss changes, what do we need to discuss changes, that kind of thing. So I think that's important.*

Regarding the use and importance of this tight apparatus of governance, Daryn (GIB lawyer) noted:

> *As a lawyer I think that governance is a great thing to have … a lot of project managers go "Well why do we need it? Why does it need to be so long?" The answer to that is, "When things go wrong, that's when you need it." Because the both parties are not wanting to talk to one another, both of them have "You're not doing this, you're not going that" but then we can return to the project and say "Well you agreed in terms of the governance schedule that you will meet on this basis, you will discuss with these people." That's how you sort of can force a supplier that's not delivering to come back to the table to then focus their energy and channel it in the right way.*

On this issue he further elaborated:

> *It is because of the unknown, you do not know what the relationship is going to be, so the best thing is to have something formalistic so that if something does go wrong you can always accommodate each other by going back to the schedule. If the services are going fine they probably will not do this, there will probably be a small communication from the bottom to the top to say everything is okay, they* (meaning the supplier's team) *are meeting the service levels, nothing needs to be done. But it is when problems happen that a good complex governance schedule like this is important.*

Daryn (GIB lawyer) put even more emphasis on his view that governance was more relevant during turbulent times in the outsourcing relationship:

> *But the governance is important because you need to have some kind of structure if things are not going fantastic, what happens then? You need to always make the supplier and the project manager aware that they should not skip over these sections because it is not important now, but during the life of the project these*

can be extremely important. So that is, you have to keep narrowing that focus to say "No don't forget the governance, don't forget the governance". … It is the same way as you get project descriptions and people never think about what happens on termination. So they never put in the detailed process that governance, how the services are taken back. At the start everybody is happy, it is a new relationship, everyone thinks the services are going to be fine. Then suddenly the relationship is bad we want to terminate but there are no provisions on how to get the services back. In the same way I think governance is important because during the life of the project you need to be able to also manage how the services are going and governance is the only way that you can do it.

Bart (GIB director of risk) commented that the outsourcing partners should not pay attention to governance only during the difficult times of the relationship. He suggested that close monitoring and governance could enhance communication and a tighter fit between the outsourcing partners:

These meetings, these processes … they are useful not only during bad times … this is very common in the outsourcing industry, ignoring governance because things go well. … All these processes can actually help you boost your relationship, communicate better, collaborate better and leverage the relationship towards innovation.

Rao (PV Head of integrated service delivery) also emphasized that from his experience, outsourcing clients were not really utilizing the governance processes unless there were problems. Similarly to Bart (GIB director of risk), he suggested that governance procedures could bring the outsourcing parties closer and enhance their relationship:

Not every customer takes his governance calls very seriously. Some of our customers, as long as there are no escalations, everything is running smoothly, they do not even participate in most of the governance calls. So, governance in these cases is implemented only through tough times. … This is not right. … My recommendation to our partners is that whether we expect something good or bad we should have these governance calls. There are a lot of things we can share with each other, understand the way we are operating so that we do not get into escalations. … In a smooth operating environment the governance mechanisms are there to help you improve yourself.

Daryn (GIB lawyer) also noted that because it was difficult for both parties to outline their expectations and secure their interests from the beginning of their co-operation, a detailed apparatus of governance constituted a safeguard, a type of re-assurance:

> *So a detailed governance is put up at the outset to ensure that if the relationship does go bad, if it doesn't turn out to be what everybody thought it would be, at least there's a very formalistic process that everyone can say "Fine let's adhere to this process, let's go through this very structured method and see if we can fix something that has gone wrong". That's the only real reason what I can see is to have such a formalistic governance process at the start.*

Regarding the importance that the outsourcing parties place on the governance they are going to have, Daryn (GIB lawyer) maintained that:

> *Governance is probably one of those areas that takes a back seat when you are doing negotiations because both parties are focused on the price, the delivery of services and service levels, those kinds of things. So those are what is important because project managers have certain targets to meet and suppliers have got certain revenue targets to meet so they are always at the front of everybody's minds.*

Governance did not take a back seat only during negotiations. Andrea Walker (consultant to GIB) emphasized that in his experience a very common mistake among clients was that they engage into outsourcing arrangements without investing in proper governance first:

> *A big mistake that clients make is that they will get to the service commencement date and they have made absolutely no investment at all in their own processes, their own governance structures or their own governance organization.*

Similar to the comments made by the lawyers within GIB, Eric (GIB Global technology outsourcing vendor management) noted that outsourcing governance was extremely important in the financial sector for legal reasons. He further emphasized, however, the importance of allocating responsibilities and the escalation structures in order to address problems:

> *We are a very regulated industry, so in order to have the authorization to do outsourcing we need to have strong governance in place. If not, the regulators are coming after us. … So yes, we need strong governance because we are very regulated but you know. … I think it is good … it is best practices … having a clear responsibility and clear escalation means actually at the end of the day better productivity because people know what to do, they do not worry to reinvent the wheel each time something happens. … So even if it is a little bit boring and a little bit not so fancy, it is something that is important in order to avoid a situation where the responsibilities are not clear and the people are trying to fix problems the wrong way.*

Bart (GIB director of risk) noted that, regarding governance, there were two areas of major importance. These included the decision-making structure (i.e. who makes the decisions) and accountability. He further highlighted that the successful governance structure required cross-divisional representations in steering committees (e.g. from IT, operations, front office, middle office, and so on) and, in particular, representations of all stakeholders. On the issue of accountability, Bart (GIB director of risk) further elaborated and noted that a governance structure was useful if someone was made accountable for the success or failure of the IT services. He added that, within GIB, ownership is very well defined and this ensures that governance structures are successful.

Most participants in our research acknowledged the role of the contract as being critical in the outsourcing relationship. The contract in essence set out the rules of the game and provided a legal safeguard for the outsourcing partners. Eric (GIB Global technology outsourcing vendor management) emphasized the importance of the contract and actually underlined its role in making the working relationship work independent of the people involved: "People may change. … So to have a good managed relationship which is not dependent on people you need to have a framework."

A number of interviewees recognized that while the contract is the basis of the engagement, it cannot address all the issues involved in the outsourcing deal. Rao (PV Head of integrated service delivery) highlighted the constrained ability of the contract to cover all aspects of the relationship and emphasized the need not to focus on the letter of the contract (i.e. what it is written) but more importantly to the spirit of the contract:

When you start executing you realize that the contract has covered some areas and has not covered other areas—has not examined some features. It is important for the very contract to know the spirit ... how do I interpret tomorrow if I end up having issues. The contract, because it is a legal document, we theoretically want to be very specific on how we put matters in. But I have seen most of the contracts falling short—they will never cover 100%. So it is important for the parties to understand the spirit of the contract, not just only the letter. Otherwise, when the relationship is going through turbulent times, you may end up in conflict.

A number of interviewees agreed that the contract played a role in the generation of transparency between the outsourcing parties. As an example, Bart (GIB director of risk) commented:

The contract sets a formal apparatus of governance that sheds light upon the development the outsourcing relationship ... it makes it more visible, more transparent and it certainly facilitates the venture through good and bad times.

A number of interviewees agreed that the contract facilitates relations of trust between the outsourcing partners through the transparency it creates. Rao (PV Head of integrated service delivery) made a more explicit link between governance and trust and argued that "the governance in place HAS to facilitate trust, otherwise you are not working with the right governance".

Carsten (GIB IBIT Sourcing and Vendor Management of IT portfolio) went a step further and illustrated that in essence, governance mechanisms should be aimed at creating transparency:

Governance mechanisms really ought to create transparency. Whenever you look or think about sourcing you recognize that the more you are able to create transparency across your sourcing portfolio the better you become in supporting issues, managing issues. Thus governance is important.

Mani (PV Global account manager) noted the importance of keeping a rigorous and well-documented governance process for keeping track of the progress of the arrangement:

All these governance meetings are documented in terms of what is discussed, what is agreed and then we track certain things. We go back next week and say what did we decide?. … What have we achieved?. … Then we say that we have achieved this, we haven't achieved this, why we haven't achieved this and what else we need to do in order to achieve what was agree. … There is a fairly rigorous process of governance all the way up, from the execution layer to the strategic layer. It is very well documented and tracked.

However, Carsten (GIB IBIT Sourcing and Vendor Management of IT portfolio) recognized that there had to be a relative balance in the amount of details that will be kept:

You have to make sure you are not over-governing things. You need to have proper governance structures in place to get issues to be on top of information, to recognize issues early up front, but not getting too much details.

Eric (GIB Global technology outsourcing vendor management) elaborated on this issue and illustrated that over-governance can be a bad thing if there was too much bureaucracy:

Over-governance can become a problem if you are not flexible, if you are putting someone in charge of governance that is becoming very bureaucratic. … Bad governance or ineffective governance would be governance that would become bureaucratic, completely disconnected from the business and the services, existing for itself… that would be very negative.

Regarding the role of SLAs and KPIs, Daryn (GIB lawyer) underlined their role in the creation of clarity on what exactly the service was that the supplier needed to provide:

So here you have a service, here you have a KPI or service level and it is black or white whether the supplier meets it.

However, he did acknowledge that in practice things are more complicated:

But again, I think the problems comes in when you start to get to the practical nature because it is all great when it is legal and it is black and white but when you have got a service delivery there are often situations where it is not only the supplier's fault.

He also gave an example to illustrate that it is possible that a supplier depends very much on the customer to reach a specific SLA:

It might be the case that GIB had to give a document or had to write something and has provided it a day late so therefore the supplier is a day late. So when they get to the end of the service level it is not completely their fault, there is a joint, you know, things happen, days to go, time delays that results in the supplier not meeting the service level. So when GIB comes to the supplier and says 'Well look you have not met the service level' the supplier's answer will always be 'Yes but there was a dependency on you so therefore it is the two of us together that have done this'. So then service levels are not always followed to the letter.

A very complicated SLA may turn out to be completely ineffective simply because it cannot be understood. On this issue Daryn (GIB lawyer) noted:

I tend to see a lot of service level regimes that are so complicated that when you come to try and understand what they mean the poor people on the ground cannot understand or can't actually effectively use them because they're too complicated.

He added:

I have seen service levels where they've got a huge matrix of different results and there are ten or twenty factors that go into determining whether or not a service level has met a particular result and because there are so many individual moving parts to the service level that for a person to actually work out whether the service level has been met, they have to do all these tiny evaluations and sometimes it just does not work because if something goes wrong in one of them it means you effectively cannot get the end result.

According to him the idea is to have as least information as possible necessary to measure a service level. Those are the effective service levels. Daryn (GIB lawyer) noted that he had seen service levels without consequences, which for him constrained their effects:

"*So you can have a fantastic service level framework that says, you know, 'The supplier will do this, this and this' but then there is no mention to what happens*

> *if the supplier does not. … So, what is the result of supplier not meeting the service level and that is sort of left blank and, I mean, service levels are only effective if there's a consequence.*" Along this line, having a good service level framework is not enough. The type of consequence they establish constitutes a motivator for supplier performance as well.

While SLAs and KPIs are absolutely critical for the governance of the venture, the ways they are defined can produce different pictures regarding the status of the outsourcing venture. Carsten (GIB IBIT Sourcing and Vendor Management of IT portfolio) suggested that the SLAs and KPIs of the bank with a number of vendors, including PV, were weakly defined. On this basis, the SLAs were green, but the performance of the vendors was not necessarily adequate and the bank not necessarily receiving the service it needed. Rajesh (PV X-RAY Global transformation manager) gave an example where GIB was not receiving a proper service although PV was reaching the SLAs that were defined in the contract:

> *I know that there are KPIs between GIB and PV where if there is a major incident it has to be resolved by PV within 24 hours. But the user's expectation will be that if there is a major incident it should be resolved in two hours. Thus, the KPI was not tied into the business expectation but contractually we did not have a problem and we would not be charged a penalty if we addressed the incident within 24 hours. … But again, the user would not be happy … even if we solved the issue within 6 hours, the user will be dissatisfied because the expectation is that the issue is addressed in two hours.*

According to Rajesh (PV X-RAY Global transformation manager), the SLAs and KPIs in relation to the X-RAY project were properly defined and they were really reflecting the business expectations.

Whereas Carsten (GIB IBIT Sourcing and Vendor Management of IT portfolio) illustrated the case that SLAs were achieved, yet the delivery of the service was not adequate, Rao (PV Head of integrated service delivery) illustrated that the opposite could also happen. Along these lines he explained that it was possible that the supplier does not reach the defined service levels, yet the delivery of service was good. Along these lines, he went a step further and noted that SLAs should be evaluated in conjunction to the satisfaction of the customer:

> *I will give you a 95% SLA which may be very good. But what happens when the other 5% of the service is not delivered to the customer? Thus, customer satisfaction is one of the things which may not come up directly to the SLA. … If I go to a customer and ask how is my service, even though I have not achieved my SLAs but if I am keeping my the customer informed that these are the roadblocks I have achieved and keep them updated constantly, satisfaction may be high.*

In practice, however, Andrea Walker (consultant to GIB) noted that either the vendor does not interrogate the KPIs, or the customer does not define them. In such cases, the customer and the vendor do not know the expectations of the engagement. KPIs are the means for identifying what is expected of the vendors so that the engagement can run smoothly. Carsten (GIB IBIT Sourcing and Vendor Management of IT portfolio) highlighted the importance of KPIs and SLAs by suggesting that they are the ultimate way of detecting performance issues. More specifically, he mentioned that the reason for the underperformance of staff augmentation models is that there are no SLAs or KPIs. For this reason it is very hard to detect performance issues upfront, as these will be related to single persons only.

With regard to the effectiveness of KPIs and SLAs as tools of governance, Carsten (GIB IBIT Sourcing and Vendor Management of IT portfolio) noted:

> *They are as effective as you define them. A broad SLA will not really help you to manage anything, but if you define proper KPIs, you can easily measure the downtime of the system- and you should put that into the SLA to see what happens when there is a downtime of the system.*

He also illustrated very vividly how complicated the definition and functionality of SLAs and KPIs may become:

> *It is more difficult to measure the quality of code. In the IT world it is not easy to say this code is really great because it is rather subjective than objective. But it is easy to measure that the production of the system was down for 3 hours. … You can also define timelines around delivery … which means that if you are late one or two weeks* (meaning the supplier) *this will happen, if you do not tell us upfront that will happen etc.*

On the same issue, Daryn (GIB lawyer) highlighted that SLAs constituted a great tool of governance, yet they were very hard to define in order to make them effective:

> *So I think it is a very good tool and should be used more often but it's very difficult to define them and it gets quite complicated when you're trying to put out which is more important, how do you fit it together.*

All three GIB lawyers that participated in the research emphasized the importance of termination and step-in rights for the protection of the client but also for the control of the behaviour of the supplier. Mark (GIB lawyer) elaborated on this issue and highlighted that termination provisions have to be very clear so that the client does not get locked-in in the contract. He further commented on the challenge of transferring the services to a new supplier:

> *Then termination provisions are no good without good exit provisions ... all of that good stuff about the supplier having to help you transfer the services to a new third party supplier. Now suppliers do not like that because they have to cooperate with their competitors. They have to cooperate with their competitors in a scenario where the competitor knows that you have effectively terminated the contract, so it's not ideal. But you need to have them because if there is no cooperation there is no handover of materials, hand over of know-how, hand back of confidential information, you know, tying up of new infrastructure, network, transfer of data and all of that stuff, then you are scuppered, you are in a difficult position.*

Mark (GIB lawyer) illustrated that there can be some more implicit forms of control and he identified the visit to the vendor's site as one of them. He explained that this was a common practice for the bank in order to control the behaviour of its vendors:

> *If there has been a poor performance for a certain period of time or a breach, we effectively send in some of the senior people in Investment Banking IT, or the Investment Banking Operations department, fly them to India, fly them To Sri Lanka, or China, or whatever, Hungary, or wherever the services are being performed and literally have the sit outside there watching you. I mean that is*

a very effective remedy. And if under their quasi management the supplier is still not able to get the services back up to speed, then you terminate after that.

Regarding the nature of governance executed by the strategic layer, Rao (PV Head of integrated service delivery) noted that it is dynamic in nature. This dynamism relates to the issues being discussed and the overall objectives of governance. Rao (PV Head of integrated service delivery) explained that:

The requirements of GIB depend upon the market requirements. Now there is a downturn, and probably cost is going to be a major factor. … The business drivers keep changing. … Depending on the business drivers GIB expects a specific performance.

Similarly, Eric (GIB Global technology outsourcing vendor management) illustrated that governance should be questioned, reviewed, and adjusted when necessary:

Like most processes, I think you need to regularly challenge your governance mechanisms. So even when you think that they are okay, that they are doing the work, you need to take a fresh view and try to see for example … are they necessary? Is it not an over head?. … You need to very regularly re-open the box and try to have all the people look at and say "Okay, is this really what we want?. … Can we improve it?." … You always have to go back.

In addition to the changing objectives of governance, Rao (PV Head of integrated service delivery) mentioned that governance is also dynamic regarding the way that the strategic layer of governance is connected to the direction and execution layers:

There are a lot of issues we discuss each quarter. We continuously keep changing. How do we resolve issues, how do we spot issues, how do we escalate issues from one level to another, we find small gaps here and there. We put mechanisms of how our weekly escalations should flow into the monthly run … and the monthly run into the quarterly run. There are small changes that keep happening.

Andrea (GIB Vendor decisions/Relationship management) explained that the scope of a project may change, and as a result of that, governance processes may also be required to change:

> *Today we have 130 applications. When they become 200 we will have to step back and look at the governance structure. We will probably have to change that—but I do not have the answer right now on how it should change. Depending on how the program grows we will decide on the governance. … Governance is not static, it has to be dynamic, it has to be extremely dependent on the kind of applications that are in the portfolio.*

Regarding the three layers of governance (i.e. execution, direction, and strategic layers), a number of participants suggested that the roles and divisions of each governance programme must be clearly defined. If they are not, there is a big potential for conflict. As Mani (PV Global account manager) highlighted:

> *It is extremely critical to define the common structure, each rule, each role that is part of the governance of the particular program. The roles and responsibilities should be very clearly defined. If you introduce unnecessary layers that are not required, it really has the potential to kill the program.*

Furthermore the same manager underlined that for governance to be efficient, each governance layer has to remain with its own space of action. More specifically he noted that:

> *If you have a situation where someone is senior, whose role should be part of the strategic or direction layer of governance and he gets involved in the execution layer … this is absolutely bad, this should not happen. If that happens one they do is participating in a conference without really having the appropriate information in hand, which is wrong. Similarly someone from the execution layer should not be participating in the governance of strategic reviews and things like that. … These things have happened in the past. It is very important to define who participates in which governance program. What are the issues that get discussed. You do not want to discuss small project issues in the strategic forum. … If you do that, you end up discussing small issues which are not worth of anyone's time. It is important for the appropriate governance that the appropriate roles and responsibilities for each governance stays.*

Mark (GIB lawyer) illustrated that the escalations of small issues can be particularly embarrassing for the outsourcing relationship:

> *If a member of the GIB Board has to meet with a member of the PV Board to discuss a small operational problem that has escalated because nobody has been able to resolve it, it is embarrassing I suppose.*

On a similar basis, Rao (PV Head of integrated service delivery) highlighted the importance of governance at all levels for the facilitation of the outsourcing relationship:

> *My suggestions is, if you have a strong governance and implement it ruthlessly in both sides, 90% of your problems will never get escalated, are never going to get raised. Your engagement will run very smoothly and tremendous amounts of value adds will come out of it. The most important thing in any relationship, whether it is at the project/program/business line/engagement level is governance.*

A number of interviewees recognized the role of governance in the facilitation of a common understanding between the outsourcing partners. Mani (PV Global account manager) commented:

> *These are forums where you discuss what the client wants to do and what the supplier understands. The purpose of this is that there are no differences between what GIB expects from PV and what GIB thinks PV expects.*

Rao (PV Head of integrated service delivery) elaborated on the importance of governance in the alignment of visions between his company and GIB:

> *Alignment of visions. … This is what we do in our quarterly stirring committee meetings. This consists of two parts. In the first part, we discuss how we have done in the past. In the second part we discuss what our vision of our account is. … At the same time, GIB is sharing with us at which direction they are moving and what is expected from us. We constantly align our objectives and goals to make sure that both are working towards achieving those objectives. This is why the KPI information is very important.*

Mani (PV Global account manager) highlighted that the empowerment of people distinguished a governance from a reporting mechanism:

> *There is a chance that a governance structure may simply become a reporting mechanism. You don't want that. You really want people in these roles to be empowered. Reporting is fine—you don't mind to report there is a problem. But if you are not empowered to fix the problem, the governance is not important. … If somebody is reporting that there is a problem, then he should be empowered to take these decisions that will fix the problem. Its only then that governance makes sense.*

Relationship Between GIB and PV

The following sections provide details of the evolution of the relational aspects between GIB and PV. We focus upon issues such as the prior history between the outsourcing parties, their mutual interest in the relationship, and issues of co-operation, communication, dependency, and senior management involvement, as well as cultural issues.

GIB and PV maintained a very long relationship before the X-RAY project. Mani (PV Global account manager) noted that there are interpersonal relationships between the two organizations that exist over the last 20 years. He commented on the importance of these long-lasting relationships: "After all, people work with people. … There is a lot of good in the organizations working together for a long time. … There is a feeling of comfort." Rajesh (PV X-RAY Global transformation manager) further noted that GIB had created in the past an organization called GIB Software which was an offshore captive. That captive was bought over by PV (a stake of 49% was bought in 2001 and the remaining 51% was bought in 2004). Along this line, a lot of PV employees are part of the old GIB Software organization.

Rajesh (PV X-RAY Global transformation manager) elaborated on the way that PV tried to demonstrate its willingness to co-operate with GIB and get a good understanding of its needs:

> *We gave GIB the feeling that we want to work closely with them and we want to make the project a success. … We wanted to show them that we would go to*

> *any extent to ensure that their expectations from us would be met. … We wanted to ensure that all issues would be covered in the proposal and this is why we put a lot of effort into understanding what the business wanted from GIB IT and in effect what GIB IT wanted from us.*

Mani (PV Global account manager) noted that PV had a very good understanding of GIB's systems. According to him, this was a very important reason why PV won the contract over its competitors and also a significant factor for the effective development of the venture:

> *We have a very long relationship with them. We knew our understanding was much better than some of our competitors. We knew a lot of these applications … we had actually created some of these applications. There was a good understanding of the technology and the applications. … These were important reasons why were chosen and we were capable to perform well.*

Rajesh (PV X-RAY Global transformation manager) also elaborated on the importance of the knowledge that PV possessed with regard to GIB's technology:

> *We used to already support about 35%–40% of this portfolio, so this gave us an edge over a few other competitors. … We could use this experience to our advantage because we had demonstrated a lot of competency in the support of these applications. … So we came with the background that GIB was already happy with our service on 40% of these applications. … For this reason we could leverage some of the benefits of that deep relation outside into the wider portfolio.*

GIB placed a lot of emphasis on the involvement of people. As mentioned, a significant requirement by GIB during the supplier selection process had been that the people who were involved in the bid would be involved also in the delivery of the service. PV had a clear commitment that the people who were involved in the bid would be fed all the way through into the programme. The two organizations appear to be highly committed to each other. Mani (PV Global account manager) mentioned:

GIB is fairly committed to PV and also the other way around. … The contracts are essentially structured to ensure that in the relationship, when one partner is doing well and is benefiting from something, the other partner also benefits … and also if GIB does something bad and PV has a problem from that, we share their problem. It is a very symbiotic relationship.

Rajesh (PV X-RAY Global transformation manager) also elaborated on the importance of both outsourcing parties committing the necessary resources:

If any of the two parties decides that they are not going to stay committed, this program will fail. This program is based on a very close partnership model. … Contracts, really there are no hard and fast rules between us and GIB in the sense that we have been expected to do a lot of things by contract, but we just can not fault lack of commitment. … But vice versa, which is what we expect from GIB, a lot of this is not by contract, because you expect things like approvals would be done on time, there will be a close working relation, there are trust-based subjective softer aspects. … So if GIB did not have the commitment on it, eventually they would see that the performance on X-RAY is coming down, which has not happened. … On the other side, we can not be under committed because if we are under committed, it is too large a program and it will fail.

Rao (PV Head of integrated service delivery) noted that for the alignment of visions to come about, the venture had to benefit both parties. More specifically, he noted:

When there is benefit to both organizations there is going to be collaboration. … The other thing is that when you start working with the partner and you see them delivering products and working hard to deliver to you, obviously the trust factor will improve in the engagement. That trust factor will ultimately lead to higher collaboration levels.

Andrea (GIB Vendor decisions/Relationship management) did not think there would be significantly lesser levels of dependence if GIB had chosen to outsource to multiple vendors: "If you look at having multiple vendors for an application you are not that different in terms of what you would have to do to move from one to another for a different level of service."

He acknowledged that having multiple vendors can be safer if the need to change a vendor comes about, but he suggested that having one vendor that would breed better cost was a risk that the bank was willing to take:

> *So, for example, if I've got my Level 1, Level 2 with one vendor and Level 3 CTB with another. … I will still have to go through a transition exercise to take one piece off one of those vendors and put it onto the other. You could argue that there is more safety in it because you already have some people that are knowledgeable on the application, but I think it is a risk we were prepared to take because it gave us a good low price for a set of applications that we wanted to spend less money on, but without losing the service.*

In terms of the level of dependence on PV, Andrea (GIB Vendor decisions/Relationship management) noted that in the case of termination of their agreement it would be costly for the bank to move to another vendor. He suggested, however, that the decision to move to another vendor would be primarily influenced by the prices that PV would offer in order to run the service:

> *In every outsourcing relationship, down at the bottom line you have to think about: "Well how do we get out of this in the end?" It is a very interesting situation really because there is a risk in it. … To get out of this contract would take a year's work to do because we would have to go through exactly the same as we went through at the start but with another vendor coming in to take it all off. … So when we get to the decision point, obviously the pricing would be up for review and you can see that PV would be in quite a powerful position to request a reasonable amount of more money to have it for another three years. Equally if we chose to change vendor there is a transition cost that we would have to pay so we do not just pay run the bank costs, as it would be with PV, we pay for the cost of transitioning which is hundreds of thousand of euros. … So then you have got the risk of moving all your applications somewhere else. It will be fascinating to see how that works out because a lot of it will depend on the commercial attitude of PV at the point in time. If they make a fair offer to us for the next three years I do not doubt that we will take it providing we are satisfied with the service.*

On the issue of dependence, Carsten (GIB IBIT Sourcing and Vendor Management of IT portfolio) noted that there was a level of dependence for both sides. The bank depended on PV for the smooth continuation of the service and the avoidance of transitioning periods to new vendors and PV depended on the bank because it is one of its major customers:

> *If they decide to go away GIB cannot work … and it GIB decides to go away from them it will need a transition. But there is a dependency on both sides. … GIB makes big revenue to them, it will have a big impact on PV's revenues to lose GIB as a customer … this is why they are highly committed and they are trying to deliver.*

Rajesh (PV X-RAY Global transformation manager) also recognized the mutual dependency between the two organizations. He added, however, that PV was dependent on GIB also in terms of knowledge production and references to other customers:

> *So GIB is largely dependent on us to get it right for their portfolio because we manage so much of their risk. We are dependent on the business and their support for so much or our work because that's the basis of our revenues. It's the basis for our, you know, promoting to other customers, also in terms of learning and so on. So there's always a huge amount of dependency.*

Mani (PV Global account manager) suggested that the levels of trust between GIB and PV were very high since the two organizations had been working together for approximately 11 years. He noted that a lot of projects had been renewed multiple times with PV—which is a strong indication of their good working relationship with GIB.

On the issue of trust, Philip (PV X-RAY European programme manager) noted that GIB is confident that PV was honestly reporting problematic situations:

> *I think that in certain circumstances if we have had a failure that we are not in a position to be able to resolve, we have been able to go over there they trust that we have done our best to resolve the issue and then go over and say "Look hands up guys, we are having trouble trying to fix this, we need your help".*

Mani (PV Global account manager) further noted that there was not only organizational trust but also people trust. Philip (PV X-RAY

European programme manager) also commented on the high levels of trust between people and illustrated how supportive his counterparts at GIB were:

> *On a personal note, speaking with some of the GIB managers they have said to me "If you ever need any help, even though we are expecting not to be involved, come over and shout if there is problem. It might be something that we are aware or of something that we have a point of view on." … So that is very good for the venture … that means that we are building the relationship with the GIB management. … Because you need to be able to say "I need your help in this" … or "I do not know, I really do not know the answer to that and thus I need your support" … If I am comfortable to be able to go over and do that, then they will feel the same kind of trust … they will trust in the fact that I can go over there and say to them "I have got a problem".*

Rao (PV Head of integrated service delivery) went a step further and highlighted that the relationships were particularly important for the development of the relationship. Simon (senior GIB manager in operations) also commented on the role of the relationships at the senior management level: "As a company, our senior management and PV's senior management are very close … they have a very good communication line … and this provides a very good forum to discuss issues."

Andrea (GIB Vendor decisions/Relationship management) commented on the role of transparency and openness in the generation of trust. He further highlighted the responsiveness by PV as a factor that was facilitating the relationship:

> *Transparency helps a lot and they have been pretty open and honest with us. I am not convinced that other vendors would be as open and honest and I think that this helps the relationship a lot. … If I go to the vendor management and say "These things are not working" they take it onboard, they come back and they will say and actually right down a number of things. … They will analyze what they did wrongly and what they are going to do about it.*

Andrea (GIB Vendor decisions/Relationship management) additionally noted that he appreciated when the vendor was open and honest even when confronting problematic situations:

They have acknowledged that they had a fault in some cases, they have revealed things to us that we did not know they were wrong, but that was good. … I was quite amazed actually at some of the things they told us voluntarily … but I like it.

Carsten (GIB IBIT Sourcing and Vendor Management of IT portfolio) noted that there had been situations where GIB was running into problems with PV, but he noted:

I would only blame them for half of the times and blame us for not being able to define a proper delivery framework that they can deliver. Whenever we have done that they have started to deliver.

He further noted that when problems remained within the lower levels of the hierarchy, the relationship did not get very seriously affected. In cases that problems got escalated to the Chief Information Officer (CIO) level, Carsten (GIB IBIT Sourcing and Vendor Management of IT portfolio) maintained that this would definitely affect the relationship between the two organizations.

Philip (PV X-RAY European programme manager) argued that the role of culture was particularly influential in the development of the client-supplier relationship in offshore outsourcing. He pointed out that together with the cost factors, it was essential that outsourcing clients pay careful attention to which company is more in line with their own culture:

If you are going for an outsourcing vendor like PV which is located in India, or a outsourcing vendor in Brazil, or China, their management culture is different from a client located in the US, Australia or in the UK. The management culture is very different in each of the locations. That really matters. So the way the outsourcing vendor in Brazil would react is different from the way an outsourcing vendor in China or India would react. … It is thus particularly important that an outsourcing client, when deciding on their vendors, that they look for vendors who are more in line with their own management culture. … So if you outsource in Eastern Europe for example, there will be a cost factor, you would not get the rate you would get in Brazil, China or India … but the relationship will be significantly better because you are more in line with their culture.

Contrary to Philip (PV X-RAY European programme manager), Carsten (GIB IBIT Sourcing and Vendor Management of IT portfolio) noted that there were some ongoing but understandable cultural issues between PV and GIB. Sunu (GIB X-RAY product manager) took the same position as Carsten (GIB IBIT Sourcing and Vendor Management of IT portfolio) and additionally illustrated that in a global business environment, cultural differences were always going to be present, but organizations needed to be flexible and accommodating:

> *Cultural issues should not be a big problem … but you have to realize, you have to understand that there is a difference in the culture. As long as you understand that, then I do not see that as a big problem. … In that global business environment you should be able to be working with people with different cultures anyway … you should be accommodating.*

David (PV client solutions partner) commented that GIB and PV managed to make this programme a win-win situation and that is why it had turned out to be so successful:

> *In this program GIB has been able to lower its cost. … We have achieved our objectives in terms of making money, or making the appropriate amount of money that we wanted to out of the contract. We have a bigger footprint in production support in the bank which offers us opportunities to expand into other areas, so it is a win for PV.*

It appeared, however, from the interviews, that the margin of PV on this programme was relatively small. It could thus be assumed that PV had been either viewing the successful execution of this project as a pathway for more projects within GIB or that it aimed to charge higher prices during the contract renewal period.

PV Performance

A number of interviewees within GIB suggested that they were very satisfied with the performance of PV in relation to the X-RAY project. Sunu (GIB X-RAY product manager) suggested that PV had demonstrated repeatedly an effort to provide added value for GIB. He noted however that they were obviously trying to provide added value within the space of their own interests:

> *PV would always try to provide added value because they want future revenue from GIB. … PV as a company would always try to compromise, but there is a thin line between making a compromise and then making a touch decision … because you cannot keep on making compromises … for then your profit is seriously impacted.*

Sunu (GIB X-RAY product manager) noted that there was a big pressure from the markets for cost reduction and thus the space for PV to provide added value for GIB was very limited. However, according to him, their performance was satisfactory in relation to the price they were charging GIB:

> *The banking industry is very much pressurized at the moment … there is a huge pressure for cost reduction and nobody will be spending too much money … it is reasonable that you are not going to have a first class performance with a very minimum spending. … GIB probably pays the minimum but PV as a company will try at least to provide a medium class service.*

Regarding the choice of GIB to be comfortable with receiving a medium quality of service, he explained:

> *The GIB management knows that "Okay, I am paying only this much money, so I am not going to get the first class quality but I am fine with this because these applications are not strategic".*

Bart (GIB director of risk) further indicated that although "PV is not able to provide any sort of innovative solutions … it is still okay, they are not paid to innovate".

Regarding the PV performance, Simon (senior GIB manager in operations) also suggested that it was satisfactory. He mentioned that probably the response time of some people might be quicker, but overall he felt that the service was good. GIB has nominated X-RAY for an award, which was another very strong indication that it had been a successful project.

However, Bart (GIB director of risk) noted that compared to other vendors, including Indian suppliers, PV was losing its strong hold in the IT solutions market. The reason was that PV was quite good in providing low-end products and services. However, it was relatively weak in providing value-adding service. Bart (GIB director of risk) further opined, when comparing PV to Tata Consultancy Services (TCS), that:

> *TCS has a much stronger focus on delivering solutions up the value chain. TCS has a scalable/flexible business model. But they are trying to push the boundaries in terms of value add. They give an integrated view of the world because they are both at the low level and they are trying to push up to the higher level of the value chain.*

References

Willcocks, L. P., & Craig, A. (2008). *The Outsourcing Enterprise: Building Core Retained Capabilities*. Logica Internal Report.

Willcocks, L., Cullen, S., & Craig, A. (2011). *The Outsourcing Enterprise: From Cost Management to Collaborative Innovation*. London: Palgrave.

5

Inside Domestic Outsourcing with Multiple Suppliers

Introduction

DUTCH is an integrated financial service company based in the Netherlands. It offers a wide range of financial services including insurance, banking, and mortgage products to consumers, businesses, and institutions. DUTCH is the product of over 15 years of mergers and acquisitions between co-operative and competing insurance companies. From 2012 it was hiring more than 22,000 employees in more than 10 business and service units.

In 2004 DUTCH engaged in its first IT outsourcing venture with Supplier A on mainframe operations. Supplier A was an international IT service provider specializing in managing and transforming the IT operations of its customers. It was based in France and offered a variety of services ranging from data centres, workplace solutions to infrastructure, and information security solutions. It serviced different industries, including the financial services, automotive, chemical, consumer products, and the public sector. It employed 50,000 people in more than 40 countries and had operations in France, the Netherlands, the UK, other EMEA (Europe, the Middle East, and Africa) countries, Asia-Pacific, and the USA.

E. Lioliou, L. P. Willcocks, *Global Outsourcing Discourse*, Technology, Work and Globalization, https://doi.org/10.1007/978-3-319-74045-4_5

The outsourcing venture between DUTCH and Supplier A progressed efficiently and resulted in significant cost reductions for DUTCH. The company thus decided to develop its outsourcing scope and at the end of 2007, it expanded its outsourcing contract to Supplier A and started two more outsourcing ventures—one with Supplier B on networks and one with Supplier C on office automation.

Supplier B was the leading telecommunications and information and communications technology (ICT) service provider in the Netherlands. It offered products ranging from the internet, wireless telephony, and TV to consumers to integrated ICT services to business customers. Supplier B was once wholly owned by the government. Its privatization started in 1994 and was completed in 2006.

Supplier C was a global supplier of information and communication technology services. It offered workspace management, security, communication, application, and technology transformation services. It was headquartered in the Netherlands and employed about 25,000 people. As from October 2007, Supplier C became part of Supplier B.

Outsourcing Decisions

This section provides an outline of GIB's objectives when engaging into the outsourcing arrangement, the scope of the outsourcing project, as well as issues around the selection of the supplier.

Outsourcing Objectives

The first IT outsourcing venture of DUTCH in 2004 was with Supplier A on mainframe operations. The main reasons DUTCH decided to engage in this IT outsourcing venture were related to the reduction of cost and fact that the mainframe operations were not part of the company's core business. It was thus considered that outsourcing was a good strategy to utilize the technical expertise and competencies of a supplier who specialized in this area. It does appear that DUTCH had a long-term vision of putting some innovative elements into their business through outsourcing, but in practice they did not place significant emphasis on this possibility back in 2004. Previous research shows that organizations that engage in IT outsourcing for the first time tend to have a relatively immature and constrained view on IT outsourcing, and thus they are inclined to focus on the reduction of cost and neglect some more strategic considerations that could be significant for the future. DUTCH was not an exception.

The company was satisfied with the cost advantages it was realizing; it renewed the contract with Supplier A and got engaged in two more IT outsourcing arrangements in 2008: with Supplier B on networks and Supplier C on office automation. It appeared that at this time there had been a more thorough consideration of the strategic possibilities with IT outsourcing. Paul Piebinga, the DUTCH Group IT service manager said in a press release at the end of 2007:

> *This outsourcing of ICT will allow us to respond more rapidly to the changing demands of our customers. Outsourcing these activities will also guarantee the continuity, stability and reliability of DUTCH's production processes. ... DUTCH aims to be the best, most customer-orientated and most innovative financial services provider in the Netherlands. These strategic objectives are supported by the targeted use of ICT systems.*

From our findings, however, the CIO that was in charge in 2008 maintained a cost reduction approach to IT outsourcing. A few months after the signing of these deals the DUTCH CIO changed and it appears that the new CIO was more focused on the realization of the strategic possibilities of IT outsourcing. John (client director at Supplier C) described the approach of the new CIO in comparison to his predecessor:

> *The last CIO actually did the outsourcing very much from the perspective of reducing cost. This CIO looks at it and says: "Okay, I have earned this money, but now I want added value, now I want future commitment in developing an idea where are we going, now I want to have a partner ... we need more, we always want the cost reduction but we want a strategic partner in this". This is a very different attitude on the contract.*

Arno (DUTCH sector manager for sourcing arrangements) also commented on the intention of the new CIO to be innovative. John (client director at Supplier C) underlined the role of the CIO into the realization of the IT outsourcing objectives:

> *The current CIO identifies the fact that you have to be cost efficient but actually likes the idea of being—technology wise—advanced. And he is the one that, of course, has to marry those two ideas. … So that is something that he is trying to do … to manage those two differences—cost efficiency and innovation—into one forward path. He is really trying to bring those two together, that is a main task I actually see him do that at the moment.*

While the new CIO appeared to play a role in taking this more strategic approach to IT outsourcing, it has to be acknowledged that an organization such as DUTCH relatively inexperienced in IT outsourcing tends to face a lot of issues before reaching the point of exploiting more strategic benefits. As further illustrated later on, DUTCH was very much struggling with operational issues in its IT outsourcing arrangements and thus it became very hard to focus on more strategic aspects such as the achievement of innovation.

A further challenge in the exploitation of strategic benefits in outsourcing related to the pressure to focus on the cost aspects of the venture. Arno (DUTCH sector manager for sourcing arrangements) suggested that DUTCH had a big financial loss in 2008 and thus it became very much cost-oriented in the management of its IT outsourcing relationships:

> *In 2008 DUTCH had a huge loss, so finance came on all of the agendas of the DUTCH company. So now, finally, we are also managing projects using financials. So meeting project budgets but also have the proper hygiene in place. … We all now know that we also have financial responsibilities to meet.*

Outsourcing Scope

The entire 2007 deal with the three suppliers represented a combined value of more than €415 million. All three contracts were medium term and would run for five years.

Supplier A would provide the data centre services for DUTCH and focus on the availability, continuity, and security of the service. The contract between DUTCH and Supplier A was worth €145 million.

Supplier B would provide communication services including land lines, mobile communications, and data networks. The contract between DUTCH and Supplier B was worth €150 million.

Supplier C became responsible for the management and further development of the workstation infrastructure. The company provided workstation systems for the entire DUTCH staff. The contract between DUTCH and Supplier C was worth €120 million.

Supplier Selection

In its entire previous outsourcing history, DUTCH had not engaged in a rigid supplier selection process. In other words, they had never performed a formal request for proposal (RFP) process that would allow them to compare different service delivery options. It appears that DUTCH chose to work with companies that it already had a business relationship with. This happened both in 2004 when DUTCH chose to outsource its mainframe operations to Supplier A and in 2008 when it chose to outsource its network to Supplier B and its workspace automation to Supplier C. Harry (DUTCH sector manager on IT operations) remarked:

> *In 2006, when we started thinking about outsourcing it took us quite a long time to decide the providers we were interested in and we made a very important decision back then. We decided not to do a large RFP in the market. We decided to choose the suppliers where we had a relationship already.*

The basic reason that DUTCH wanted to engage a multi-sourcing arrangement in 2008 and did not give the entire to deal to Supplier A was the issue of over-dependence on one vendor. For this reason, they did not want to bundle the service at that stage. Harry (DUTCH sector manager on IT operations) further explained that at the same time DUTCH was highly interested in creating partnerships with its vendors:

> *We did not want one single supplier. We wanted three suppliers because we did not want to lock in on one supplier. … So we said "Let's divide our infrastructure into three parts and have one supplier for data center, one for network and one for office automation" … and on each of these parts we tried to see which is our main supplier where we had the best relationship with, because we were convinced, seeing all the different outsourcing in the market at that moment, the only way to make it successful is when you try to establish a real partnership. That was our goal when we started.*

Nevertheless, Harry (DUTCH sector manager on IT operations) expressed his dissatisfaction about the choice of DUTCH to work with three outsourcing vendors and he illustrated that working with a number of suppliers makes it difficult to create real partnerships:

> *I am not very happy about the fact that we chose three partners. I think when you make a principal decision about outsourcing it is better to take one partner where you really say "we are partners", and where you also discuss this partnership more thoroughly. … I think that is one of the main issues why this (our present arrangement) is so difficult to make work.*

Harry (DUTCH sector manager on IT operations) also added that he was not sure if DUTCH would carry on its outsourcing to three suppliers because the effort to improve the performance of Supplier B and Supplier C took a lot of management and control costs.

Regarding the choice of the specific vendors, Edward (DUTCH IT director) acknowledged that for Supplier A and Supplier B, he did see the rationale for choosing to work with them. He appeared, however, more sceptical about the selection of Supplier C:

> *For Supplier A, it is more or less understandable in terms of the fact that they already had a sourcing contract on the mainframe side and they were doing well on that contract. We were very satisfied with their performance and naturally they would be the first party you look at when you want to outsource platforms. … Supplier B was of course already a very important business partner for us in terms of telecommunications. … The selection process in Supplier C. … I do not have it on the table nor do I care too much because I am just managing the existing situation. But I have my suspicions this was not a very careful, scientific auditable process.*

Similarly to Edward (DUTCH IT director), Harry (DUTCH sector manager on IT operations) illustrated that the choice of Supplier A and Supplier B did make sense to him but also expressed his concerns over Supplier C:

> *Supplier A was already in place because we had already outsourced our mainframe with them. We already had an experience with Supplier A in an outsourcing way of thinking. … Supplier B our connectivity partner … a large part of the network was already in the hands of Supplier B. Thus, we had a large understanding with Supplier B. … So Supplier A very logical, Supplier B logical—while also we did not have any outsourcing experience with them— …. Supplier C really to be honest … a bit strange. … I am not sure where that came from. … I know we did business with them but from my point of view, we did not do business with them on the workstations until then. … So that was actually a rather strange decision afterwards. … I am not sure who made that decision.*

It was interesting to find out that, in 2007, when the Supplier C contract was signed, the company appeared to have a bad image in the market. A number of our research participants expressed their scepticism about the extent that Supplier C was chosen for good business reasons. It turned out, however, that the DUTCH IT director that signed the Supplier C contract in 2008 went to work to Supplier C a few months after the closing of the deal.

The next sections provide an overview of DUTCH's as well as the suppliers' capabilities for the management of the venture.

Client and Supplier Capabilities

In this section the capabilities of the client and the vendor are illustrated. The frameworks that were utilized are the same as in the previous case studies, namely the 'nine core IS capabilities framework' (Willcocks and Craig 2008) and the 'twelve key supplier capabilities' framework by Willcocks et al. (2011).

DUTCH's Capabilities

From our evidence, DUTCH was lacking important capabilities that put significant constraints on the efficient management of its complex multi-sourcing venture. More specifically we will focus upon issues of IS/IT governance, business systems thinking, relationship building, designing technical architecture, making technology work, informed buying, contract facilitation, contract monitoring, and vendor development.

Leadership: IT governance is particularly important for ensuring that the IT function is successfully integrated and delivers value to the business side. DUTCH was the product of a lot of mergers and acquisitions between organizations. It thus consisted of a number of business units that had their own IT history and architecture. The integration of these different IT architectures was particularly complex and made IT governance a great challenge for DUTCH. John (contract manager from Supplier C) very vividly emphasized "You have a very kaleidoscopic IT world within DUTCH itself which is reasonably unmanageable. If you want to outsource that … it really becomes a mess."

The main companies within DUTCH concerned with information and communication technology challenges were Interpolis and DUTCH IT. These two companies appear to have a different attitude towards the acquisition of IT. John (client director at Supplier C) mentioned:

> *Interpolis has always been used to be the top of the bill … have the best of breed and actually invent things. … DUTCH IT on the other hand is more like "lets be a fast forward, but lets be very economical about it". … The first guys mind about the technology and the latter mind about the money. … This creates a very messy situation by default. … Edward (DUTCH IT director) does realize this predicament and he is trying to marry these two things more or less.*

As illustrated later, in addition to the challenge of integrating the diverse IT architectures within DUTCH, the different attitude of Interpolis and DUTCH IT in the acquisition of IT created issues in the internal management of DUTCH's IT outsourcing ventures.

Business systems thinking: This capability is about "ensuring that IT capabilities are envisioned in every business process" and that the technology aspects of business problems are being identified. A major expectation from DUTCH from its suppliers was that they were proactive and that they came up with proposals on how they could contribute to DUTCH's business. Along these lines, DUTCH itself was relatively weak in terms of business systems thinking and that it was a benefit it expected to acquire through outsourcing.

Relationship building: Facilitation of communication and co-operation between business and IT units within an organization. Within DUTCH it appeared that there were tensions between the business units and the IT departments. Michael (DUTCH IT demand manager) noted that IT was being viewed as a cost centre rather than a strategic enabler for the business. He also noted:

> *If you are not capable of explaining your challenges as an IT business to the primary business of DUTCH itself as customers, you are always in reaction mode. This is a major challenge for DUTCH.*

John (contract manager from Supplier C) illustrated also the additional challenges that the diverse customers within DUTCH pose towards the acquisition of IT:

> *DUTCH is not one customer. DUTCH is a group of customers with their own history. … And these customers do not always concur with what one part of the company has thought and what DUTCH has contracted.*

Architectural planning and design: This capability refers to the creation of a coherent IT architecture that will be accommodating current and future business needs. As mentioned, DUTCH had a diverse IT architecture which was complex to integrate. Michael (DUTCH IT demand manager) noted:

> *The directors of Interpolis and DUTCH IT had an important decision to make three years back: "Do we first integrate the two different companies or do we bring it through the external service providers and let them integrate?"*

> *… The latter one is the one that was chosen at the time … and it had an impact on the way you can give steer to these external service providers. … They were saying "you send me a not integrated file, so we have to take some time to go through the level that we need to reach". … This choice weakened our position.*

It thus appears that DUTCH was itself not capable of creating a coherent IT architecture, and it decided to deal with this challenge through outsourcing.

Arnold (DUTCH sector manager for sourcing arrangements) added that the retained organization in terms of technical expertise was very poor and that at this point (mid-2010) DUTCH was unable to review its technical design:

> *We have architects but, for example, we do not have a controlling architect. Those guys have gone. And what we now run into is doing a project which is a called a "project start architecture". Currently we do not have the capability to review the technical design. This is something DUTCH still should have in place because then you have a project end architecture … and currently DUTCH is unable to close the loop.*

A further problem was that DUTCH had not been investing in its IT infrastructure, and it did not have a good understanding of the processes it was outsourcing. Edward (DUTCH IT director) elaborated on this issue:

> *We had not properly invested in the environment that we were moving to the vendors. We did not have the proper assessment levels, maintenance levels and we did not know what we were outsourcing to them. Consequently in the first phase of the contract there was the verification phase. And what happened was "We do not know what we have given to you, can you please tell us?"*

It thus appears that DUTCH was basically trying to hand out to the suppliers some IT areas that it could not manage on its own.

Making technology work: This capability is mainly related to the facilitation of business needs not properly satisfied by technical approaches. Although DUTCH faced a lot of issues into making technology work, it appears that there was a lot of informal communication and exchange directed towards the effort of making technology work.

Informed buying: Analysis of market opportunities. DUTCH did not go through a very formal RFP process to exploit potential market opportunities when it was engaging with the three large IT outsourcing contracts back in 2007. It appears, however, that the company was by mid-2010 much more active in seeking potential market opportunities, especially because it had entered a period in which it was reconsidering its current IT outsourcing contracts.

Contract facilitation: Ensuring the success of current contracts on a day-to-day basis. Edward (DUTCH IT director) illustrated very vividly that this was a major challenge to an organization that had not done much outsourcing before. He explained that a lot of time, effort, and experience are needed before an outsourcing customer becomes competent in facilitating and managing its outsourcing ventures. He highlighted that vendors have a big plus in that respect:

> *So what you typically find is that in the level of professionalism, in terms of service level management, the vendors have a ten mile advantage over the organization … that is executing the outsourcing. And thus, organizing in the fastest possible way a professional manner of conducting vendor management and service level management is a must-do from the client organization …. Because this is not the way internal organizations are managed.*

He also added:

> *Even though some internal service providers are using service levels and semi-contractual agreements internally with their own internal customers, it is not the same as when you are an outsourcing part and you have a separate P&L responsibility, experienced sales people and account representatives … it is a different ballgame. But that is what is making it very difficult for organizations to adjust and adapt. … I have seen organizations taking at least two to three years to get up to par with their supplier. … And these two to three years they have paid a lot of extra money for things they should not have bought and so on.*

While the 'innovation tool' constitutes an important mechanism to motivate the suppliers, it appears that DUTCH had been relatively week in influencing vendor behaviour, primarily for two reasons:

1. The firm had so far had a poor retained management capability, and the suppliers to some extent have taken advantage of it.
2. There were contractual gaps and/or misspecifications that do not incentivize the suppliers to perform.

Contract monitoring: Holding suppliers to account against both existing contracts and developing their performance according to the standards of the service market. DUTCH was doing relatively poor in that respect. It appeared that because the company did not have a very good control of the processes it was outsourcing, it later on faced a lot of challenges in monitoring its contracts, ensuring the performance of the vendors, and making sure that it was receiving standards more typical of the competitive service market. DUTCH was making important progress towards developing its contract monitoring capability. DUTCH was by mid-2010 more active in benchmarking and very focused in developing its governance structures. It had put effort in introducing much more detailed metrics than ever before, as a way of gaining more control over the outsourcing arrangements.

Vendor development: Long-term potential of the suppliers to provide value. DUTCH was very much concerned about the potential of its suppliers to provide added value for its business. As elaborated later, DUTCH was interested not only to make sure that its vendors were able to adhere to their service levels and deliver operational performance but also to leverage their potential to provide added value to its business.

Suppliers' Capabilities

In this section we will assess the suppliers' capabilities for service delivery. We will use the categorization developed by Feeny et al. (2005) and will examine the suppliers' delivery, transformation, and relationship competencies. More specifically the *delivery competency* is based on the supplier's ability to respond to the customer's ongoing needs. The *transformation competency* is based on the supplier's ability to deliver radically improved service in terms of both quality and cost. The *relationship competency* is based on the supplier's willingness and ability to align its business model to the values, goals, and needs of the customer.

Supplier A Capabilities

Delivery competency: Supplier A appeared to be doing well in terms of delivering the required service. Although there had been some performance issues towards the end of 2009, it appeared from our interviews within DUTCH that they did consider Supplier A as a supplier that possessed the right expertise to deliver quality service to DUTCH. Harry (DUTCH sector manager on IT operations) illustrated that DUTCH demonstrated continuously a problem-solving attitude and exerted effort to understand and address operational issues in co-operation with DUTCH: "They sit with us and they try to find out 'what is the problem, what do we have to do, what do you have to do' … and together we make it work."

Transformation competency: While a number of interviewees within DUTCH recognized that Supplier A possesses important technical capabilities, it appears that they were somewhat concerned with their potential to transform current business and provide value-added service. Liam (Consultant to DUTCH) explained:

> *I think they are technically quite good. The problem is that they do not have an insight into the business processes in such a way they would be seen as a professional advisor. So Supplier A is good at hosting services instead of advisory services.*

Arnold (DUTCH sector manager for sourcing arrangements) also felt that although Supplier A was considered the best supplier for data centre management, they did not fully come up to the expectations of DUTCH:

> *For data centre management Supplier A is of course the best. And we are disappointed because we have a long-term relationship with Supplier A … and we had this relationship even before the outsourcing initiative. So how well should Supplier A understand the data centre position of DUTCH? They should be very well aware. They should know what the relationship is between service application, locations and so on. And now when they are building scenarios and finding how to move a data centre from location A to location B, what we see is that they are struggling … and it is disappointing because they even have a separate organization called Move ICT, dedicated to data centre movements … and again they are still struggling.*

Similarly to Arnold (DUTCH sector manager for sourcing arrangements), Edward (DUTCH IT director) said:

> *They had a specific area in the past where they had an existing relationship and that was in mainframe services. Now they are a general hosting provider. So that means that they are also now maintaining other platforms and data centre locations themselves … they are basically maintaining all the storage and what we are seeing is not so much a deviation from the agreed day-to-day service levels, but a not flawless execution in projects.*

Relationship competency: From our findings it appears that there was a mutual interest from DUTCH and Supplier A to make their outsourcing venture successful. As later discussed, the business between the two organizations had been growing—there was a good relationship at the senior level and a cultural fit in the way of conducting business. However, it appears that Supplier A did not do particularly well regarding customer development. At this time (mid-2010), the two organizations were still negotiating their potential for aligning their visions. Marco (DUTCH contract manager for Supplier A) noted on this issue:

> *Supplier A wants new business very badly. We are one of the biggest clients for them and there was, until a couple of months ago, also the vision regarding DUTCH that they will get a lot of new business, talking about a lot of millions. … And there you see the second thoughts on our board level, then based on the incidents and relation right now, that maybe we do have to ask Supplier B or another vendor to get a more strategic role and make Supplier A one of the two or three strategic vendors instead of the biggest one. So that is the real change.*

Supplier B Capabilities

Delivery competency: From our interviews it appeared that it took Supplier B quite a long time to get to the point of delivering the required service to DUTCH. As discussed later (in the more detailed discussion below on the relationship between DUTCH and Supplier B), this delay was related not only to the delivery competency of Supplier B but also to the messy situation they inherited from DUTCH. Another issue was that Supplier

B was doing well in terms of delivering standardized products to DUTCH but not in terms of responding to non-standard requests.

Transformation competency: Supplier B had been concerned for a long time with operational issues in service delivery and had not been able to demonstrate their ability to transform DUTCH's business. Edward (DUTCH IT director) mentioned:

> *The fundamental problems that they had with their day-to-day performance has been keeping them from thinking about business transformation or innovation altogether. And the type of innovation they are doing currently is very basic, it is focused on stability-improving activities ... and we are wearing the entire team out by just focusing on those stability programmes.*

However, John (client director at Supplier C) mentioned that in his view Supplier B was a company that had a forward-looking view of the service it delivered:

> *Supplier B has been under a lot of market strain and competition and thus it is a company that is far more in a position to try to envisage what are the products of tomorrow etc etc and they beat the customer on that.*

Relationship competency: As detailed below (in the more elaborate discussion on the relationship between DUTCH and Supplier B), DUTCH is an important customer for Supplier B but was not ranked among its top ones. There also appears to be a cultural misfit between the two organizations that hindered the development of a good relationship. By 2010, DUTCH was interested to see what the vision of Supplier B was on the services they were providing and what their proposition on adding value to DUTCH's business for the coming years would be.

Supplier C Capabilities

Delivery competency: From the beginning of the outsourcing venture, Supplier C was doing very poorly in terms of service delivery. A major reason for the underperformance of Supplier C had to do with the internal organization of Supplier C. John (contract manager from Supplier C) brought as an example the way that his company is dealing with the management of incidents. He illustrated that it was a complicated process with a number of people involved in it whose roles and responsibilities seemed to be unclear. As a result the incident management process had not been generating any positive results:

> *You get for instance an incident management process. You got an incident agent. You got an incident coordinator who should, who is supposed to instruct the incident agent. Then there is an incident manager who has to talk to the incident coordinators. Then there is … believe it or not … there is another incident manager and still now you have got four people but from those four people none solves the incident. … They are not responsible for solving the incident. … And then you got line management. You got a line manager and you got a team coordinator and a team manager and you have got a team coordinator and somewhere in the line there is probably someone who has to solve the incident. This makes it all a very slow process which means that incidents are not solved in time.*

John (contract manager from Supplier C) also noted that the delivery of service was overall very complicated due to the fact that many Supplier C divisions were involved:

> *I think in speaking about governance, it has got something to do with the way Supplier C is organized because there is not one department or one division within Supplier C who was responsible for service delivery to DUTCH. We have got workplace management service, global service center … so different divisions are responsible for service delivery. So from each division, you got a service delivery manager and there is one integral service delivery manager covering all the others. So that makes it intricate.*

He also highlighted that these divisions have budget problems with one another:

> *One other aspect of the different divisions within Supplier C, responsible for service delivery is also that you got a budget problem. Who is going to pay for what? So when they discuss the kind of service that has to be delivered, there is always a discussion about money. … And below service delivery there is all*

kinds of departments with their own budgets. So team managers don't want to pay for another team. ... So the question, the problem always is shoved around.

John (contract manager from Supplier C) further noted that the problems that Supplier C faced internally were getting exacerbated as a result of the merger with Supplier B. He mentioned that there was a lot of movement of people, new top management, and that Supplier B had a different working style than Supplier C.

Transformation competency: Supplier C had been struggling very much with operational issues and has not managed to demonstrate its competency to transform the business of DUTCH. From DUTCH's side, it appeared that even in the case that Supplier C managed to demonstrate a better delivery competency, they would still not want to carry on working with Supplier C. John (client director at Supplier C) accepted that his company was very reactive as a business: "Supplier C is a typical outsourcing partner. ... A customer has a problem and they respond to that. He has a problem, they respond. It is very much a reactive type of business."

Relationship competency: From our interviews it appears that Supplier C had a very poor competency in developing its outsourcing relationships. A number of indications in support of this conclusion will be presented later, during the discussion of the evolving relationship between DUTCH and Supplier C. However, it is worth mentioning that Supplier C appeared to be relatively passive in developing its relationship with DUTCH. Our interviewees within DUTCH repeatedly expressed their dissatisfaction with the arrogant attitude within Supplier C and their non-responsiveness. Furthermore, it appears that there was not a special connection at the senior level that could facilitate the relationship between the two organizations. In some way, it appeared that Supplier C had given up on its potential to extend the outsourcing relationship with DUTCH.

Contracts

The three contracts followed the same structure and provided information on areas such as the general agreement, the sourcing period, the IT services to be provided, security issues, audits and benchmarks, a change plan, personnel issues, intellectual property issues, financials and confidentiality issues, details for the acceptance of service, details of invoices, pre-employment screening, and project management issues.

DUTCH's governance structure included three levels: the operational level (issues of discussion involve day-to-day business and service levels), the tactical level (this level dealt with a more general overview of management of processes and their impact), and the strategic level (discussions between directors regarding the vision and strategic direction of their organizations).

Apart from the formal key performance indicators (KPIs) and service level agreements (SLAs) that each of DUTCH's vendors was expected to achieve, there were some softer criteria upon which the suppliers were being assessed. Within DUTCH these softer criteria appeared to be more important as of mid-2010. These soft KPIs called 'strategic performance indicators' (SPIs) were also contracted and were concerned with issues such as on-time delivery, on budget, and so on. DUTCH had credits on the KPIs and bonuses on the SPIs. According to Liselore (DUTCH lawyer), the SPIs were not really used the way they were meant to, and they were not focusing on issues such as innovation.

Additionally a risk/reward mechanism was applied in all three contracts. Each IT service (e.g. internet connectivity) was translated into a specific value called service credit. The objective of service credits was to stimulate the providers to achieve and meet the agreed services. At the same time service credits served as a compensation for the underperformance of other IT services (e.g. hosting service). The starting point to assess the service credits were the critical KPIs. The KPIs were divided into a percentage of the service credit. Example: hosting service = 10% of the service credit. All service credits were aggregated into a risk pool which is 10% of the monthly revenue. To weight each KPI, the following raking was applied: KPI = n% × risk pool. When KPIs are achieved, a bonus or penalty will be executed. If they did well and vendors innovated, they received a larger part of DUTCH's innovation budget.

Another mechanism within the contract for governing and steering the behaviour of suppliers was the 'innovation tool'. More specifically, there was an innovation budget both on the DUTCH and on the vendor side. Inside DUTCH there was also a mechanism to decide what part of its budget would be used for innovation projects and what part for other kinds of projects. The innovation board at DUTCH decided how this budget was going to be spent. If the vendor performed well, then they got a bigger share of the DUTCH part of the innovation and contributed less themselves. More specifically, the SPIs were attached to the outsourcing goals, and based on the scores on these indicators, the budget was split between DUTCH and its suppliers. In other words, DUTCH had a reserve of money and the vendors had placed some kind of presales money into the contract. This mechanism was meant to incentivize suppliers, as DUTCH would spend more on the innovation projects with the vendor that was performing well. By mid-2010, however, this mechanism had not been implemented completely because of problems of getting reports on KPIs and SPIs. It also appears that the suppliers of DUTCH were not particularly geared up to achieve innovation.

The customer satisfaction survey was another formal procedure aimed at controlling the outcomes of vendor performance. However, according to a number of our DUTCH interviewees, the customer satisfaction survey was constructed in such a way that it did not reflect the real performance of Supplier C and Supplier B. In other words, while the customer satisfaction survey produced a relatively satisfactory image, it did not reflect the real situation with Supplier C and Supplier B, just because of its content and structure.

The overall contract structure applied was as follows:

1. Governance model
   - (a) KPIs: performance indicators based on the balanced scorecard
   - (b) Innovation (budget) (4.25% of the annual revenue of the previous year) can be upgraded when the performance is achieved
   - (c) Audit plan (bundled set of audits)
   - (d) Complaints, escalations
   - (e) Meeting structures at strategic, tactical, and operational levels

     Including agenda, time frame, and frequency

(f) Reports

Performance on processes (architecture, security, service management)
Only one person is allowed to fulfil one role/function
Vendor employees must be authorized by DUTCH when they want to work for the client DUTCH (pre-employment screening, including interviews)

2. Indicators

   (a) Strategic performance indicators

   Related to strategic goals (agility, execution power, managing cost level)

   (b) Sourcing objectives
   (c) Innovation budget
   (d) KPIs and critical KPIs (related to service delivery)

3. Personnel

   (a) All roles and responsibilities at both DUTCH and provider side are described and explained. At DUTCH the following roles are identified: sector manager, client service manager, sourcing manager, vendor manager, product manager, and operation manager. At the provider side we recognize the following roles: client executive, commercial director, client operations manager, security officer, and service delivery manager
   (b) Meeting structures are defined at strategic, tactical, and operational levels and are organized based on an agenda

4. Conflicts

   (a) Mediation

5. Operational Level Agreements

   (a) The Operational Level Agreements describe the operational agreements between DUTCH and their providers (e.g. type of IT service, performance metrics, and price)

   (b) Measurement methodology is based on the weight of various determinants (business balanced scorecard model) like service delivery and pricing
   (c) Service delivery coordination agreements are based on consciously implemented processes related to integrating IT services
   (d) Two important documents are well described and explained. First, the SoW (statements of work) and second a FA (financial agreements)

6. Transition plan
7. General agreements
   (a) Changes, pre-employment screening
   (b) Project management
8. Security agreements
9. Financials
   (a) Audits and benchmarks: including processes and procedures applied
10. Exit plan
11. Service improvement plan

The next sections provide details of the evolution of execution in each of the contracts, with a focus on the areas that appeared to be problematic. It is worth mentioning that DUTCH is an organization that culturally tended to favour the role of informal governance in the execution of its contractual arrangements. With this in mind, the role of informal governance in complementing the formal contractual arrangements will also be illustrated.

Supplier A Contract

The Supplier A contract was signed in 2007 and it basically constituted an evolution of the previous contract between the two organizations back in 2004 that was already running smoothly. The only significant change was that the contract grew in terms of size, and more services were outsourced to Supplier A. Irene (engagement manager from Supplier A) mentioned that DUTCH made significant miscalculations, especially regarding the storage capacity it needed, and the value of the contract increased by 66.7%:

> *They did not know how much hardware they had in their data centers. The contract was signed for 120 million over five years and it turns out to be 200 million. … Storage is the bigger part of the contract and they miscalculated by an enormous percentage. DUTCH IT merged with Interpolis and because they were going to outsource they did not pay attention to the merger. … They thought it is going to happen in the outsourcing and they did not look at the south of Holland. So they did not know their numbers.*

It can be assumed that the neglect of DUTCH to do a more accurate calculation of its requirements reduced its negotiating position on the contract. Edward (DUTCH IT director) additionally appeared to have concerns over the current pricing system with Supplier A. However, Marco (DUTCH contract manager for Supplier A) mentioned that in 2009 DUTCH went through a benchmarking procedure on the Supplier A services and they managed to push the prices down: "We sat together with a formal benchmarker and we made this a joint project … after some negotiations they put their prices down."

Furthermore, the two organizations had a very good prior history and DUTCH did not put particular emphasis on the details of the new contract. Although the contract between the two organizations lacked some precision, it appeared that this did not become an obstacle for their co-operation. The two organizations were discussing openly and they did progress to some contractual amendments in time. Nevertheless, the relationship between the two organizations was good—Supplier A was demonstrating a satisfactory performance and for a long time it appeared that the contract played a relatively secondary role in the management of the ongoing outsourcing venture.

Marco (DUTCH contract manager for Supplier A) and Irene (engagement manager from Supplier A) were very much in favour of not managing the venture too rigidly on the basis on the contract. Marco (DUTCH contract manager for Supplier A) illustrated that while he was very knowledgeable on the contract, he preferred to stay away from it whenever possible:

The contract is the basis which you can rely on but it must not be part of your work as a vendor manager the whole day. Yes, I know it from the first to the last page and sometimes I have big discussions about it but it is not on a daily basis. … I try to keep as much away from it as possible but what we do is updates. … It is very important that you keep it updated. If we have for example hidden service or things that were not foreseen and sometimes it costs money for DUTCH, I try to attach this change to the contract. … The contract is a living document.

In a similar vein, Irene (engagement manager from Supplier A) recognized the importance of people in the execution of the contract and highlighted:

I do not think that if I have a very good contract, everything will then be okay. You do not get rid of your problems if you only have a good contract, you need very good people. … Once you have to pull the contract off the shelf, it is too late already because then the relationship has not worked.

Marco (DUTCH contract manager for Supplier A) additionally mentioned that there were some meetings with Supplier A that are outside the contract that were very significant for the smooth operation of the venture. He suggested that this sort of informal governance was very significant and he recognized this as a difference with how Supplier B and Supplier C were managed:

At Supplier A we also have the incident and the problem meeting … these are not part of the contract but we do it anyway to get discussion and things working. … So apart from the formal governance, there is a lot more informal governance with Supplier A than the other two vendors. … In the Supplier A relationship people find each other more easily. … My way of working is that people can contact each other.

It appears, however, that while this sort of informal governance appeared to work fine for DUTCH and Supplier A, some operational cracks in the

Supplier A performance in late 2009, together with their overall delay to progress into the transformation stage of the venture, directed the attention of the DUTCH senior management back to the contract. Edward (DUTCH IT director), while accepting that, to some extent, part of the problem was the lack of a realistic plan in relation to the timelines of these projects, did claim that DUTCH had not given proper incentives to its suppliers, including Supplier A, to meet these timelines:

> *If we had contracted it differently and said "this is the date that you are responsible for migrating the services to the FMO and our prices are dropping at that moment", they would get pressured. … Now all the pressure and the issues are with DUTCH, not with our vendors. … They have all the reasons for some time to stay in the PMO (present mode of operation) or PMO Plus instead of moving to the Future Mode of Operations. … So basically there is not a natural alignment of incentives. … From a contractual perspective, we did not establish the proper incentive to move to PMO Plus or FMO.*

There appeared to be another significant obstacle in the progress to the transformation stage. By 2010, DUTCH was having financial discussions with Supplier A regarding investment in the new data centres. Arnold (DUTCH sector manager for sourcing arrangements) mentioned that DUTCH was not prepared to make an additional investment. Similarly, Edward (DUTCH IT director) noted that DUTCH's intent of outsourcing had to be contractually clear:

> *So one of the big reasons why we wanted to outsource was to have a variable cost and a "demand-capacity" type of service …. Consequently it is rather irritating to be confronted with a supplier that basically says "Well, if you want machine X, Y or Z, I want you to guarantee that you will use it for three years otherwise I will not do the investment." … We said to them "What? This is not the way we wanted it". So we are now getting back into contract study and adaptation to the contract because we feel that we further need to clarify what the original intent of the outsourcing was and this should be contractually clear … crystal clear.*

It thus appears that there was a lack of clarity or even most likely a lack of completeness in the contract that allowed for some manipulation of what had been agreed, and this worked in favour of the vendor.

According to Irene (engagement manager from Supplier A), the main problem she had observed with the current contractual arrangements of DUTCH was that at times there was a lot of battling over responsibilities between the four parties (DUTCH and the three vendors). She suggested however that a contract can never be complete: "Of course you cannot put everything on paper. We tried that. You first put something in the contract then the reality sets in. And also the issue is where does our contract stop?." On this basis she said that the definition and redefinition of obligations and responsibilities in outsourcing arrangement was an ongoing challenge.

Supplier B Contract

At the time when the contract with Supplier B was signed, back in 2008, DUTCH was not very focused on using formal governance mechanisms and relied solely on the relationships of the people for the management of the venture. Edward (DUTCH IT director) noted:

> *We took a bit too large a jump back in 2007 … because we thought that in outsourcing and a partnership relation, you do not have to write every detail down … and that is what we did, we did not write down every detail.*

The venture with Supplier B did not start very well, however; there were a lot of operational problems and the Supplier B performance was very low. For these reasons DUTCH realized that it had to go back to its formal governance processes and put significant effort into putting down the details of the outsourcing venture.

One of the main issues with the Supplier B contract was that it did not establish clear measurement procedures in relation to the Supplier B performance. For this reason there had been a lot of disagreement between the two organizations regarding particular figures of performance. Gabriel (DUTCH contract manager for Supplier B) illustrated a very typical situation that used to come up:

> *We saw an SLA performance of 50% and Supplier B was saying "it looks like 50%, but there is this … and this … and this" … and they spoke it up to 80%, which is the minimum performance they should achieve.*

Jacob (DUTCH outsourcing operations for Supplier B) added that what he found particularly frustrating was that the two organizations ended up talking about ratings and not actual methods of performance improvement:

> *We said the performance had to be 80%. We show them the rating and it was 70%. … They were always saying to us 70% is not correct … it is actually 85%. … So we are not talking about how we can get the performance to a higher level, but we are talking about the rating.*

At this point the two organizations appear to have addressed the challenge of establishing a common measurement system. Gabriel (DUTCH contract manager for Supplier B) noted the process of trying to understand DUTCH's operations and processes in order to be able to measure them generated significant knowledge that people within DUTCH did not have:

> *In the short saying, garbage in is garbage out. Now we have tried to manage our own garbage and I think we are able to manage it. … We know where the real garbage is and we are wiping it away … the performance and the control mechanisms helped us.*

It appears that the contract lacked clarity not only in respect to measurement procedures but also in relation to the actual service levels that Supplier B should provide. The deal was that the service levels that Supplier B had been able to give during the first six months of the co-operation would be measured and those would be the contractual service levels. Edward (DUTCH IT director) suggested that you have to have an extremely trustworthy relationship with your vendor to do something like this.

In addition to the lack of clarity in relation to the measurement procedures and the service levels, there were other parts of the contract that led to different interpretations. Jacob (DUTCH outsourcing operations for Supplier B) elaborated on this issue: "If you ask five people to read the contract … they will come up with five different understandings … that is a major problem we have with the contract." As a result of this lack of clarity and preciseness, the contract is currently being rewritten, and one of the main areas being improved is the product catalogue.

Another major issue was that the contract with Supplier B was not complete. More specifically, the contract did not cover important areas such as business continuity, disaster recovery, or security management. These omissions were particularly important, taking into account that there were regulations that actually make these processes obligatory. It is also significant that an organization has to set down a clear process on how it is going to recover its operations in the case of a disastrous event. Michiel (engagement manager from Supplier B) noted that DUTCH has been relying on informal governance regarding the areas of business continuity, disaster recovery, and security management, but they now realized that they had to put them down contractually:

> *Supplier B is a very large organization and I am mitigating this risk internally at Supplier B currently. … So I know that there are large risks for DUTCH and when a large problem occurs they will say "please help us and we are friends, partnership etc." … So although it is not contracted that way, they will ask us for those measures when it occurs. … So I am setting proactive offers for them right now and we are mitigating these risks … but they still have to establish these processes contractually … not just on the pressure of regulation, but also because they need to know what they are going to do with their business, the up-time of their internet … or the call centre functionality in case of urgency.*

He also added that DUTCH had important internal problems back in 2008 and they were very busy with getting the performance straight. This is why they did not do something about the processes of business continuity, disaster recovery, and security management back then.

Michiel (engagement manager from Supplier B) noted that in the beginning they had too much informal governance that was actually hindering the two organizations from working effectively:

> *We started to have more meetings in addition to the ones that the contractual governance had established … by the second half of 2008, we had so many meetings that people in my team were in meetings for about two-quarters or three-quarters of a week with DUTCH just to talk without doing any actions. … March 2009 we decided to go back to the contractual governance.*

Michiel (engagement manager from Supplier B) suggested that by following very rigid governance procedures a supplier may become a bit more inflexible. However, keeping a close and documented control of the work is at the benefit of the customer:

> *When you are trying to bring something under control, you have to work according to a governance, according to rules … and we are understanding better certain products, what they do, how old they are, when they need to get replaced. … These documentation processes where not here when DUTCH tried to outsource. … And the effect was always more inflexibility. … But when we are documenting the work, we are getting a better quality for less money.*

Michiel (engagement manager from Supplier B) noted that although formal governance did not fit his own personality, he had learnt that

> *When you look at the huge amount of questions, requests, thoughts and actions related to outsourcing … you cannot do anything other than follow formal governance process.*

He mentioned that he very often received informal requests from DUTCH, but he understood that he often had to say no.

The contract also included some misspecifications related to the infrastructure that Supplier B was receiving. In particular, the versions that Supplier B would undertake were older than the ones mentioned in the contract. These misspecifications enabled Supplier B to charge DUTCH more and certainly this caused a lot of dissatisfaction within DUTCH.

Supplier C Contract

Similar to the Supplier A and Supplier B contracts, the Supplier C contract lacked details as well. Edward (DUTCH IT director) mentioned that DUTCH progressed to the outsourcing of workspace management too fast without having a good control of the processes they were outsourcing. This, in turn, created a lot of tension with the supplier:

> *When we outsourced our workspace management systems … we did this too fast and there were a lot of things that we did not know how they worked and we were*

asking the supplier to explain to us, while it should be the other way around. ... This meant that we were actually not in control ... and when you are outsourcing, you should know what you need functionally and ask your provider to do it. ... And we had a catalogue with services which was really far from complete. ... We should have been more accurate because if you outsource garbage, you get garbage back.

The performance of Supplier C was not satisfactory and two years after signing the contract, the venture was still in transition. To make matters worse, the venture with DUTCH was still at the stage of 'present' mode of operations, while the company was paying at the rates of the 'future' mode operations, for a service it did not receive. Although the performance of Supplier C had been consistently bad and the venture very problematic, it appears that DUTCH was not able to terminate their contract without incurring significant cost because it could not build enough evidence to claim termination for cause. According to Rob (DUTCH contract manager for Supplier C), there was an informal agreement that enabled DUTCH to terminate the contract without having too many restrictions when handing the service to another supplier, but he was concerned about this option as there was nothing on paper:

There is a gentlemen's agreement ... yes. But when you try to affect this agreement—meaning the contract—*you are not sure whether they are going to be flexible. There is nothing on paper. If we look at the contract we cannot just stop right now. It is not possible. ... We have not built enough evidence to be able to claim termination for cause. ... So we really have a gentlemen's agreement ... 'if you want to stop, that is not a problem' ... but this is not on paper. ... It is made on the board of directors level, which is a gentlemen's agreement ... nothing signed.*

Along these lines, Rob (DUTCH contract manager for Supplier C) suggested that it would be better for DUTCH to search for other suppliers. Yet he was concerned that the termination of the contract with Supplier C would cost a lot of money:

We are facing a lot of problems which to an extent means that we may have to break the contract ... it should be better to take things out and put it with another supplier. But in terms of how the contract restricts us to do those things, it is very difficult. ... So I think that the whole swap from one supplier to another will cost us a lot of money.

Rob (DUTCH contract manager for Supplier C) additionally mentioned that the governance between DUTCH and Supplier C had been improved in terms of establishing the right communication structures but also in terms of documentation. He noted that it was important to have the right people in place but also the appropriate documentation:

> *We have sort of adapted the governance to get a smoother form of communication between Supplier C and DUTCH … and it works very well. … But you also have to grow within the governance, not only in making sure that the right people are talking to each other, but also in terms of building quality reports, quality documentation. … We have seen that the quality of the notes that we used to make was not really enough. … So it is not only a matter of having the right people, but also the quality of content.*

Another issue was that DUTCH and Supplier C were using different measurement systems. John (contract manager from Supplier C) more specifically mentioned "The numbers DUTCH uses differs from the numbers Supplier C uses. So we always have these discussions about what the figures represent." He further mentioned that another problem was that they did not have common definitions on what an incident was or what certain levels of priority represent.

Rob (DUTCH contract manager for Supplier C) mentioned that they used to run into a lot of problems into Supplier C because they were using general metrics for performance, and thus it appeared that there were no problems to report. He highlighted, however, the need for the disaggregation of data: "With our current reporting we are getting only one figure and no matrix. … Once we are connected to their service management tooling, it is going to be much better in getting reports on detailed figures."

When the two organizations started their co-operation, they agreed on working with the service management tool that was used at DUTCH. Rob (DUTCH contract manager for Supplier C) elaborated:

> *Suppliers however have their own service management tool. … So they have to work with our tooling … and our tooling was going from customer to the Supplier C work-group. … And under Supplier C there were a lot of sub-work groups. … In the end, we could only get reports about the total service that*

> *Supplier C provided us. … We have a lot of services … we have workspaces, mail etc etc … normally you would expect that you should expect a report that addresses all the different service. This was a problem, we only had one general figure. … So it was very difficult to analyze which were the problematic areas. … It took us a lot of time to get into deeper modes of analysis.*

Harry (DUTCH sector manager on IT operations) illustrated an example where the measurement of the Supplier C performance was not precise. What happened was that there was not a very clear agreement about when Supplier C performance should begin to be measured:

> *When we started to work with Supplier C, we measured the time from when a service request enters DUTCH IT until it is sorted out. We measured the total time. Of course, Supplier C said "we did not agree on this total time, we agreed on this part of it, where my work is. … You have to measure me on my performance and this part of the deal."*

He further noted a major mistake that DUTCH made—the service levels they agreed with Supplier C were not in line with the total service levels to their end customers.

DUTCH'S Outsourcing Relationships

The following sections provide details on the evolution of the relational aspects between DUTCH and its suppliers. We will focus on issues such as the prior history between the outsourcing parties, their mutual interest in the relationship, and issues of co-operation, communication, dependency, and senior management involvement, as well as cultural issues. While there will be a brief reference to performance issues, these will be discussed in further detail later on.

Relationship Between DUTCH and Supplier A

The Supplier A contract was the first IT outsourcing venture for DUTCH, signed in 2004. As already mentioned, the two companies had already had a business relationship before 2004, which played a major role in the selection of Supplier A. The prior relationship between the two companies had been also particularly significant in reaching common ground and solving problems during the early stages of their outsourcing relationship. Thus, while the performance of Supplier A was not reaching the desired levels at the beginning of the outsourcing venture, the two companies worked closely and the performance results improved and got stabilized later on. Marco (DUTCH contract manager for Supplier A) described the development of the relationship: "The experience was not really good in the beginning, the transition phase was behind … but after a year things significantly improved. … The business case, the return on investment was huge and it stayed huge." On this basis and despite the problems in the first period of the outsourcing venture, the contract grew very significantly from 2004. DUTCH became one of the biggest clients of Supplier A in the Netherlands, while Supplier A became the number one vendor of DUTCH.

Regarding the development of the DUTCH-Supplier A outsourcing relationship, Harry (DUTCH sector manager on IT operations) indicated the importance of communication and close co-operation between the two organizations when they were facing problematic situations:

> *I think Supplier A really tried to make it work as a partnership … and of course we had our issues, and of course there were problems … moments where we said "Well, Jesus. … Supplier A this was a very crappy job you did there." And we had a lot of discussions with them, but in essence, you could talk with them and discuss "well, what do we have to give, what do you have to give, where do we make it together work for our customers within DUTCH?"*

Edward (DUTCH IT director) underlined the growth of the contract between DUTCH and Supplier A as an important factor in the development of the outsourcing relationship and also the fact that Supplier A appeared to have good profit margins from the contract:

> *They are in a good deal, they are making their profit, that is clear … and they are in a growing deal. … Because we have difficulties managing our demand which means that storage and server capacity which is basically the heart of the*

contract, just keeps on growing at a rate where you have to be satisfied as a supplier. And they also admit that DUTCH is a) an important account for them and b) is also an account for them where they still have some financial flexibility and they do not have the feeling that they are at the rock bottom.

Irene (engagement manager from Supplier A) commented extensively on how much her company values DUTCH as a customer. Similar to Edward (DUTCH IT director), she stressed the importance of the size and profit margins of the contract in the development of the relationship with DUTCH:

Well, if you have a good relation with the customer and you make money out of the contract, if those two things are together, then it is a good contract. And it is a large contract. It is one of the largest contracts that we have. It is one of our biggest customers which is also important because if you have a good contract but it is a small one, it does not mean anything for the company. But the DUTCH contract means a lot for our company in the Netherlands.

A number of interviewees indicated that there was a very good working relationship between the DUTCH and Supplier A people. It also appeared that the good and long-standing relationship between the engagement managers of the two companies played an important role in more turbulent times. Irene (engagement manager from Supplier A) also added the importance of favourable relationships at the senior level in the smooth execution of the venture:

We are lucky there because Edward (DUTCH IT director) is a friend of our managing director in the Netherlands. … They have an emotional bond so they can always speak.

She mentioned, however, that for day-to-day operations, this connection at the senior level does not matter much:

This relationship could not help if I screwed up the contract and relation every day. But it works when we have difficulties, especially these kinds of discussions about whether we can do business outside the current contract … then it does help.

Irene (engagement manager from Supplier A) also said that there had to be a mutual give and take from the two organizations. Along these lines, she indicated that her organization was willing to be lenient with DUTCH as long as DUTCH is lenient with her organization:

> *We have a very good relationship and I realize that the vendor manager that we work with now sometimes gets accused that he is too easy with us. But I assure you, yes, he probably is a bit easy with us, he does leave me 10,000 here and a little bit there, but I do that as well, I do that in not telling that I want every cent from him. … And we are not looking with a magnifying glass. … So we are trying to be lenient but if the atmosphere gets worse then I will be stricter. It is not going to earn anybody any money. And it is probably going to make the operation worse as well.*

It also appears that DUTCH and Supplier A had a shared interest and a mutual dependency in the relationship. DUTCH appeared to be heavily reliant on Supplier A on the grounds that the size of the deal was big and the services contracted to Supplier A were particularly important for the smooth execution of its operations. As an example, all the new DUTCH servers were placed in the data centres with Supplier A from 2008. According to Marco (DUTCH contract manager for Supplier A), the exit strategy of DUTCH out of the contract would be very difficult. From the Supplier A side, it did appear that they have a dependency and a high interest in DUTCH, in the sense that it was one of their top three customers in the Netherlands. Furthermore, Supplier A saw the potential for doing more business with DUTCH in the future, especially in the area of applications. On this basis, Marco (DUTCH contract manager for Supplier A) maintained that Supplier A had very good incentives to exert effort in their relationship with DUTCH.

Michael (DUTCH IT demand manager) also noted that there was a fit between the Supplier A and the DUTCH culture and that they both saw their venture as a partnership directed towards obtaining results: “Their culture fits the DUTCH culture. … Supplier A seeks to make it a partnership with a goal. … There is a mutual desire to get the best results.”

Gabriel (DUTCH contract manager for Supplier B) emphasized also the fit between DUTCH and Supplier A and explained that both organizations sought more relationship-based approaches to conducting business: "Supplier A likes soft, flexible and more relationship orientated interactions, unlike some other suppliers. … So that suggests that there is a better fit between DUTCH and Supplier A."

Despite the good relationship between DUTCH and Supplier A, both companies had more recently been receiving financial pressures that affected the smooth development of the outsourcing venture. On the one hand, DUTCH made a significant loss in 2008, something that presumably made it more sensitive to issues of cost. From the Supplier A side, Irene (engagement manager from Supplier A) mentioned that although the profits that its company were making on the DUTCH contract were high, she still received big pressures from the Supplier A mother company in France:

> *What is particularly problematic at present is that we are still struggling with the relation between the Dutch company and the French. … The French are asking us to provide numbers and today they want them horizontally, tomorrow they want them vertically. … My numbers are good, I am making an enormous amount of profit … but they put an enormous amount of stress on us to reduce costs and do whatever you can think of. And that takes up a lot of our time which we should be spending on the customer.*

Although in the first round of the interviews, all research participants commented very highly on the Supplier A performance (and actually brought it in juxtaposition to the evolvement of the relationship and the performance of Supplier B and Supplier C), they had a rather different attitude during the second round of discussions. It appears that there were some incidents in the period between November 2009 and January 2010 that created some turbulence in the relationship.

More specifically, there was an incident that resulted in some data loss that had never appeared before. That was a major issue that put the relation under a lot of stress. Furthermore, the two organizations had been having some financial discussions regarding the movement of the DUTCH servers to Supplier A (this movement would be in parallel to reaching the future mode of operation in the Supplier A contract). In particular, Supplier A was expecting DUTCH to make an investment in this operation that DUTCH was not prepared to make. Arnold (DUTCH sector manager for sourcing arrangements) noted that it was highly probable that Supplier A was receiving pressure from its mother company in France but that they were not open to discussions on this:

> *We, as DUTCH, do not want to invest. We do not want to own any property in a data center. They see that we have presented that point of view for several months already and they still are asking us for a certain amount of money to do the investment. … So … "Okay then Supplier A, do you have an internal conflict within the Supplier A organization? Is it that Supplier A Netherlands is not allowed to do the investments themselves?" We do not know. So we have asked Supplier A to share their problem, but they are not willing to.*

Marco (DUTCH contract manager for Supplier A) indicated that these financial discussions in relation to the movement of servers had not been moving very well and that there was a lot of finger-pointing from the DUTCH boards to Supplier A. He emphasized that although he was doing his best to smooth the relationship between the two organizations, the venture was undergoing a lot of turbulence, and despite the long-term effective co-operation with Supplier A, he appeared to be uncertain about the future of the venture:

> *On the one hand, I am a little bit in the middle of course, and that is my role and I see that the Board is not that realistic all the time. So I am trying to manipulate them a little bit so they act differently and just get real and see what Supplier A has done in the past four years. But there is, at this moment, so much pressure from the business, also from the head office on financial result but also on the problems themselves, that there is just a little bit space to manoeuvre. And I am not sure where it is going to. … So at this point, it can be go up again but also it can go down and we get the same relation as we have with some other vendors and problems with it. … So I hope that we have learned that despite of this kind of periods, that we can give the relation the more strategic role that it had before … but I am not sure at the moment. So you see that Supplier A is the biggest vendor and the most strategic at the moment, but the Board is also looking also at different vendors and there is a Dutch saying that the grass always seems greener than where you are and that is what is happening now.*

Edward (DUTCH IT director) also noted that although the performance of Supplier A is better than those of Supplier B and Supplier C, he had been observing some cracks there as well. This message appears to have been communicated to Supplier A, as Irene (engagement manager from Supplier A) pointed out that the DUTCH people had been getting very grumpy over a few months with their performance:

> *Basically in our servers nothing has changed. We are still doing well … the figures are good … but still they are very grumpy towards us, which I think in the end it obviously is not going to improve the relation … it is not going to earn the money … perhaps it is even going to cost them more money because if they are getting grumpier, we are getting grumpier. And you are tighter on your money … watching more closely that nothing slips through the mazes.*

Marco (DUTCH contract manager for Supplier A) underlined that although his organization was less satisfied with the Supplier A performance compared to a few months before, Supplier A performance results on the current business would improve. However, he highlighted that the DUTCH board was having second thoughts about giving more business to Supplier A, as their primary strategic vendor.

Relationship Between DUTCH and Supplier B

The contract with Supplier B was signed in 2007. Supplier B was selected as an outsourcing partner for DUTCH in networks because the two organizations had already had a business relationship and because Supplier B was the largest network provider in the Netherlands.

The development of the relationship between DUTCH and Supplier B had been rather patchy. An important reason for this appears to be that although the contract with Supplier B was big in terms of its value, DUTCH is not ranked among the top customers of Supplier B. Jacob (DUTCH outsourcing operations for Supplier B), the DUTCH contract manager of the Supplier B deal, commented on this issue and it appeared that he considered it an important reason for the lack of attention by Supplier B: "I believe that they see us as one of their customers. … Just a customer because they have bigger customers. So we are one of their customers. That is how it feels." He also noted that Supplier B did not act in a style of a partnership in the outsourcing arrangement with DUTCH: "DUTCH was looking for a partner … we are partners, we do it like partners. But that is not the case, the practice is that Supplier B sends at the end of a month a bill … it is not really a partnership."

Another very important issue that hindered the development of a good working relationship between Supplier B and DUTCH appeared to be a cultural clash between the two organizations. A number of interviewees within DUTCH identified the difference in cultural attitudes as a major reason for the unsatisfactory relationship between the two organizations. Along these lines, they characterized the culture of Supplier B as being arrogant. Their reasoning was that Supplier B had a monopolistic market position in the Netherlands. Gabriel (DUTCH contract manager for Supplier B) emphasized: "Supplier B is the largest network provider in the Netherlands. … Sometimes they behave as if DUTCH should be thankful for the time they spend."

Arnold (DUTCH sector manager for sourcing arrangements) elaborated on this element of arrogance in the Supplier B culture and tried to bring it in conjunction with the DUTCH culture:

> *They had a monopoly position. They were the largest vendor in the Netherlands on networking and voice. So there is a course of arrogance in their culture. And in their culture it is "Either the Supplier B way or the highway." … On the other hand, we as DUTCH, we feel unique … this is also part of typical customer behaviour of course. … We are unique, we are special. … So there you have two cultures which of course eventually collide.*

He further mentioned that although in terms of some of their technical approaches Supplier B might be right, he had a lot of issues with their behaviour:

> *We did some self reflection because you have to be honest. Looking at the infrastructural services, you are talking about commodities. And contracting commodities with vendors is also stating "I apply your best practice". … So I think for infrastructure services it is the Supplier B way. … But then of course talking about behaviour the "Supplier B way" is "leaning on the chair and just waiting for something to happen. … And then, uh, we have a disruption, lets fix it and*

customer, you have to be very pleased of course if we fix it within the SLA." ... But hang on. I thought you had a network operating center with monitoring capabilities in place, didn't you see this coming? That is the right behaviour ... being proactive.

Another issue with the culture of Supplier B was the fact that they had a culture of working in a very formalized and standardized way, something that came in conflict with the informal way that DUTCH preferred to be contacting business. More specifically Michiel (engagement manager from Supplier B) from Supplier B explained:

DUTCH is possibly more informal and relationship-based ... and Supplier B is much more procedurally organised and you know it is very much focused upon standards, the standards have to be kept. This was a problem in the relationship.

On this issue Michael (DUTCH IT demand manager) noted:

It is the culture of the company I guess ... not to be stepping aside from the standard process and try to help somebody. They always go back to the standard process. I understand why, but it is horrible to work like this. ... And the more you push, the stiffer they get.

This formalized way of conducting business by Supplier B appeared to be connected to its government background. However, Supplier B's bureaucratic procedures appeared to be very annoying within DUTCH. Michael (DUTCH IT demand manager) noted that Supplier B was always taking tremendous amounts of time to deliver, while Rob (DUTCH operations) mentioned that the biggest problem he had with Supplier B was that he did not know how he could 'activate' their speed to do something. On this basis non-standard demands or the request for specialties became very complicated for the client. More specifically Rob noted:

When you put something in a back office through to Supplier B, three months later something will come out, you know what comes out and you know what it costs. But it lasts for three months. If you want speciality, "I want within that factory ... a private line with fibre optics ... within two weeks" they are not able to manage that. That's really difficult for them.

On this basis Supplier B was not particularly successful in accommodating the non-standardized requests from DUTCH. While the DUTCH research participants wanted Supplier B to be more efficient in delivering their non-standard requests, they did accept that it was immature for DUTCH to have this culture of non-standard delivery. Gabriel (DUTCH contract manager for Supplier B) highlighted:

DUTCH wants everything as a speciality, really everything has a high priority and it's not standardised. We contracted PDC where all our products are designed, because we wanted to take standard products from Supplier B and Supplier C. The ink wasn't even dry and we had a speciality.

Gabriel further noted that in his view, an important expectation from the side of Supplier B and Supplier C might be that DUTCH changed its culture to be making constantly non-standard requests:

What Supplier B and Supplier C would want from DUTCH is to ask for standardized products ... where we describe the product, negotiated the price and do not ask any specialty apart from that. Because this is how they are managed, how they are structured, this is how their culture is.

Jacob (DUTCH outsourcing operations for Supplier B) also identified as a problem that to some extent the senior management in Supplier B and DUTCH did not have a very close relationship:

Another problem is that if you want to be a partner the senior management has to have a relationship ... you have to go few times and rent a boat, go to the sea and have a nice day and understand each other, talk with each other. Now we are only talking about service levels, about the contract. ... There has to be an understanding in a more human way.

Despite all these problems in the relationship between DUTCH and Supplier B, it appears that Supplier B was changing its attitude as the contract renewal period approached and was trying to exert extra effort in order to satisfy DUTCH. Gabriel (DUTCH contract manager for Supplier B) noted on this issue: "What I see in Supplier B is that at the moment there is a switch to positive commitment to DUTCH, because they really, really do not want to lose DUTCH as a customer." Although DUTCH was not among the very top-ranked customers of Supplier B for deserving 'special treatment', it appeared that it was an important account for Supplier B that they would not want to lose. Gabriel (DUTCH contract manager for Supplier B) noted that a very positive development since September 2009 had been the change of focus from the operational to the technical level:

> *A couple of months ago we only spoke with Supplier B about incident A or incident B and their capability of solving it within the time we contracted. … This time, we speak with Supplier B about what innovation can be done in their product lines to help DUTCH innovate. … It is a small step we have made but at least it appears that we are moving to a higher level with Supplier B. … Out operational focus is decreasing and the focus on the contract and its benefits is increasing … we had not spend any time on the contract, what is in it in the last two years.*

Although Gabriel (DUTCH contract manager for Supplier B) admitted that Supplier B had improved its performance, he noted:

> *I feel frustrated that it lasted for such a long time to get Supplier B in the performance level that we ask of them, because this is the moment where tactical governance is executed, and after that, the strategic governance. … We should have done that more than a year ago, so that is my frustration. … We lost more than a year in the outsourcing deal.*

In addition to the delay for this performance improvement, it is also important to note that to the frustration of our interviewees within DUTCH, a change in the arrogant attitude of Supplier B had not materialized.

Relationship Between DUTCH and Supplier C

As already mentioned, the contract with Supplier C was signed in 2007 and a number of DUTCH interviewees had been sceptical about the choice of Supplier C as an outsourcing supplier. DUTCH had already had a commercial relationship with Supplier C, but Harry (DUTCH sector manager on IT operations) noted:

> *I know we did business with them but from my point of view, we did not do business with them on workstations until then. So that is actually a rather strange decision. I do not know where it came from.*

The choice of Supplier C appears to be related to personal relationships and politics, and more specifically to the two DUTCH executives that signed the contract and six months later on were hired by Supplier C. It may well be that with this genesis, and with the sponsor of the deal also leaving, the venture was at risk from the start.

Regarding the DUTCH-Supplier C relationship, Rob (DUTCH contract manager for Supplier C) mentioned that a major problem was that the attitude of the Supplier C people towards DUTCH was not good. More specifically, it appears that the Supplier C people did not have a problem-solving attitude. Rob (DUTCH contract manager for Supplier C) elaborated on this issue by making a comparison between Supplier A and Supplier C attitudes:

> *I also worked together with Supplier A and they have a completely different attitude. … Lets say that Supplier A treats the customer more like a customer and Supplier C does not. … If I would define a KPI on attitude, Supplier A would get seven out of ten, while Supplier C only three. … And we do have the same contract structure, but as you understand, it has to do with ownership. If you do an outsourcing of the workspace, you really want to get a company that takes the contract to solve your problems. Supplier C does not solve problems. What happens is that we ask a question and we get two questions back.*

He added that Supplier C had an attitude of pointing the finger at DUTCH and blaming them for everything:

> *We were always the ones that did not do it well or right. … It was never Supplier C. It was always the customer that did not ask the right question, or the customer that did not do something on time. … It was never Supplier C.*

It thus appears that the two parties were not particularly competent in solving conflicts and managing problematic situations. Harry (DUTCH sector manager on IT operations) also noted that from the beginning of their outsourcing venture with Supplier C they had real problems in defining what the two organizations had agreed and they had to be always going back to the contract. According to him, for this reason this venture could not progress as a partnership.

Harry (DUTCH sector manager on IT operations) also mentioned that DUTCH tried to keep control of its architectural decisions. That proved to be a problem in the development of the relationship because the DUTCH architects had a different point of view from the Supplier C people, which led to disagreements:

> *I think it is still a very good idea to let the architects work in our company and let them choose the right way forward. But also, these architects have a DUTCH way of thinking. And of course, Supplier C had a different mindset. … These conflicts made discussions about a partnership very difficult. … Supplier C said "Well, in our future mode of operation this is the way we have to go" … and our architects were saying "No, we want to go there". … So we said to Supplier C that "it is nice that they have this environment which they can deliver for their customer but we want a slightly different one".*

Interestingly, Rob (DUTCH contract manager for Supplier C) mentioned that Supplier C was doing financially very well in the DUTCH account. And that was exactly the reason why they did not pay serious attention to the issues that DUTCH faced:

> *I know that financially they were actually in a very good position, because what I learned is that in terms of profit and loss, as long as their customer is green … there is no response. If you ask something, there will be no response. … Internally in Supplier C, above all these client directors there is a man who is vice president, who is responsible for the twenty-five largest accounts. … So as long as his light is green, you do not get any attention. It starts when financially the light becomes red. There is no profit for Supplier C anymore, so they start paying attention.*

Rob (DUTCH contract manager for Supplier C) added that the situation with Supplier C was too problematic for DUTCH and at some point they had to go outside the normal governance structure and address this person. That was the only time DUTCH got his attention. So Rob concluded that "So it is the financials, that is the metric that they are using in the management of the outsourcing … as long as they are getting their profit, they do not really care".

Arnold (DUTCH sector manager for sourcing arrangements) suggested that Supplier C had a very important problem in its internal organization, because they were having issues with other customers as well:

> *It is not just DUTCH … the perception of all their customers is actually the same, they get below what they expect. … I believe that there will come very difficult times for Supplier C. … And I believe also that they will lose a lot of contracts in the next coming two years.*

Arnold (DUTCH sector manager for sourcing arrangements) explained that the workload for DUTCH was really big, due to the inability of Supplier C to deliver:

> *Normally, in our organization, we should be with something like thirty-two people to manage the Supplier C service. … We actually need fifty-six to handle it because nothing goes as it should go. … We work now one year and ten months with them … and what I have to say is that it is really too much work to work with Supplier C.*

Arnold (DUTCH sector manager for sourcing arrangements) also noted that there was not a good fit between what DUTCH expects for its suppliers and the cultural attitude of Supplier C. More specifically, he mentioned that Supplier C does not have a culture of being proactive:

> *When you look at some cultural aspects within Supplier C, for example … taking ownership, being proactive, presenting improvement plans by it self and not because DUTCH asked for it. … There is this cultural aspect that has also been discussed with them. … So meeting the service levels on regular business is not enough for DUTCH. … We are now focusing on their "cultural performance" and we have agreed that Supplier C will use the first quarter of 2010 to prove their added value for the DUTCH organization.*

Staff transfer towards Supplier C included 100 full-time employees. This transfer proved to be problematic, predominantly because employee unions were very powerful within DUTCH. What happened was that the people that should be transferred to the suppliers actually stayed within DUTCH and consequently their knowledge was not passed on. Edward (DUTCH IT director) elaborated on this issue:

> *There were difficult discussions with the unions and employee representatives in terms of what are the social terms and conditions … and what happened was that less people that could be assigned for the work were actually transferred to the vendors because at the last minute we decided to basically offer everybody a job somewhere else in DUTCH. So if you do not want the fallout, you have the possibility to apply for another role within DUTCH.*

While the Supplier C participants mentioned that DUTCH was an important customer for their company, it did feel like that to some extent Supplier C was giving up on the possibility for renewal. It felt like a lot of people thought "we are not going to get a renewal here anyway, so what is the point?" It appears that unless there is some dramatic action at senior levels in Supplier C, the Supplier C employees in the DUTCH contract would be demotivated.

Supplier Performance

Supplier A Performance

For a long time, the performance of Supplier A appeared to be satisfactory in terms of reaching their service levels. Marco (DUTCH contract manager for Supplier A) mentioned as a reason why Supplier A performed better than the other two suppliers—the longer co-operation between DUTCH and Supplier A. However, he mentioned that it was additionally very important that people in the interface between DUTCH and Supplier A were not moving, which was not the case with the other two suppliers. He explained that Supplier A had a very good team that was already working at DUTCH and also an operation manager that had been involved in this arrangement since its initiation. According to him the phase of transition is particularly critical for every outsourcing arrangement and he emphasized that it was very important for the partners to keep the team close and stable:

> *So that's one of the unique things you have to do as you outsource … that at the start, in your transition, try to keep for a period of time the team together to deliver to the customer … and then try to decide what you are going to do latter with the services and the people.*

Irene also made a similar comment and suggested that the basic reason why Supplier B and Supplier C were underperforming was related to the way that they were organized. In the case of Supplier A, there was the group of people that came from DUTCH plus a group of people who were from Supplier A. These people were involved in the ongoing management and governance of the venture and they had a voice through her. In the case of Supplier B and Supplier C, the people in operations were working from the factory and the engagement managers from Supplier B and Supplier C did not have proper communication lines with them:

> *In Supplier B and Supplier C they put their people in the factory, they do the work from the factory but my counterparts at Supplier B and Supplier C can not say anything to these people. I think that this has been the key to our success because we have been more flexible in adhering to the customer's needs.*

Edward (DUTCH IT director) discussed, however, his dissatisfaction with the performance of Supplier A during the period November 2009–January 2010, as there were some important incidents (including a data loss) that had a major effect on DUTCH's operations. It appeared that Supplier A was not fully coming up to DUTCH's expectations:

> *If you are a hosting provider and you are managing storage for a financial institution like Supplier A, your ability to handle changes professionally, execute projects professionally is critical to the business continuity … and we are seeing too much problems there.*

He also maintained that there had been a considerable delay in completing the movement of the DUTCH data centres into the Supplier A data centres. The two organizations were still in the beginning of these projects and there were also significant discussions regarding the investment that each party would make.

Supplier B Performance

The performance of Supplier B was not satisfactory when the venture started. Gabriel (DUTCH contract manager for Supplier B) gave an example and mentioned that for the DUTCH centralized service desk, Supplier B should have achieved a first-time resolution of a level of 75% that was negotiated in their contract and it achieved only 35%. As mentioned above, for a long time there were a lot of operational problems in managing the outsourcing venture and especially issues regarding the measurements of the service. A major problem for the underperformance of Supplier B appears to be that a lot of the people that were transferred to Supplier B went back to DUTCH. The outcome was that knowledge did not go to Supplier B but remained within DUTCH.

Although the performance of Supplier B improved, it appears that this had taken them too long to achieve. According to the contract, Supplier B should progress from the 'present mode of operations' to the 'present mode of operations plus' until July 2008. However, the company did not manage to do this until May 2009 and a number of interviewees within DUTCH expressed their frustration at this loss of time. Gabriel (DUTCH contract manager for Supplier B) more specifically mentioned:

> *It is disappointing that it lasted for such a long time to get Supplier B in the performance level that we asked from them, because this is the moment where I start to fill the tactical governance and after that, with Edward (DUTCH IT director) the strategic governance. We should have done that more than a year ago, so that is my frustration. We lost more than a year in the outsourcing deal … it is very important that Supplier B and DUTCH come together and exchange their strategic view for the coming years, what is DUTCH doing in health care, insurance or banking and what is Supplier B can do to help*

> *DUTCH enlarge their power in the insurance market … we could not have such discussions until now … we were overwhelmed with operational problems.*

Gabriel (DUTCH contract manager for Supplier B) acknowledged that an important reason why Supplier B could not perform was related to the very own DUTCH infrastructure which was outdated:

> *We have given the management to Supplier B and said "now that is your problem". We are saying to them "you now have to reach the service levels" and that is not fair. So if you are really a partner, you have to say "okay we give you the rubbish, please helps us to get the rubbish on a good level and then we are talking about the service levels".*

It appears that Supplier B had subsequently improved its performance but not quickly enough. They missed their committed improvement deadlines two times and subsequently by late 2009 were openly renegotiating with DUTCH on the current contract.

Supplier C Performance

The performance of Supplier C had been unsatisfactory for a long time. Rob (DUTCH contract manager for Supplier C) said that for a long time there was a lot of finger-pointing between the two organizations regarding responsibility and the improvement plans were not fruitful enough:

> *They always said we do not do it right … and we said you do not do it right. So these discussions lasted for three or four months and finally we got some improvement on the service levels, but still way below the 80% we expected.*

A major reason for the underperformance of Supplier C appears to be that the DUTCH staff that were transferred to Supplier C in mid-January 2008, by July 2008 had been moved into the Supplier C factory. As a result, the knowledge, the motivation, the incentive, and the relationship they had with DUTCH had gone completely. Thus, while new people were coming into DUTCH from the suppliers' companies, DUTCH was not operating a formal governance structure precisely when it really needed to have some level of stability in its processes.

No one really explained why that happened, why those people went off the contract, and relatively soon after they went into Supplier C. This could be attributed to different reasons, for example, some re-organizing inside Supplier C, the redistribution of workforces, and probably some people that were particularly good were used for other contracts. While it is difficult to explain why these people left the contract, their movement clearly impinged adversely upon the relationship. Having the same people would have stabilized the relationship, would have established the commitment of the workforce, and would have enabled them to build knowledge of their client. This knowledge was lost during transition because of the change of people in these roles.

Another reason that might explain the consistently bad performance of Supplier C appears to be that at some stage in its history the company decided that it was not cost-efficient enough and that it needed to reduce its cost base. For this reason the company needed a re-organization with better processes and a way of accounting where money went and who earned what. It appears that Supplier C became very internally focused, and while trying to re-organize itself, it neglected the fact that it was servicing a particular set of customers. Thus, a number of interviewees within DUTCH, although they appeared to appreciate the technical capabilities of Supplier C, were highly concerned about its delivery capabilities. For them, that was a major obstacle in the development of the relationship between DUTCH and Supplier C.

At the operational level Supplier C had a client team dedicated to facing its top four or five customers for service delivery. DUTCH is one of them. However, this team appeared not to have any significant power to get the resources to serve customers properly.

In January 2010, Supplier C improved its performance and managed to reach its service levels. Yet, DUTCH was not satisfied with their overall performance and their potential for achieving business transformation. Arnold (DUTCH sector manager for sourcing arrangements) said:

They are now on target, but we realize it took DUTCH more than 13 months to achieve that level. You can imagine that we are not satisfied with the performance of Supplier C. So the board of directors of both companies have met and discussed. ... Because meeting service levels on regular services is one achievement, but when you look at the level of business change ... this is in deep red.

On this basis, a number of interviewees appeared to be pessimistic regarding the prospects of Supplier C to improve its performance. At this point, DUTCH was seriously considering a contract exit.

References

Feeny, D., Willcocks, L., & Lacity, M. (2005). Taking the Measure of Outsourcing Providers. *Sloan Management Review, 46*(3), 41–48.

Willcocks, L. P., & Craig, A. (2008). *The Outsourcing Enterprise: Building Core Retained Capabilities*. Logica Internal Report.

Willcocks, L., Cullen, S., & Craig, A. (2011). *The Outsourcing Enterprise: From Cost Management to Collaborative Innovation*. London: Palgrave.

6

The Transaction Cost Economics Discourse

Introduction

This chapter presents analysis of the three case studies and five outsourcing contracts from a transaction cost economics (TCE) perspective. The TCE analysis takes place at two levels: in the first level of analysis we focus on the constructs of asset specificity and frequency and assess the predictive power of TCE over the decision to keep the IT activities in-house, outsource using a contract as a tool of governance, or outsource based primarily on relationships. In the second level of analysis we perform a similar assessment, but we also included the construct of uncertainty.

The LION Outsourcing Contract from a TCE Perspective

Asset Specificity and Frequency

The services outsourced from LION to FDL included the development, support, and maintenance of systems for savings and loans products.

E. Lioliou, L. P. Willcocks, *Global Outsourcing Discourse*, Technology, Work and Globalization, https://doi.org/10.1007/978-3-319-74045-4_6

Systems development was seen as a service that required knowledge that was specific to the LION business. Systems support and maintenance were viewed as a more generic kind of service. The research participants further indicated that the provision of these services required particular familiarity and knowledge of the Dutch regulatory environment. LION was the primary customer of FDL in the Netherlands and thus we tend to believe that this factor was contributing to some relative increase in terms of asset specificity. Liam (LION demand manager) additionally highlighted that at the beginning of the outsourcing venture there was a 'get-to-know' period, where the two parties had to set out and align their processes:

> *At the start we defined a lot of procedures, we had to learn how all these procedures worked. For instance, if we ask for a change from FDL, it has to go through a specific procedure here within LION. … It has to go through the procurement department, it has to go through the finance department … another guy has to give approval on that … etc etc … and then it goes to FDL. And FDL gives us a proposal on our request for change and this is how it goes … we all had to learn how these procedures work. … That was the first year, we were learning. … The second year was to grow into a more mature level and to improve these procedures because what we saw is that some of these procedures did not work or could be more efficient.*

In time, as the two parties accumulated learning and experience around their work processes, they went a step further to improve them. In this direction, the two parties created a document of working practices that would provide a basis for the coordination of their activities.

In terms of the frequency of the transactions, systems development was seen as a relatively frequent activity. There was a rather important amount of interaction between the two firms in terms of systems requirement identification. Systems support and maintenance were generally viewed as ongoing and frequent transactions.

On this basis, the outsourcing deal included a sizeable amount of services that required knowledge specific to LION, as well as an important amount of processes to support the interactions with LION. On the other hand, the interactions between the two organizations appeared to be relatively frequent, in the course of a three-year period. For the above reasons, it appears more proper to classify the transaction as 'mixed recurrent'.

Uncertainty

Environmental Uncertainty

LION was facing significant challenges in defining the volume of services it needed on the savings and loans systems development, support, and maintenance. A major reason is that financial markets are highly unpredictable and that the demand for certain products and services changes rapidly. This volatility in the market environment is a significant driver for outsourcing within the financial service industry, particularly in IT-related products and business processes. As Bamse (LION business manager) indicated:

> *In an organization like ours, if you only develop for your own organization you need people to do that of course and you have them on your payroll. And there are times when they do not have anything to do and there is times when they have too much to do. There is never a smooth line in the work. An outsourcing vendor has more flexibility in putting the right people, at the right time, in the right company.*

On this basis, the scalability of demand was an important driver for LION in the decision to outsource its savings and loans systems development, support, and maintenance. In the contract with FDL, it is very specifically mentioned that LION is outsourcing various IT functions in its savings and loans products in order to achieve a number of objectives, including scalability.

Nevertheless, the financial industry went through a period of recession during 2008 and a lot of institutions in the sector, including LION, incurred significant losses. The financial stretch that LION had been going through as a result of the economic crisis in 2008 made it compulsory for the firm to cut into its cost-structure and reduce investments on systems development. Back then, LION negotiated with FDL to change their outsourcing cost model. The two organizations had a transparent discussion on the salary and compensation rates of the onshore and offshore workforce and decided that the most efficient way to go forward would be the reduction of the number of Indian employees. It appears, however, that LION was still under pressure to reduce the volume of services outsourced to FDL on the savings and loans area. The disadvantage for LION was that reducing the size of the contract was most likely going to increase the pricing.

Research participants did not appear to be particularly concerned with issues of technological uncertainty in the area of the savings and loans products. LION did not regard this area as key for the generation of strategic competencies and thus tended to downplay the influence of technological changes. On the other hand, it might be that LION was relying on the outsourcing vendor to handle issues related to technological changes.

Research participants within LION were concerned about the future of the venture with FDL. FDL is an American company and LION is its major customer in the Netherlands. The problem? Volumes that LION needed from FDL in the Netherlands were declining, as a result of the financial crisis. For this reason some of the LION managers explained their fear that FDL might decide at some point to 'pull the plug' in the Netherlands. For this reason, LION was also looking at other suppliers. It appears, however, that a major challenge for LION was to identify a technically competent supplier that would also have experience with the Dutch regulatory environment.

Internal Uncertainty

Within the LION organization, there were many issues stemming from requirement uncertainty that increased the transaction costs with FDL. According to the research participants, LION had difficulty in translating its business requirements into systems requirements but also in identifying the exact scope of projects. Rajesh (consultant from FDL) noted on this issue:

> *Proper requirements management was not done properly … even the project management may not have a clue about what they really wanted actually. It was difficult for them to collect their system requirements and turn it to a business requirement and send it to us actually.*

Furthermore, LION was very often changing its requirements, which inhibited the effective coordination of processes with the offshore team. Boris (LION lawyer) explained:

> *After the assessment of services you are supposed to have an idea of the scope … but this is never the case within LION, because scope can change until you have signed the contract and after. … So one of the big issues with any contract is that you need fixed requirements. If you know that they are hard to fix, like the LION case, you need a very firm change process and you have to stick to that.*

While these issues were important and were causing disturbances in the execution of operations, it appears that the two organizations put the right processes in place in order to handle 'requests for change' relatively smoothly.

Furthermore, within LION the communication lines between the different disciplines of the organization did not operate particularly effectively. The size of LION made it particularly challenging to organize the flow of information which makes the execution of work harder. In terms of contract management and facilitation with an external vendor, LION had to increase the professionalization of its internal organization.

Behavioural Uncertainty

In relation to the assessment of the performance of the vendor, it appears that LION was not facing issues. The assessment of the service levels and the overall methodology against which the supplier's performance would be assessed was clearly established by the contract between the two organizations. LION and FDL seemed to have very explicit governance process set-up, and according to the research participants, there were not any penalties or too many examples of serious escalation.

LION and FDL had a long history of co-operation before signing the outsourcing arrangement. For this reason, LION had a good idea of the FDL capabilities and its way of conducting business. The prior history between the two firms provided LION with significant indications regarding the positive evolution of the venture. FDL had convinced LION in relation to both its skill set and its ability to perform. Haresh (account manager from FDL) noted on this issue:

> *We made it very clear to LION that we are very trustworthy … the other suppliers were by far the cheapest in terms of cost savings, but we were by far the lowest risk because we had the skill set and we had a track record with LION. … This is what convinced LION to work with us.*

On this basis, the prior history between the two firms constituted a mitigator of the possibility that the FDL would behave opportunistically.

Furthermore, it appears that FDL valued LION very much as a customer. LION was one of the top institutions in the financial sector and thus it added to its suppliers' reputation, including FDL. For this reason, FDL would want to keep LION satisfied as a client.

Type of Contract

The contract between LION and FDL included a lot of details in relation to the outsourcing arrangement (including the scope of the outsourced services, the service levels, the methodology against which the supplier's performance will be assessed, time frames, pricing, and so on). The contract served as the original point of reference between the two parties, suggesting that it was neo-classical in character. Martin (LION service manager) noted:

> *FDL is very good at doing what they need to do. … They have a very good contract management organization, knowing the contract by heart. … They will do perfectly what we agreed and they will not do what we have not agreed. The issue is that colleagues, they do not just do what they agreed. … If FDL was a partner they should also do what they think is necessary for LION. … Our people who are managing the contract of FDL, maybe sometimes think that*

FDL will think for us and do more than just the asked things ... for this reason there might be gaps at these points in the relationship.

Nevertheless, there were also some relational elements in the outsourcing venture that were going beyond the contract. As examples of the relational nature of the contract, when LION underwent serious financial pressure to reduce the hours of application development, it engaged in a very transparent discussion with FDL and changed the cost-structure of the contract accordingly. Furthermore, the evidence is that FDL demonstrated a clear intention to be transparent and trustworthy in its communications with LION.

Critique of TCE in the LION Case

First Level Analysis

LION outsourced a set of 'mixed recurrent assets' to FDL. According to the theory of transaction costs, in order to achieve a successful result, LION should have outsourced the systems development, support, and maintenance of its savings and loans products using a relational contract. Instead, the outsourcing venture was carried out with the use of neo-classical contract that included some relational elements and it was still very successful.

While it is hard to say which option would be more successful than the other, we tend to believe that the use of a neo-classical contract was the only way to go, given LION decided to progress with the outsourcing venture. Although the inclusion of some relational elements in the venture was possible (and actually did happen), it appears that the creation of a strong relational contract, where both parties would mutually invest on the relationship, was less likely to evolve.

The primary reason is that the savings and loans products included a set of functions that were not regarded as particularly strategic within LION. Along these lines, it seems that the organization itself had adopted a 'resource-based approach' and consequently did not have a great interest investing in activities less significant for the generation of distinctive competences. On this basis, since there did not exist a mutual interest to create a strategic venture, where mutual investments would take place and a pattern of commonality and unity would emerge, the generation of a 'relational contract' (i.e. a venture where behaviour would ultimately be stirred by the spirit of the venture) was improbable. Taking into account the economic climate that was still putting important pressure on LION to maintain a reduced cost-structure, we tend to believe that it is highly unlikely that the firm would decide to create a relational strategic partnership with FDL.

Along these lines, according to the theory of transaction costs, LION should not have outsourced its savings and loans products unless it developed a relational contract with the vendor. Nevertheless, in practice the firm very successfully progressed with a neo-classical contract with some relational elements with its vendor. The performance of FDL appeared to be satisfactory and a number of research participants commented highly on its technical competencies and ability to deliver. Although a few challenges during the lifetime of the venture were mentioned, we did not get any research participants within LION complaining particularly about the performance of FDL, except they needed to be a bit more proactive and entrepreneurial.

Second Level Analysis

LION certainly constitutes a case where asset specificity was present to a non-trivial degree. The element of uncertainty appeared also to be significant, as a number of interviewees within LION repeatedly emphasized their concerns in relation to the highly volatile environment that their firm operates in (environmental uncertainty). There were also issues regarding the availability of suppliers and more importantly of suppliers that would be competent with the Dutch regulatory context (environmental uncertainty). Some other challenges included requirement specification and the level of professionalization within LION in terms of contract facilitation (internal uncertainty). Consequently, according to transaction cost theory—which takes into account the constructs of both asset specificity and uncertainty—LION should have kept the activities in-house.

Nevertheless, the LION case demonstrated a different logic that led to a very successful result. Environmental uncertainty was actually identified as a major reason why LION wanted to outsource its savings and loans applications in the first place. More specifically, and similar to many institutions in the financial sector, LION faced challenges in predicting its demand for IT. LION actually managed to address this challenge by outsourcing to an external vendor and also building enough flexibility into the contract in order to make adjustments according to its needs. It also appears that LION had signed the contract for the right period. Considering its constrained ability to predict its volumes, LION rightfully did not commit itself to a long-term contract.

Additionally, it did not appear that keeping the activities in-house, like the theory of transaction costs prescribes, would have brought a better result. A major reason is that the activities chosen to be outsourced were non-strategic for LION and thus investing in these activities was not adding significant value to the firm's operation. By outsourcing, LION managed to maintain a lower cost-structure that was also flexible enough to accommodate volume uncertainties. Furthermore, it seems that in terms of technical and delivery competencies, LION had selected the right supplier for the services in the savings and loans area, and FDL had already demonstrated these competencies in its prior business relationship to LION. This observation is particularly indicative, signalling the usefulness of theories within the strategic management literature (namely the resource-based view of the firm) in explaining sourcing decisions.

Additionally, FDL wanted to expand its business within LION. This was a further motivation for FDL to demonstrate good performance. Currently, it appeared that FDL already had a big stake in LION, something that concerned the LION boards. FDL kept growing its business in LION and by 2010 there were serious fears of vendor lock-in. However, getting over-dependent on one supplier generated the risk of enhancing its power position and increasing the possibility that the supplier would engage in opportunistic behaviour.

The GIB Outsourcing Contract from a TCE Perspective

Asset Specificity and Frequency

According to the research participants, PV would be hosting a set of non-strategic applications servicing a group of users that did primarily back office and some middle office activities. The idea was that by outsourcing the management of these non-strategic applications, more GIB management time could be allocated to the more strategic applications. Furthermore, research participants and especially Andrea (Vendor decisions/Relationship management) noted that the management of these non-strategic applications did not require particularly sophisticated skills or knowledge. On this basis we decided that the transaction should be classified as 'non-specific'.

In terms of frequency, it was suggested that the management and support of these applications were ongoing, suggesting the transaction to be 'recurrent'.

Uncertainty

Environmental Uncertainty

GIB interviewees emphasized that environmental uncertainty was a major concern for all firms operating in the financial sector. Changes in the market, customers' preferences, and technology were some of the primary challenges that financial firms had to be constantly coping with. Outsourcing of IT services had actually been viewed as a good strategy to cope with these types of uncertainties.

According to the interviewees, volume uncertainty was not a major issue in the outsourcing venture. Although around January 2009 the X-RAY project doubled in size (raising the number of applications that would be hosted by PV from 150 to 300), there were no particular concerns around this major increase. It seemed that PV was flexible enough to accommodate changing volumes by PV. However, it was a contractual obligation for GIB to contact PV on time to report significant changes in volume requirements, so that PV could do its best to accommodate them.

However, the bank was particularly sensitive to regulatory requirements, and thus in the contract there were several contractual clauses that requested the supplier to adhere to any regulatory changes. As an example, the service levels of the project could be amended from time to time in light of any changing regulatory practices or any new industry-wide procedures.

Regarding technological uncertainty, it turns out that firms in the financial sector were actually using outsourcing and consequently the expertise of specialized suppliers in order to satisfy their own requirements while minimizing risk. Bart (GIB director of risk) noted on this issue: "Outsourcing is a way to tackle technological uncertainties … you can also exploit technology in a way that benefits your business."

Internal Uncertainty

The year 2005 constituted a milestone in GIB's approach to IT outsourcing because the company decided to enhance its governance processes and make them more rigid. By that time, the firm had recognized that having a strong governance mechanism in operation was of critical importance to realizing the benefits of IT outsourcing. On this basis, in 2005 GIB started to work extensively on its IT outsourcing governance mechanisms and processes. By 2007, the firm managed to establish a strong IT outsourcing governance apparatus that since then has only been fine-tuned.

IB had a very integrated approach to contract monitoring and was trying to make sure that this function was taking place on a cross-division basis. Furthermore, GIB was very effective in setting down initial requirements and estimating what processes could be influenced through IT outsourcing and how. Additionally, GIB was particularly strong in terms of contract facilitation and monitoring. On this basis, internal uncertainty in GIB appeared to be pretty low.

Behavioural Uncertainty

In the case of X-RAY, there were no particular difficulties in measuring the performance of the vendor. The interviewees did not mention any significant deviances from the contracted SLAs.

Regarding the reputation of the two organizations, they had been doing business together for a long time. Firstly, in 1999, GIB had created an organization called GIB Software which was an offshore captive. This captive was taken over by PV in 2004 and a number of PV employees were part of the old GIB Software firm. There were interpersonal relationships between GIB and PV that developed over the previous 20 years. In particular Bart (GIB director of risk) noted the long-standing relationship between the two firms:

> *GIB maintained a long relationship with PV. … We know PV very well … the people, the management. … We knew that support and maintenance of applications was something that they are good at.*

On this basis, the two firms maintained a spirit of relative closeness. Furthermore, the two firms had established numerous outsourcing projects and PV was recognized as a strategic vendor to GIB. GIB was satisfied with the performance of PV, and according to a number of research participants within GIB, the deal was really cost-effective for the bank. This long history of co-operation appears to be an important factor in limiting the possibility for vendor opportunism. PV was highly interested in keeping GIB satisfied, not least because it was its number one customer.

Type of Contract

The contract between GIB and PV was very thorough and included a lot of details in relation to the outsourcing arrangement. The contract served as the original point of reference between the two parties, and we can define it as neo-classical. However, it seems that there were also some significant relational elements in the outsourcing venture that were going beyond the contract. From the interviews it turned out there was a lot of co-operation and support between the two firms. As examples, Philip (PV X-RAY European programme manager) illustrated:

> *I think that in certain circumstances if we have had a failure that we are not in a position to be able to resolve, we have been able to go over there they trust that we have done our best to resolve the issue and then go over and say "Look hands up guys, we are having trouble trying to fix this, we need your help".*

Mani also commented on the co-operative behaviour that GIB demonstrated:

> On *a personal note, speaking with some of the GIB managers they have said to me "If you ever need any help, even though we are expecting not to be involved, come over and shout if there is problem. It might be something that we are aware or of something that we have a point of view on." … So that is very good for the venture … that means that we are building the relationship with the GIB management. … Because you need to be able to say "I need your help in this" … or "I do not know, I really do not know the answer to that and thus I need your support". … If I am comfortable to be able to go over and do that, then they will feel the same kind of trust … they will trust in the fact that I can go over there and say to them "I have got a problem".*

Critique of TCE in the GIB Case

First Level Analysis

The performance of PV was very satisfactory and a number of interviewees within GIB said their firm received good "value for money" services. GIB outsourced to PV a set of 'non-specific recurrent' assets. According to the theory of transaction costs, GIB should have outsourced these assets through a classical contract. However, the firm performed the outsourcing through a neo-classical contract (with some relational element as well) and the result was very successful. From the interviews it did not appear that a standardized classical contract could accommodate the GIB requirements. It appeared that flexibility was important for the execution of the venture.

Second Level Analysis

The assets that GIB outsourced to PV were 'non-specific recurrent' and the level of uncertainty surrounding the transaction appeared to be medium. The uncertainty around the transaction stemmed primarily from environmental factors and more specifically with exogenous forces that could influence the requirements or the volumes that GIB needed. However, the theory of transaction costs suggests that for non-specific recurrent transactions, the most appropriate form of contracting remains the classical. However, from the interviews it did not appear that a classical contract would have been enough to accommodate the X-RAY project.

As mentioned, there were significant exogenous factors that impacted the volume of services. For this reason, some flexibility at the contractual level was desirable and it seems that a neo-classical contract was the most effective governance structure to progress. From the interviews it turned out that GIB had contracted the right services under the X-RAY project for the right time. The level of environmental uncertainty that surrounded transactions in the financial industry made some degree of contractual flexibility mandatory even in circumstances of low asset specificity.

DUTCH's Outsourcing Contracts from a TCE Perspective

Here we present an analysis of the DUTCH outsourcing contracts to Supplier A, Supplier B, and Supplier C. Firstly, we will examine the three ventures in terms of their asset specificity, frequency, and the type of contract. Regarding uncertainty, some of the challenges that DUTCH had been facing were related to all three vendors. For this reason these challenges will be discussed in a separate section.

Supplier A Contract

Asset Specificity and Frequency

The data centre services outsourced to Supplier A were perceived as of low asset specificity. The research participants tended to view these services as commodity services that played a support function in the operations of DUTCH on an ongoing basis, suggesting that the transaction should be classified as 'non-specific recurrent'.

However, there appeared to be some issues stemming from dedicated asset specificity that were raising the transaction costs. More specifically, Supplier A wanted DUTCH to invest in the new data centres that will be hosting its applications. It also seems that Supplier A required from DUTCH to commit to using specific equipment for three years in order to do the investment. On the other hand, DUTCH did not seem to be willing to commit in terms of either investments or time frames. Arnold (DUTCH sector manager for sourcing arrangements) explained:

> *We, as DUTCH, do not want to invest. We do not want to own any property in a data center. They see that we have presented that point of view for several months already and they still are asking us for a certain amount of money to do the investment.*

The two firms had not agreed on these issues contractually when the deal was signed and started their venture using a relationship-based approach. Nevertheless, these investments on dedicated assets that need to be made on the new data centres appear to be rather significant. We tend to believe that the research participants tended to underestimate the specificity of the transaction with Supplier A, especially when the contract on the data centre services was signed. For this reason, we decided to classify this transaction as 'mixed recurrent'.

Type of Contract

At the beginning of the outsourcing venture, the type of contract between DUTCH and Supplier A appeared to be highly relational. As illustrated in the DUTCH case study, the firm had a relationship-based approach on its outsourcing ventures and was geared towards the creation of partnerships with its suppliers. On this basis, DUTCH did not engage in formal processes and details when it was setting its outsourcing contract with Supplier A. According to the interviewees, the original contract between the two organizations lacked significant details and was signed in a spirit of 'partnership'. Some more details were built into the original contract later on and it appears that there was ongoing activity towards making the relationship with Supplier A more formal.

On the one hand, it appears that there was still a significant relational element between the two firms. Marco (DUTCH contract manager for Supplier A) and Irene (engagement manager from Supplier A), the two engagement managers of this contract, commented extensively on the long co-operation between DUTCH and Supplier A. On this basis, and although the venture has run into turbulence since the end of 2009, Marco (DUTCH contract manager for Supplier A) suggested that DUTCH was still a very important partner to Supplier A. In particular, he noted:

> *On the one hand, I am a little bit in the middle of course, and that is my role and I see that the Board is not that realistic all the time. So I am trying to manipulate them a little bit so they act differently and just get real and see what Supplier A has done in the past four years. But there is, at this moment, so much pressure from the business, also from the head office on financial results but also on the problems themselves, that there is just a little bit of space to manoeuvre in. … So I hope that we have learned that despite of this kind of periods, that we can give the relation the more strategic role that it had before … but I am not sure at the moment.*

Irene (engagement manager from Supplier A), on the other hand, emphasized how much her company valued DUTCH as a client.

However, it seems that after some incidents of unsatisfactory performance that Supplier A demonstrated towards the end of 2009 and in the light of the coming negotiations regarding investment in new data centres, DUTCH sought to make this relationship more formalized. At this point, the relationship between the two firms appeared to be stretched and the engagement managers of the two firms were trying to establish some common ground. However, Edward (DUTCH IT director) the IT director emphasized the need to maintain the intent of the venture contractually clear, implying the necessity to use the contract as the ultimate point of reference in the venture.

Supplier B Contract

Asset Specificity and Frequency

The network services outsourced to Supplier B were perceived as assets of low asset specificity. These services were viewed as commodities—although they were significant for the everyday operations of the firm, they were of low strategic importance. This is an indication that the transaction be classified as 'non-specific'.

It is worthwhile noting that research participants emphasized that DUTCH had a culture of making very customized requests to Supplier B, which is an indicator of some relative increase in asset specificity. Furthermore, because the infrastructure of DUTCH is rather complex, the two firms needed to make particular investments in order to improve the capability of DUTCH's network. Arnold (DUTCH sector manager for sourcing arrangements) elaborated on this issue:

> *We have to make some investments because again, the infrastructure of DUTCH is based upon mergers, acquisitions, so we did have some single point of failures in our infrastructure, just be connected to each other. … So Supplier B stated that we have to do some investments regarding monitoring capabilities but also redundancy and so on in order to improve the capability of our network.*

While these issues indicate some increases in asset specificity, we considered that these should not be particularly significant. We thus decided to categorize the transaction as 'non-specific' in terms of asset specificity.

Regarding the frequency of the transaction, research participants perceived the telecommunication services as ongoing activities. For this reason we will categorize the transaction as 'recurrent'.

Type of Contract

In the beginning of the venture, DUTCH appeared to have a relational contract with Supplier B. The contract between the two firms did not contain a lot of details in relation to their agreement and was relatively incomplete. Edward (DUTCH IT director) explained:

> *We took a bit too large a jump back in 2007 … because we thought that in outsourcing and a partnership relation, you do not have to write every detail down … and that is what we did, we did not write down every detail.*

As an example, the contract was missing, among others, important details on disaster recovery. In essence the contract was signed in the spirit of partnership between the two firms and for some time it was not used as point of reference in order to guide their venture.

However, the venture did not proceed in the desired way and very soon DUTCH started to put efforts towards formalizing its relationship with Supplier B. The two firms started to fill in the omissions, gaps, and misspecifications inside the contract. Particular focus was given to the measurement procedures and service levels. Other important areas included the product catalogue and the disaster recovery plan.

By 2010, Supplier B had demonstrated significant performance improvements. The interviewee also suggested that Supplier B had additionally exhibited signs of proactive behaviour. While there appear to be some relational elements in the venture, we see the agreement as being established on a more formal basis.

Supplier C Contract

Asset Specificity and Frequency

The services outsourced to Supplier C were related to the management and further development of workspace infrastructure. The research participants viewed these services as commodities, suggesting asset specificity to be low. Although DUTCH had a culture of making non-standard requests, which increased the overall specificity of the transaction, it seems that this increase was relatively small. It appears that these non-standard requests could have been accommodated by the establishment of some special processes (i.e. relative increase in procedural specificity) and that they did not require highly sophisticated knowledge that would be relevant only to DUTCH (i.e. human asset specificity is low). For this reason, we categorize the services outsourced to Supplier C as 'non-specific', in terms of asset specificity. Furthermore, research participants within DUTCH perceived these services as ongoing activities, and thus in transaction cost theory terms these ought to be classified as 'recurrent'.

Type of Contract

Initially, the contract with Supplier C was purely relational. DUTCH progressed to the outsourcing of workspace management too fast without having a proper retained management function for the processes they were outsourcing. Edward (DUTCH IT director) illustrated this situation:

> *When we outsourced our workspace management systems … we did this too fast and there were a lot of things that we did not know how they worked and we were asking the supplier to explain to us, while it should be the other way around. … This meant that we were actually not in control … and when you are outsourcing, you should know what you need functionally and ask your provider to do it. … And we had a catalogue with services which was really far from complete. … We should have been more accurate because if you outsource garbage, you get garbage back.*

The original contract lacked details and the venture was expected to be conducted in the spirit of a partnership. The relationship between the two firms was not effective in terms of providing motivation for performance; moreover the cultures of the two firms appeared to clash. The performance of Supplier C was consistently bad and DUTCH decided to put significant effort towards making agreements more formalized. On this basis, a number of amendments of the original contract were made.

The performance of Supplier C was not improving, however, and DUTCH decided to refer to the vice president of Supplier C. The performance of Supplier C remained consistently bad until the beginning of 2010 when it started to demonstrate some small signs of improvement.

While there were formal controls put in place, it appears that these were constrained to spotting poor performance and that they were not actually changing the performance or the vendor's behaviour. At this point it is hard to say where the arrangement was heading, though according to the research participants the possibility of termination appeared to be particularly high. In particular, Rob (DUTCH contract manager for Supplier C) noted:

> *We are facing a lot of problems which to a good extent means that we have to break the contract … it should be better to take things out and put it with another supplier. But in terms of how the contract restricts us to do those things, it is very difficult. … So I think that the whole swap from C to (another supplier) will cost us a lot of money.*

It seems that people within DUTCH were frustrated by not being able to motivate Supplier C to perform either through the contract or through a relationship approach.

Uncertainty

Environmental Uncertainty

As noted, for our purposes environmental uncertainty is delineated into volume and technological. Issues of volume uncertainty appeared to concern mainly the relationship between DUTCH and Supplier A, in terms of the volume of services that DUTCH would need. Research participants within Supplier A indicated that their organization was unable to clarify its needs in relation to data centre service management. From the Supplier A side, Irene (engagement manager from Supplier A) became more specific and explained that the miscalculations were essentially made on the storage capacity that DUTCH needed. From the interviews, there were no particular reasons why DUTCH did not make a good estimation of its data centre service requirements. It rather seems that DUTCH was not very much into utilizing formal processes. Along these lines, DUTCH settled on making rough estimations without engaging proper measurements in order to reach a more valid assessment.

The miscalculation of DUTCH was very significant. The contract with Supplier A was signed for €120 million over five years and it turned out to be €200 million, resulting to a 66.7% deviance.

From the interviews, it appeared that among other reasons, DUTCH got engaged into the three outsourcing ventures with Supplier A, Supplier B, and Supplier C in order to address technological challenges and changes in a more effective way. The idea was that external suppliers would be able to handle technological challenges more efficiently and that DUTCH would be able to benefit from their expertise and insight. On this basis, a number of research participants commented that a major attitude that DUTCH expected from its suppliers was the demonstration of proactiveness.

Another indication that DUTCH was outsourcing its IT mostly for reasons of technological uncertainty comes from the press release by the DUTCH Group IT services manager, back in 2007 when the three contracts were signed. In that press release it was stated that a major reason that DUTCH got engaged into these major outsourcing deals with Supplier A, Supplier B, and Supplier C was related to the expectation that the outsourcing of information and communication technologies would allow DUTCH "to respond more rapidly to the changing demands" of its customers. In other words, IT outsourcing was actually a strategy for DUTCH to address particular technological challenges and uncertainties in a way that would allow it to be more flexible and responsive to the changing demands of its customers.

Internal Uncertainty

In the case of Supplier A, it did not appear that there were particular challenges in terms of requirement uncertainty. It did appear, however, that there were issues with Supplier B and Supplier C since DUTCH tended to be constantly making very specialized requirements. It seems that there was some lack of discipline around requirements which probably had something to do with the decentralized structure and culture of DUTCH. While Supplier B had trouble accommodating the non-standardized requirements of DUTCH, it did manage to accommodate them, though with some time delays. In the case of Supplier C, the situation was worse. The internal organization of Supplier C was not stable, and consequently their ability to accommodate non-standard requests from DUTCH was limited.

The internal organization within DUTCH at the time that these outsourcing contracts were signed appeared to be relatively weak. A major problem had to do with the diverse mindsets that existed within DUTCH. DUTCH is the product of a number of mergers and acquisitions, resulting in a diverse infrastructure and varying philosophies on how IT should be managed. Consequently, the complexity of the tasks was significant, affecting especially the work of Supplier C. John (contract manager from Supplier C) more specifically noted:

> *You (have) got a very kaleidoscopic IT world within DUTCH itself which is reasonably unmanageable. If you want to outsource that … it really becomes a mess.*

Furthermore, DUTCH did not have a good command of the IT environment and also did not have proper measurement and control mechanisms in place. As an outcome, the contracts that it signed were not complete and effective in shaping the behaviour of the vendors. Edward (DUTCH IT director) noted:

> *We had not properly invested in the IT environment that we were moving to the vendors. We did not have the proper assessment levels, maintenance levels and we did not know what we were outsourcing to them. Consequently in the first phase of the contract there was the verification phase. And what happened was "We do not know what we have given to you, can you please tell us?"*

In contrast, by not establishing proper measurement and control mechanisms, the contracts were actually not effective in preventing the potential of the vendors to behave opportunistically. This was particularly the case with Supplier B and Supplier C that for a long time were claiming much better performances than the ones they were really putting in. It also appears that for some time Supplier A was charging DUTCH higher prices than anticipated.

In time, the internal organization of DUTCH got improved and formal control processes were put in place, although the DUTCH representatives did admit to a couple of improvements that could still have been made. As examples of such improvements, some of the metrics were probably not disaggregated enough to actually challenge the supplier on exactly where they were failing. For this reason, again there were occasions when the suppliers were behaving opportunistically. Furthermore, these metrics were averaged too much so that supplier performance looked quite good at a general level. The metrics were not teasing out why there was such a level of disappointment about some parts of the supplier's performance.

Behavioural Uncertainty

Regarding measurements, DUTCH faced severe challenges in the case of Supplier C and Supplier B. During the period of transition, the existence of an inadequate retained function with limited benchmarks and measurements gave the chance to Supplier C and Supplier B (to a lesser extent) to take advantage of the situation. On this basis, Supplier B and Supplier C took many opportunities to field excuses as to why their performances were poor. In essence, they were trying to escape responsibility for their variable performances. In the case of Supplier B, a common measurement system was established and the performance of Supplier B significantly improved in time. In the case of Supplier C, while DUTCH did put some effort on the establishment of measurement mechanisms, there were still a lot of room for possible improvements. As examples of such improvements, some of the metrics were probably not disaggregated enough to actually challenge the supplier on exactly where they were failing. Furthermore, these metrics were averaged too much so that supplier performance looked quite good at a general level and failed to establish why there was such a level of disappointment about some parts of Supplier C's performance.

DUTCH chose to outsource to companies it already had a relationship with. In a sense, prior history was supposed to be an indicator of the future prospects for co-operation. For this reason, DUTCH never got engaged in a formal RFP process and chose its vendors based on its past experiences. The research participants further suggested that the reputation of the vendors was of major importance to DUTCH when it was choosing its outsourcing vendors.

On this basis, prior history and the vendors' reputation can be moderators of behavioural uncertainty between the exchange parties. According to the research participants, DUTCH had a good prior relationship with Supplier A and Supplier B which were also very reputable in their areas of expertise. For this reason, they suggested that the choice of these two suppliers on the basis of their previous performance and reputation was reasonable. However, they were very sceptical in the case of Supplier C. Firstly, DUTCH did not have an experience with Supplier C in the workspace environment, and additionally, it appears that there was a widespread scepticism in the marketplace about Supplier C around the time that the contract was signed.

Table 6.1 presents a detailed overview of the levels and types of uncertainty that DUTCH was facing with each of its vendors.

Critique of TCE in the Supplier A Case

First Level Analysis

Although the performance of Supplier A was not very effective at the beginning of the outsourcing venture with DUTCH, it did stabilize later on. For a long time after the initial 'get-to-know period', Supplier A was reaching the desired service levels and DUTCH appeared satisfied from their performance. Although some issues were reported towards the end of 2009, it appears that the overall performance of Supplier A was satisfactory, and according to the interviews, the return on investment was very significant.

DUTCH outsourced to Supplier A a set of 'mixed recurrent' assets. The theory of transaction costs prescribes a 'relational contract' for such

Table 6.1 Uncertainty challenges for DUTCH

Environmental uncertainty	Volume	Supplier A: High Supplier B: Low Supplier C: Low	Overall level of environmental uncertainty	Supplier A: High Supplier B: Low Supplier C: Low
	Technological	Supplier A: Medium Supplier B: Medium Supplier C: Medium		
Internal uncertainty	Requirements	Supplier A: Low Supplier B: High Supplier C: High	Overall level of internal uncertainty	Supplier A: Medium Supplier B: Medium Supplier C: High
	Professionalization in the IS department	Supplier A: Medium Supplier B: Low Supplier C: Low		
	Complexity of the tasks	Supplier A: Medium Supplier B: Medium Supplier C: High		
Behavioural uncertainty	Measurements	Supplier A: Low Supplier B: Medium Supplier C: High	Overall level of behavioural uncertainty	Supplier A: Low Supplier B: Medium Supplier C: High
	Reputation effects	Supplier A: Low Supplier B: Low Supplier C: High		

assets and this is exactly the strategy that Supplier A had followed. By 2010, the two organizations were in important negotiations in relation to the investments into the new data centres. Supplier A wanted DUTCH to invest in the new data centres and to commit to using specific equipment for three years. DUTCH on the other hand did not want to make such commitments. What appears interesting from a TCE perspective is that the 'relational contract' appeared to work during the period that Supplier A was managing the data centre services of DUTCH which according to the interviewees were activities of low asset specificity. As mentioned, the reason I decided to classify the transaction as 'mixed' in terms of asset specificity was related to the dedicated investments needed for the new data centres. When the two firms entered further discussions in relation to dedicated investments, they identified the need to go back to the contract and make sure their objectives and intentions of outsourcing were contractually established.

On this basis, it appears that DUTCH adopted a 'resource-based' approach and decided to outsource the data centre services, as these were considered non-strategic activities. However, it seems that DUTCH downplayed the investments it would need in the future in the case of the new data centres of Supplier A and neglected to negotiate on these. From the interviews it turns out that the 'relational contract' predicted by the theory of transaction costs was most likely not going to be sufficient for the management of the relationship. On the contrary, the interviewees mentioned that they were now going back to the contract and will engage in discussions in order to amend it accordingly. In the meantime, DUTCH was looking for alternative suppliers as well.

Second Level Analysis

The Supplier A case constitutes a case where asset specificity is present to a non-trivial degree. Furthermore, the uncertainty levels appear to be medium, primarily because of the difficulty in defining the volume of services required (environmental uncertainty) and the poor organization within DUTCH (internal uncertainty). The theory of transaction costs suggests that when asset specificity is present to a non-trivial degree, increases in uncertainty make markets more attractive to hybrids and hierarchies more attractive to both hybrids and markets. In other words, a TCE approach on the Supplier A case that takes into account both the construct of asset specificity and uncertainty would suggest that DUTCH should either keep the activities in-house or outsource using a classical contract.

However, DUTCH outsourced its data centre management to Supplier A using a relational contract and the venture was successful. From the interviews it did not appear that keeping the activities in-house would be a good option for DUTCH, since the savings that it realized through outsourcing were very significant. Furthermore, the development of a classical contract between Supplier A and DUTCH does not appear very feasible, since both organizations are very much relationship oriented.

What was learned from the Supplier A case through a TCE analysis is that an analysis based strictly on the construct of asset specificity explains the outsourcing result between DUTCH and Supplier A. However, an analysis that would consider additionally the construct of uncertainty would have led to a misleading result. From the interviews, it does not appear that there had not been increased transaction costs between the two organizations, as a result of uncertainty. As illustrated, DUTCH did not have a good estimation of the volume of services that it would need and the contract grew significantly in size. However, Supplier A did not reduce its prices until DUTCH engaged into a benchmarking procedure. It was actually the results of the benchmarking that obliged Supplier A to lower its prices. On this basis, volume uncertainty empowered Supplier A to behave opportunistically.

In time, DUTCH decided to move towards a neo-classical contract (with some relational elements) in order to reduce some opportunistic behaviour that Supplier A appeared to demonstrate, and in terms of improving performance, this appears to be the correct way to go forward.

Critique of TCE in the Supplier B Case

First Level Analysis

The performance of Supplier B was not satisfactory at the beginning of the outsourcing venture but did stabilize later. DUTCH outsourced to

Supplier B a set of 'non-specific recurrent' assets. According to the theory of transaction costs, in order to achieve a successful result, DUTCH should have outsourced its network services to Supplier B through a classical contract. During the time that DUTCH and Supplier B were co-operating through a relational contract, the results were particularly disappointing and thus the theory of transaction costs has been useful in explaining the underperformance of Supplier B through the relational exchange with DUTCH. The performance of Supplier B was low initially because DUTCH did not have a proper control of the services it would hand out to Supplier B. A further reason was that because there was not a common measurement system, there were all sorts of disagreements regarding the actual level of performance that Supplier B had reached. Furthermore, Supplier B and DUTCH had a different style of conducting work. DUTCH was much more into following a relational approach, while Supplier B tended to be formally oriented. Although the underperformance of Supplier B was partly a result of DUTCH's culture to be making non-standard requests, it does appear from the interviews that Supplier B was taking advantage of the fact that DUTCH did not have a proper retained management capability in place. The performance of Supplier B started to rise only when DUTCH put proper measurement and control mechanisms in place and put significant effort in establishing processes to run the venture in a more formalized way.

It was only when the venture started to move towards a neo-classical contract that the performance of Supplier B got better. This development is in line with the theory of transaction costs, in the sense that the theory of transaction costs would predict that a more formalized approach would have benefited the arrangement. However, it is still not easy to make assumptions about whether a classical contract, which is the type of contract that the theory of transaction costs prescribes as the most successful option, would work better than a neo-classical contract. A number of interviewees within DUTCH accepted that their culture of making non-standard requests needed to be disciplined, but it does not appear that this would be enough to make the creation of a classical contract between DUTCH and Supplier B feasible (i.e. to fully define the processes inside a contract and standardize it). The reason is that the three vendors need to be co-operating in the delivery of their service and at times they need to be making specific adaptations in their work. Consequently, while some discipline in the DUTCH culture would breed desirable results, it appears that some flexibility at the contractual level would still be needed.

Second Level Analysis

Supplier B constitutes a case of outsourcing non-specific recurrent assets. The level of uncertainty appears to be medium and is related primarily to uncertainties around requirements, the level of professionalization in the IS department of DUTCH, the complexity of the tasks, and also some measurement difficulties (internal uncertainty). According to the theory of transaction costs, in the case of non-specific assets, classical contracting prevails and the degree of uncertainty does not alter this. On this basis, a TCE approach that considers all the dimensions of the transaction would again prescribe a classical contract between DUTCH and Supplier A.

The construct of uncertainty appears to be explaining much of the transaction costs that DUTCH faced while it was operating on a relational contract with Supplier B. It appears that the high levels of internal uncertainty within DUTCH, in terms of requirements, empowered Supplier B to delay the delivery of service and occasionally charge higher prices. Furthermore, there was also significant measurement uncertainty because of a lack of a common measurement system between the two firms. Additionally, some of the matrixes that DUTCH was using in order to evaluate the overall performance of Supplier B were too aggregated and did not provide a good guide to the performance that Supplier B demonstrated. On this basis, Supplier B was able to underperform and question the evaluation that DUTCH made in relation to its performance.

Critique of TCE in the Supplier C Case

First Level Analysis

DUTCH outsourced to Supplier C a set of 'non-specific recurrent' assets. In the beginning of their venture, DUTCH was co-operating with

Supplier C through a relational contract. This approach resulted in an unsatisfactory result and the supplier performance was consistently bad, to the point where the exit clause could have been triggered in fact if DUTCH had wanted, even though they were still at transition. The theory of transaction costs would usefully predict that a relational contract in the case of 'non-specific recurrent' assets would not be appropriate and would suggest a classical contract.

Even when DUTCH started to make the relationship with Supplier C more formalized and moved towards a neo-classical contract, the performance of the venture did not improve significantly. It actually appears that with Supplier C nothing could work and that the venture was destined to fail. From the interviews it does not appear that a classical contract would work. The people within DUTCH suggested that the venture was not performing because Supplier C itself was in chaos. It seemed to be related to the way that Supplier C was organized in terms of silos and not being really customer focused but being mainly product focused. It thus appears that the venture with Supplier C would not work in any case, unless Supplier C did some internal re-organization.

Second Level Analysis

DUTCH outsourced to Supplier C a range of 'non-specific recurrent' assets. The uncertainty levels surrounding the transaction appear to be significant. There were issues regarding requirements, the level of professionalization in the IS department of DUTCH, the complexity of the tasks (internal uncertainty), measurement difficulties, and also reputation effects (behavioural uncertainty). The theory of transaction costs suggests that in the case of non-specific assets, classical is the most appropriate form of contracting. On this basis, a TCE analysis that considers all dimensions of the transaction would be useful in explaining why the venture with Supplier C did not work.

First of all, DUTCH tended to make non-standard requests, something that empowered Supplier C to manifest its constrained ability to deliver the desirable service to DUTCH. Furthermore, Supplier C demonstrated intense opportunistic behaviour as a result of the weak organization within DUTCH. Some of the metrics DUTCH was using for performance evaluation were not disaggregated enough to actually challenge the supplier on exactly where they were failing. Additionally, these metrics were averaged too much so that supplier performance looked quite good at a general level. Another problem: DUTCH did not have a good understanding of the services it was outsourcing to Supplier C. The choice of Supplier C as an outsourcing supplier appears also not to have been made on a solid basis. While interviewees within DUTCH found good rationales for the choices of Supplier A and Supplier B, they could not explain why Supplier C was chosen. While there was a prior relationship between DUTCH and Supplier C, this was not on work automation, for which the new contract was signed. A number of interviewees expressed their scepticism about the extent that Supplier C was chosen for good business reasons. It turned out, however, that the DUTCH IT director that signed the Supplier C contract got employed later by Supplier C. On this basis, the existence of high levels of internal and behavioural uncertainty within DUTCH empowered Supplier C to behave opportunistically, as the theory of transaction costs would predict.

Summary: Applying a TCE Perspective

The first level of analysis that considered only the constructs of asset specificity and frequency was predictive partially in the DUTCH-Supplier A case (i.e. successful relational contract at the start of the venture). It does not appear however that the DUTCH-Supplier A case would remain successful in the long run, and at some point in the relationship a neo-classical contract (with relational elements) started to work. In the rest of the cases, the first level of analysis was not useful in predicting the most efficient outsourcing decision.

In the case of LION-FDL, a relational contract was prescribed, but the firms created a successful neo-classical contract (with relational elements). In this case, the creation of a relational contract that the theory of transaction costs prescribes did not even appear feasible.

In the case of GIB-PV, a classical contract was prescribed, but the firms created a successful neo-classical contract (with relational elements). The classical contract did not appear adequate to accommodate the requirements by GIB.

In the DUTCH-Supplier B case, a classical contract was prescribed, but the firms, after a failed relational venture, progressed to the creation of a neo-classical contract. The creation of a classical contract did not appear to be promising for the evolution of the venture, in terms of its constrained flexibility.

In the DUTCH-Supplier C case, a classical contract was prescribed, but it appears that DUTCH chose the wrong vendor and no type of governance could be effective.

Table 6.2 demonstrates a summary of the results of the first level analysis regarding the predictive power of TCE.

The second level analysis considered all dimensions of the transaction (i.e. asset specificity, frequency, and uncertainty). In none of the cases, the theory of transaction costs appeared to be predictive of the best form of governance.

In the LION-FDL case, the theory of transaction costs would prescribe that LION kept the activities in-house. This option, however, does not appear that would have been the most profitable option for LION. The firm outsourced very successfully its savings and loans systems development, support, and maintenance under a neo-classical contract (with relational elements).

In the GIB-PV case, TCE would prescribe a classical contract (similarly to the first level of analysis). As it was mentioned, a classical contract did not appear to be adequate in the accommodation of GIB requirements.

In the DUTCH-Supplier A case, TCE would prescribe that DUTCH keeps the data centre management in-house. However, it does not appear that this would be the most beneficial option, as the firm outsourced its data centre management with a neo-classical contract (with relational elements).

In the DUTCH-Supplier B case, TCE would prescribe a classical contract (similarly to the first level of analysis). However, as mentioned, the creation of a classical contract did not appear to be appropriate for accommodating DUTCH's needs.

In the DUTCH-Supplier C case, similarly to the first level of analysis, a classical contract was prescribed, but it appears that DUTCH chose the wrong vendor and no type of governance could be effective.

Table 6.3 demonstrates a summary of the results of the second level of analysis regarding the predictive power of TCE.

Table 6.2 Summary of results from the first level of analysis

Case study	Asset specificity	Frequency	First level TCE prediction	Predictive power of TCE
LION-FDL	Mixed	Recurrent	Relational	Successful neo-classical contract (with relational elements) The creation of a relational contract did not appear feasible
GIB-PV	Non-specific	Recurrent	Classical	Successful neo-classical contract (with relational elements) A classical contract appeared constrained to accommodate the GIB needs
DUTCH-Supplier A	Mixed	Recurrent	Relational	Initially, successful relational contract This approach did not appear to be appropriate in the long run. Progressively, the creation of a neo-classical contract appeared to be more suitable
DUTCH-Supplier B	Non-specific	Recurrent	Classical	Initially, unsuccessful relational Progressively, the creation of a neo-classical contract appeared to be more suitable A classical contract appeared constrained to accommodate the DUTCH needs
DUTCH-Supplier C	Non-specific	Recurrent	Classical	Initially, unsuccessful relational Progressively, unsuccessful neo-classical contract It appears that the venture would not work in any case as a result of poor Supplier C organization

Table 6.3 Summary of results from the second level of analysis

Case study	Asset specificity	Frequency	Uncertainty	Second level TCE prediction	Predictive power of TCE
LION-FDL	Mixed	Recurrent	High environmental High internal	Keep in-house	Successful neo-classical contract (with relational elements) Does not appear that keeping the activities in-house would have been a more profitable option
GIB-PV	Non-specific	Recurrent	Medium environmental	Classical	Successful neo-classical contract (with relational elements) A classical contract appeared constrained to accommodate the GIB needs, especially regarding the volatility of its external environment
DUTCH-Supplier A	Mixed	Recurrent	High environmental Medium internal	Keep in-house	Initially, successful relational contract Progressively, the creation of a neo-classical contract appeared to be more suitable Does not appear that keeping the activities in-house would have been a more profitable option
DUTCH-Supplier B	Non-specific	Recurrent	Medium internal Medium behavioural	Classical	Initially, unsuccessful relational Progressively, the creation of a neo-classical contract appeared to be more suitable It appears that some flexibility at the contractual level was needed
DUTCH-Supplier C	Non-specific	Recurrent	High internal High behavioural	Classical	Initially, unsuccessful relational Progressively, unsuccessful neo-classical contract Does not appear that anything would work

The above results indicate that **TCE had a very limited predictive power in both levels of analysis.** In the first level of analysis that included only the constructs of asset specificity and frequency of the transactions, we felt that our assessment was missing important elements from the social context and relationships within which the transactions were taking place. For the cases under investigation, TCE appeared to be giving rigid prescriptions for either classical (i.e. highly rigid and standardized contracts) or relational (i.e. open-ended) contracts and downplayed how formal and relational governance can work together. The second level of analysis included the construct of uncertainty and thus captured a significant element of the social environment. However, significant relational elements that can incentivize clients and suppliers to invest in the outsourcing vendors appeared again to be missing. The issue here appears to stem from the focus of TCE on the opportunistic behaviours that clients and suppliers are assumed to engage when their power position becomes stronger than that of their exchange partner.

7

A Foucauldian Discourse Perspective

Introduction

This chapter re-examines the case study evidence in the light of the selected Foucauldian concepts of governmentality, power relations, and discourse. In the course of the analysis, certain other related Foucauldian concepts were brought to bear (e.g. surveillance, power/knowledge, discipline) where, we believe, this helps the analysis and provides further insight. The analysis of discourse was only partial in this chapter, as we wish also to comment more fully on TCE and outsourcing themselves as discourses and these matters are best reserved for a more general last chapter.

A major theme running through all the case studies under review, reflecting indeed what prior and most recent empirical studies of IT outsourcing have perennially revealed, is the essential tensions/synergies and dialectical play between **contract** and **relationships** as modes of governance and management. Indeed, reflecting its importance, we devote a whole later chapter on just this theme. This is also highly interesting from a Foucauldian perspective because the Foucauldian concept of governmentality embraces both contract and relationship as techniques of

E. Lioliou, L. P. Willcocks, *Global Outsourcing Discourse*, Technology, Work and Globalization, https://doi.org/10.1007/978-3-319-74045-4_7

control, discipline (including self-discipline), and the production of power relations and knowledge. Moreover contract and relationship emerge as modes of governmentality that utilize differently what Foucault would call 'technologies' of surveillance, discipline, control, and/or transparency, all of which can be observed in the five case histories that form the present study.

A second observation from the case histories is that they emerge as shot through with **power relations** but in ways which cannot be captured by the somewhat negative and individualized view of power found in Williamson's TCE conceptualization. For example, the assumptions of seeking self-interest with guile, of vendor opportunism in the event of a small number of suppliers, and of information asymmetry being a source of power, seem to take us only so far in understanding events, outcomes, and motivations in and across the case studies.

Thirdly, one can observe a consistent, indeed persistent **discourse** emerging within each and across the case studies with regard to outsourcing. In the case study chapters, we presented what people and documents said in great detail precisely in order to allow any such discourse to emerge, to see if there were regularities, prohibitions, permissions, exclusions, and legitimations, in short to see if Foucauldian principles of discourse regulation (Foucault 1972) are applied. The documentary evidence would seem to be that there is indeed such a discourse with recurring issues, language, and regularities and that this discourse also served to discipline behaviour thought and action but also was/is a political resource that agents operating within the discourse actively seek to leverage through circuits of power relations.

In what follows we illustrate these themes and observations from the evidence collected in the case study in Chaps. 3, 4, and 5.

A Foucauldian Perspective on the LION Case

Governmentality operated in LION firstly through strong surveillance mechanisms, formal procedures, and detailed monitoring mechanisms. LION decided to outsource its savings and loans processes on the basis that these activities did not constitute a part of its core business. LION had a good command of these activities. Therefore, the firm was able to establish a good contract and efficient formal surveillance mechanisms from the beginning of the venture with FDL. In general, LION appeared to favour formal surveillance mechanisms. The Master Services Agreement (MSA) that was established between LION and FDL was detailed and had established a clearly defined scope for application development, maintenance, and support set of services. The service level agreements (SLAs) for these services, as well as the methodology for the examination of the FDL performance, were also thoroughly described. In particular, they had set a working practice document that outlined in detail the processes behind their co-operation. Furthermore, the two firms had established very clear working processes. On this basis, LION and FDL had established a thorough formal surveillance framework that made the FDL performance visible and provided a clear distinction between acceptable and unacceptable results.

The words of Haresh (account manager from FDL) made clear the importance of tight contractual surveillance as a means of governance and the effort devoted to its development:

> *Whatever contract stays longer than individuals who run the business ... either within LION or within the vendors. ... The contract is thus very important and I think we worked quite a lot, about four to five months, purely on making the contract sufficiently equipped for LION and also for FDL.*

Again Boris (LION lawyer) emphasized the importance of documentation of governance meetings and communications in order to substantiate an organization's position in cases of conflict:

> *the outsourcing parties come to legal and say that the other party did not stick to these requirements. ... Well yes, but what did you as a client do in between? Did you record all your communication with the supplier? Do you have minutes of meetings? Do you have call sheets? What do you have in order to substantiate your position?*

These are examples of the client effort invested in the microanalytics of control and discipline within the outsourcing arrangement. One can add that these modes of control were greatly enhanced by the information technologies through which they operated, thus bringing office technologies and software into the circuits of power relations operating.

Nevertheless, while strong surveillance mechanisms had been established for the monitoring of the venture, there was a strong belief among the two parties that the relationship element was also very significant. As an example of this rationality, Bamse (LION business manager) noted that the situation where an outsourcing client decides to go back to the contract in order to examine the possibility of exercising sanctions is particularly confronting. On this basis he suggested that such confrontations might be really damaging for the relationship and not beneficial in the long run:

> *If you have to go to the contract and look at the penalty part, you do not have a good relationship. In this case there is certainly something wrong and probably you can go with your legal team and you might be right but you will not benefit your long-term goals as an organization. That is a very confronting thing because a lot of people work very hard to think of good penalty clauses but I personally do not believe in them. It will not work in the long-term. Probably you need to them when there is a divorce coming basically … but you do not need them for a good relationship and work together.*

This comment illustrates a common theme encountered in the interviews of how 'productive' 'good' relationships were, in terms of achieving legitimate outcomes. The word 'partnering' was regularly used as a summary word to capture this notion. The word emerges from all the case studies as in fact loaded with other sub-notions such as flexibility, trust, reciprocity, and other-directed behaviour. A Foucauldian perspective on this discourse would suggest governmentality at work, disciplining through identifying with the 'rightness' of partnering and with agents internalizing codes of conduct that shaped subsequent behaviour.

And indeed, in line with the partnering rationality, LION needed, and did reveal, a considerable amount of flexibility in the venture with FDL. The high volatility in the European financial industry made it very difficult for LION to predict its demands in savings and loans activities. For this reason LION needed FDL to be flexible and adaptable in their co-operation. A clear indication of the partnering rationality was that the agreement between the two firms had been revisited once, as a result of the volatility of the financial industry. In particular, LION had not predicted its requirements correctly and contracted much more services to FDL than the ones it actually was making use of. The two firms revisited the agreement and discussed transparently how they could address the problem. Martin (LION service manager) elaborated on this issue:

> *FDL had an open calculation model with us where they were fully transparent in terms of what is the cost of their front office in the Netherlands and what is the cost of the offshored part of the deal towards India. … In every decision we take and every forecast we do for what is the amount that we need for system maintenance or system development, they are always very transparent and they give us the opportunity to co-decide with them. … We know what we pay for and we openly discuss the economics behind about it.*

The stresses on 'transparency', 'openness', and 'co-deciding' are indicators at the local level of how disciplinary mechanisms operate in order to regulate, render transparent, and also achieve the reflexive self-control noted as attributes of governmentality by Clegg et al. (2002).

From these comments it can be seen that, as Foucault maintained, power relations can be highly productive, not just of truth and knowledge but also of practical behaviours seen as positive and useful in the social circumstances and contexts in which they are enacted. But, following Foucault, power relations can be highly dynamic, and this can be revealed at different moments in any outsourcing arrangement. This is illustrated in the comments of Bamse (LION business manager) who mentioned that there had been some particularly challenging phases during the outsourcing venture. He gave an example where the two firms had run into serious cost and time overruns and emphasized how they worked together and smoothed their operation:

> *As an example, before we outsourced we would develop a new product and it would cost us 800,000 Euros and it would take a throughput time of nine months. And the claim from FDL when we were negotiating the contract was "we can do it in a short period of time for you, we can do it cheaper". So the*

> *first time we developed a product, they came back and it cost 1.2 million Euros and it took them twelve months. Anyone can imagine what kind of clash happened with LION at that moment. This was not what LION anticipated. … LION was very much in the offensive mode and they reacted very defensive.*

Bamse (LION business manager) noted that this was a case where the two organizations had to go back to their contract and LION actually considered exercising penalty clauses:

> *At that time we went back to the contract to find out what we had agreed in terms of penalties when FDL does not deliver on time. So it started to become a clash and we did not trust each other. … Certainly there was no partnership.*

It is interesting here how the language of partnership is utilized as a shorthand to represent what happened—"certainly there was no partnership". Such language renders those not agreeing to one's requirements as illegitimate in their claims and unfair in their behaviours. Here it can be seen how language and controlling the discourse also enter the circuitry of power relations and also can form part of the technologies of governmentality. And where soft disciplining through language, or what Miller and Rose (1990) call intellectual technologies, fails to achieve the desired effects, then more overt forms of disciplinary action—back to the contract, exercising penalty clauses—are available and become necessary to apply.

However, on the whole, the partnership-based rationality appeared to be working between LION and FDL and this can be attributed to a number of reasons. Firstly, LION regarded FDL as an expert supplier for IT outsourcing and FDL considered LION as a very prestigious client. It thus seems that each of the organizations valued the reputation and prestige of the other. Furthermore, it appeared that there were people that were key for the effective evolution of the venture on a partnership basis. Jeremy (contract manager from FDL), who was an ex-LION employee, was such a person. His contribution was major as he knew very well the processes within LION and thus he was able to facilitate significantly the co-operation. These substantive, emotional, and symbolic resources also formed part of the collective circuitry of power relations and contributed to productive relations and 'successful' outsourcing outcomes.

On this basis, it appears that, as far as governmentality was concerned, the formal and the partnership-based rationalities were co-existing in the venture between LION and FDL. It also appears that the role of people and informal relationships were important for the efficient progress of the venture (as an aside—something that TCE tends to neglect to consider).

More significantly, according to the research participants, FDL clearly demonstrated a 'partnership' style of behaviour when the needs of LION changed and thus the outsourcing arrangement needed to be revisited. LION, on the other hand, did not impose sanctions on FDL as a result of its underperformance during the integration project of Postbank and LION. The two firms worked together so that the requirements by LION got clearly communicated to FDL.

But although both outsourcing parties had demonstrated strong signs of partnership behaviour, it appears that some people within LION were still sceptical about the overall attitude of FDL. As an example, Martin (LION service manager), although as illustrated previously he did think FDL had been particularly accommodating to LION, noted if it was a true partner, it would have demonstrated a more proactive type of behaviour:

> *FDL is very good in doing what they need to do. … They have a very good contract management organization, knowing the contract by heart. … They will do perfectly what we agreed and the will not do what we have not agreed. The issue is that colleagues, they do not just do what they agreed. … If FDL was a partner they should also do what they think is necessary for LION. … Our people who are managing the contract of FDL, maybe sometimes think that FDL will think for us and do more than just the asked things … for this reason there might be gaps for these points in the relationship.*

Liam (LION demand manager) also commented on the fact that FDL should be more proactive in its engagement to LION:

> *I think they are confident that they will close another agreement because they do the work … and the work they do it perfect, no issues about that. But this is really not enough, they need to be much more proactive.*

These passages are particularly revealing in terms of the language being used to suggest that the supplier still is really not doing enough. The language again is that of partnering or rather failure to partner 'correctly'. Again the seeming commonsense 'partnering' language of business, in fact, has deep emotional and political meanings, pulling the participants into a discourse that disciplines, cajoles, excludes, and points to specific correct and incorrect responses and behaviours. These are technologies of power being revealed in seemingly simple and straightforward statements being made by case participants at the local level.

In this LION case, the microanalytics of power are revealed in the highly detailed requirements set down in the MSA, how project descriptions have to be arrived at, and the meticulously detailed scoping of tasks and performance levels. Should dynamism shake the stability of the disciplining system, for example, when changes in processes are to occur, then Boris (LION lawyer) notes the importance of documentation in keeping track. These must always be adequate, so that when something goes wrong, client one can answer in the affirmative when asked:

> *did you record all your communication with the supplier? Do you have minutes of meetings? Do you have call sheets? What do you have in order to substantiate your position?*

The favourable comments made by client respondents when they note occasions when the supplier staff were 'transparent' are typical of other studies into panoptic power operating in organizational intercommunication. And if such transparency can be allied to non-use of penalty clauses, but the reliance instead on relationships, and goal sharing, then this is to be preferred because, as Bamse (LION business manager) states about the use of overt mechanisms such as a penalty clause: "it will not work in the long term". Governmentality may work best, then, when internalized, that is, when overt mechanisms of control are replaced by discursive modes such as language, codes of conduct, and belief systems. At the same time the case reveals cracks in the applicability of this discursive mode of control. At one point we find language barriers being cited as creating challenges between the parties, though ironically it is the

Indian supplier respondents commenting on the client staff speaking Dutch. At several other points client respondents mention instances of cultural differences creating challenges for relationships and for performance (a common theme in other case studies in the offshore outsourcing literature). In effect, such barriers break into the smooth flow of the circuit of power that disciplines both client and supplier actions, rendering both 'partnering' and performance problematic.

The major complaint against the supplier in the case is that: "we do not have strategic vendors in Lion because when you have a real strategic vendor this means that you are actually running along (together) in business" (Sandro, LION contract manager). This appears to be an insight into what the outcome of a fully disciplined supplier would look like. The overt disciplinary mechanisms, including the detailed contract, SLAs, and the micro measurement put in place, would no longer be necessary (in place but rendered unnecessary), because the partnership/relationship logic would be sufficiently powerful to render the supplier flexible, transparent, and highly amenable and operating fully in the cause of the client.

This scenario seems unlikely, despite the otherwise highly approving comments made by the client respondents about FDL, especially given the considerable unease in the case revealed by LION respondents about over-dependence on FDL. This seems particularly paradoxical given that one of the prime reasons FDL was selected in the first place was because it had demonstrated significant technical expertise and knowledge. Here then is a problem for the client: how do you harness a supplier's knowledge/expertise, without becoming over-dependent and placing oneself in harm's way? In a demonstration of power relations at work, LION needs to create internal know-how that can monitor the supplier's performance and put in place surveillance mechanisms that somehow render the supplier's behaviour as transparent as possible. The concern about over-dependence becomes overt when contract renewal begins to be considered. LION respondents think of ways out of the dilemma—FDL might want to not renew, but another supplier might now be more capable. Such thinking, as emerging from the respondents' comments, reveals the circuit of power relations stripped bare.

A Foucauldian Perspective on the GIB Case

In the GIB case the same dialectic between contract and partnership modes of governmentality was played out. GIB managers were also highly concerned to have in place a full array of contractual, measurement, and control mechanisms that are highly detailed and render transparent events and supplier performance. The surveillance effects of these mechanisms and their visibility to all parties were highly disciplining and also lay down the regulation of acceptable thinking and language as well as restricting behaviour along certain channels rather than others.

Although there had been a climate of closeness, mutual dependency, and co-operation between the two firms, GIB also maintained very tight formal surveillance mechanisms with PV. In particular, the MSA set out the fundamental terms, conditions, and processes governing the relationship between GIB and PV. The MSA in essence constituted an umbrella contract, storing the function of different project descriptions which constituted individual contracts themselves. In other words, each project description, including the X-RAY one, formed a distinct contract which contained details of specific services and/or deliverables to be provided but also incorporated the terms and conditions of the MSA. Eric (GIB Global technology outsourcing vendor management) commented on the importance of the contractual governance through the MSA: "People may change. … So to have a good managed relationship which is not dependent on people you need to have a framework."

However, what Eric was referring to was not merely a 'framework' but in fact a highly detailed set of disciplining mechanisms, which increasingly in outsourcing, and also amongst GIB respondents, were referred to as 'governance', through what respondents knew as 'the rules of the game' but essentially amounted to surveillance and control to achieve governmentality. Why was this so important? Because though the systems and activities outsourced were labelled as 'non-strategic', in fact a bank like GIB is, as many respondents pointed out, highly dependent on its information systems: "if the IT systems fail and do not come back up online again it can have a catastrophic effect on the business" (Mark Millward). Also: "banks are financial institutions, but actually we are IT houses, software houses". This strategic dependency on the supplier made highly detailed disciplining mechanisms critical, in the eyes of the GIB management respondents. In the circuit of power relations, power required countervailing power, the potential for assertion required locales of resistance.

Power circulating, according to Foucault, capillary-like is ever-present and everywhere:

> *power is exercised through networks, and individuals do not simply circulate in those networks; they are in a position to both submit to and exercise this power. They are never the inert or consenting targets of power, they are always its relays. In other words, power passes through individuals.* (Foucault 2003)

If power circulates, then its operation is never just in one direction. All parties are caught in the network, and all produce, submit, and control within the dynamic configuration of these power relations that we can see GIB attempting to shape. GIB does so through building up countervailing in-house capabilities in the form of people with a range of skills including those of monitoring and management of the supplier but also through highly detailed documentation and measurement.

In this respect, the MSA is particularly illuminating for its panoptic and disciplinary qualities and intended effects. Disciplining and normalization need to act across all parties and not just the supplier(s). In the case it was interesting to observe how power relations also existed and operated—circulated—between GIB centre and its local units, as well through GIB and its supplier. The MSA was designed to discipline the 'negative' outcomes from such central-local tensions. We include in the case study chapter extensive details of the MSA's contents to give insight into the meticulous level of detail felt to be needed if these disciplining mechanisms were to be effective. One particular concern was to ensure that no change occurred without a highly detailed set of processes being passed through—uncontrolled change being particularly anxiety-inducing given a set of formalized procedures designed to achieve a specific set of behaviours. Respondents also stressed how all these mechanisms were important for when things went less well: "governance is important because you need to have some kind of structure if things are not going fantastic" (Daryn, GIB lawyer). When normalization is not working, then countervailing mechanisms are required. But to demonstrate how power relations and these specific disciplining mechanisms can also be productive, Bart (GIB director of risk) commented:

> *all these processes can actually help boost your relationship, communicate better, collaborate better, leverage the relationship towards innovation.*

Such controlling, but also productive, effects are essential parts of Foucault's conceptualization of power relations.

Playing into the broader conceptualization of governmentality operated by Foucault, what respondents called 'governance' was even more important because banks operated within a much bigger system of power relations and discourse:

> *we are a very regulated industry, so in order to have the authorization to do outsourcing, we need strong governance in place—if not the regulators are coming after us.* (Eric, GIB Global technology outsourcing vendor management)

Respondents told us that how outsourcing was conducted and managed was also already being brought into the remit of such regulation, extending disciplinary processes, the power relations circuitry, and the need for ever more detailed procedures and monitoring. The issues of external regulation and closer monitoring also applied in the four other case studies from the insurance industry that form part of this thesis, though we highlight them mainly in the current case because respondents included such matters much more in their outsourcing discourse.

The case reveals a major problematic around governmentality through constitution, contract, and measurement. Foucault himself worried about the totalizing effects of his representations of disciplinary power. His 1960s and 1970s formulations seemed to leave little room for human agency. But his later work focused more on the issues of agency, creation of psychological contracts, and what he called care of the self (Willcocks and Mingers 2004). The case study here reveals that, in fact, these totalizing effects can rarely be perfected, at least in outsourcing arrangements of any size. Despite every attempt (and GIB seemed to have invested more effort into this 'disciplining' area than most organizations represented in the empirical literature), the mechanisms cannot be all encompassing or totalizing in their effects. For example, research participants commented on the limitations of SLAs and key performance indicators (KPIs). As examples, Rao (PV Head of integrated services delivery) noted that customer satisfaction should be taken into account in conjunction with the achievement of service levels:

> *I will give you a 95% SLA which may be very good. But what happens when the other 5% of the service is not delivered to the customer? Thus, customer satisfaction is one of the things which may not come up directly to the SLA. … If I go to a customer and ask how is my service, even though I have not achieved my SLAs but if I am keeping my the customer informed that these are the roadblocks I have achieved and keep them updated constantly, satisfaction may be high.*

Rajesh (PV X-RAY Global transformation manager) also commented on the same issue and illustrated that KPIs should be in line with business expectations:

> *I know that there are KPIs between GIB and PV where if there is a major incident it has to be resolved by PV within 24 hours. But the user's expectation will be that if there is a major incident it should be resolved in two hours. Thus, the KPI was not tied into the business expectation but contractually we did not have a problem and we would not be charged a penalty if we addressed the incident within 24 hours. … But again, the user would not be happy … even if we solved the issue within 6 hours, the user will be dissatisfied because the expectation is that the issue is addressed in two hours.*

Clearly the attempt to legislate for every conceivable eventuality and problem could not work in a large-scale outsourcing arrangement like this one. The dynamism, the unanticipatable junctures of events creating unlikely challenges, and the fact that in practice the apparatus of governance was, in the words of Daryn, 'ideal' by which he meant idealistic, not least because both client and supplier staff found it the sheer size and detail difficult to refer to and interpret, let alone follow—all these things shaped a major anxiety that was also observed in the previous case.

Governmentality through legal, documentary, benchmarking and measurement modes were insufficient for achieving the performance outputs GIB required. Daryn neatly described the position reached in the case:

> *It is because of the unknown, you do not know what the relationship is going to be, so the best thing is to have something formalistic, so that if something does go wrong you can always accommodate each other by going back to the schedule.*

But as we have seen in the previous case analysis, modes of governmentality are not exhausted by formalized disciplinary mechanisms. The language of partnering, culture and individual, psychological contracts steer respondents in the direction of referring to the importance of 'relationships' and their management. One factor this language signals is the human component in outsourcing arrangements—that is, human workers as thinking, feeling, deciding, and performing agents within networks of power relations. As such human subjects are potential source of resistance, recalcitrance, or act as boosters within power relations. The dependence and uncertainty created within the outsourcing arrangement due to this 'human element' create tensions within the mode of governmentality and lead to attempts to address the potentially emerging issues in different ways that can be subsumed under the catch-all nomenclature used by every one of our respondents of 'partnering'.

Respondents made clear that GIB maintained a long-standing 'partnership' with PV. As mentioned, in 2004 PV acquired a GIB captive and thus a lot of people previously working for GIB became PV employees. A number of research participants within GIB and PV commented on the partnership rationality that existed between both firms and particularly in relation to the X-RAY project. As indicative examples, Rao (PV Head of integrated services delivery) suggested that while the contract establishes a frame in the relationship, it fell short in covering all aspects of the venture:

> *When you start executing you realize that the contract has covered some areas and has not covered other areas—has not examined some features. It is important for the very contract to know the spirit … how do I interpret tomorrow if*

> *I end up having issues. The contract, because it is a legal document, we theoretically want to be very specific on how we put matters in. But I have seen most of the contracts falling short—they will never cover 100%. So it is important for the parties to understand the spirit of the contract, not just only the letter. Otherwise, when the relationship is going through turbulent times, you may end up in conflict.*

'The spirit of the contract' is a very illuminating phrase, not least because it seems to be referred to in most of the case studies in the empirical literature, as well as by respondents in the five cases here under study. On a Foucauldian interpretation one would suggest that following the 'spirit' of the contract means achieving by other means what the contract in itself as a disciplinary mechanism is unable to enforce. In practical terms this means interpreting the contract's language to favour your own interests, or where the contract is silent, or incomplete, extending its meaning in certain directions, also in pursuit of specific interests. But a bigger interpretation would be to see this phrase as bringing together out of tension and fashioning a duality of control operated through the contract and relationship modes of governmentality, as referred to in the previous LION case. This interpretation can be pursued through the following examples taken from the GIB case chapter.

From the GIB side, Bart (GIB director of risk) noted:

> *The contract sets a formal apparatus of governance that sheds light upon the development the outsourcing relationship … it makes it more visible, more transparent and it certainly facilitates the venture through good and bad times.*

However, the contract is insufficient. Rajesh (PV X-RAY Global transformation manager) mentioned that the X-RAY project would have failed without the commitment and co-operation from both parties:

> *If any of the two parties decides that they are not going to stay committed, this program will fail. This program is based on a very close partnership model. … Contracts, really there are no hard and fast rules between us and GIB in the sense that we have been expected to do a lot of things by contract, but we just can not fault lack of commitment. … But vice versa, which is what we expect from GIB, a lot of this is not by contract, because you expect things like approvals*

> *would be done on time, there will be a close working relation, there are trust-based subjective softer aspects. … So if GIB did not have the commitment on it, eventually they would see that the performance on X-RAY is coming down, which has not happened. … On the other side, we cannot be under committed because if we are under committed, it is too large a program and it will fail.*

'Co-operation', 'commitment', 'close partnership', and 'trust-based' are highly loaded words when it comes to describing behaviour in an outsourcing arrangement. They indicate another form of technology at work, incorporating but going beyond what Miller and Rose (1990) referred to as 'intellectual technologies'. Going beyond, because there is a capture by this language not just of right thinking but also of right feeling, and moral identification that will direct behaviour and performance in the direction of 'the spirit of the contract'. Pursuing this point, it is interesting to note Mani (PV Global account manager) describing the relationship between the two firms as being 'symbiotic', highlighting the mutual benefits that they derived:

> *GIB is fairly committed to PV and also the other way around. … The contracts are essentially structured to ensure that in the relationship, when one partner is doing well and is benefiting from something, the other partner also benefits … and also if GIB does something bad and PV has a problem from that, we share their problem. It is a very symbiotic relationship.*

Rajesh (PV X-RAY Global transformation manager) also commented on the high levels of dependency between the two organizations:

> *So GIB is largely dependent on us to get it right for their portfolio because we manage so much of their risk. We are dependent on the business and their support for so much or our work because that's the basis for our revenues. It's the basis for our, you know, promoting to other customers, also in terms of learning and so on. So there's always a huge amount of dependency.*

On the issue of mutual dependency, from the GIB side, Carsten (GIB IBIT Sourcing and Vendor Management of IT portfolio) noted:

> *If they decide to go away GIB cannot work … and it GIB decides to go away from them it will need a transition. But there is a dependency on both sides. …*

GIB makes big revenue for them, it will have a big impact on PV's revenues to lose GIB as a customer … this is why they are highly committed and they are trying to deliver.

Despite the considerable array of formal surveillance and disciplinary mechanisms described in the GIB case study chapter, one has to conclude that the relationship mode of governmentality seemed to be the more important one shaping the behaviours and levels of performance GIB gained from its supplier and vice versa. There was indeed a very significant partnership style type of rationality, as Rajesh (PV X-RAY Global transformation manager) illustrated:

We gave GIB the feeling that we want to work closely with them and we want to make the project a success. … We wanted to show them that we would go to any extent to ensure that their expectations from us would be met. … We wanted to ensure that all issues would be covered in the proposal and this is why we put a lot of effort to understand what the business wanted from DB IT and in effect what DB IT wanted from us.

Mani (PV Global account manager) also noted:

After all, people work with people. … There is a lot of good in the organizations working together for a long time. … There is a feeling of comfort.

The issue of people and subjectification practices is worth discussing here, especially since Foucault himself saw his work as analysing: "the different modes by which, in our culture, human beings are made subjects" (quoted in Willcocks and Mingers 2004). He talks of three modes of objectification. The first is by how a subject is represented in modes of enquiry that give themselves the status of sciences. For our purposes the relevant enquiry modes are sociology and economics, including in TCE which has a distinctive view of the human subject in work environments. Such enquiry modes tend to enter into the thinking and design processes that then shape, for example, how outsourcing arrangements are thought about and their governance modes designed. The second is through dividing practices. For our purposes the formalized disciplinary mechanisms of the outsourcing arrangement make clear such things as 'good' and 'bad', 'proper' and 'unacceptable' performance. The third is subjects also take part in self-subjectification practices.

The quotes highlighted in the last few paragraphs show how people on both client and suppliers became willing 'partners'—meaning something much more than 'agents' or 'workers' in the outsourcing environment—in achieving performance. This demonstrates intellectual and emotional identification and commitments to producing outcomes steered along specific desirable lines. This willing participation not only reflects self-subjectification practices at work forming highly supportive psychological contracts but also, within the circuitry of power relations, reinforces those practices as each episode of 'right conduct' is recognized and rewarded either materially or emotionally.

According to the research participants, the performance of PV had been satisfactory and for this reason the formal means of discipline had not been put into action for deviations from the established SLAs or KPIs that were not considered particularly important by GIB. However, the very existence of the tight formal surveillance framework appears to have been effective mostly in creating visibility in the arrangement while producing its own (incomplete) disciplinary results.

A Foucauldian Perspective on DUTCH's Outsourcing Contracts

DUTCH forms an interesting set of cases because, although the three suppliers carry out different tasks, there are similarities in terms of size, contract length, starting time, and common client. This creates some relatively natural research controls for my purposes, making comparisons and judgements across the cases on the role of factors relatively easier than would otherwise be the case.

The cases are also illuminating because they produce different experiences and results despite so many common factors prevailing. The Supplier A experience is, from DUTCH's perspective, satisfactory and the Supplier B experience is eventually satisfactory, but the Supplier C experience is very unsatisfactory. How to explain such different results?

Again in these case studies the interplay between two modes of governmentality was observed, namely, 'contract' and 'relationship', the playing out of power relations, and ongoing discourses in which concepts and language are loaded with prescriptive, disciplinary intent. We also had access to additional documents and respondent evidence that allows a Foucauldian-informed analysis of two other issues in outsourcing that could not be pursued, given limitations on the evidence collected, in the previous two cases. The first generic issue across the three contracts here is that of multiple suppliers. The second issue is how a supplier's own internal organization may also figure in circuits of power relations and their effects. We will also comment on the imperfectibility of the disciplining of the outsourcing arrangements attempted by DUTCH.

DUTCH and Multiple Supplier Contracts

A recurrent issue in the discourse found in the literature on outsourcing practice is whether to go with one, two, or multiple suppliers). Empirical studies on outsourcing over 25 years show that by far the dominant choice has tended to be multiple suppliers—the main reasons being to maintain competition (partly to keep prices market-based), mitigate risk, and leverage 'best-in-class' capabilities of specific suppliers (Lacity et al. 2010). However, the multiple supplier choice increases transaction/management costs, adds complexity to governance, and may become a tactical rather than an integrated strategic response to the potential offered by outsourcing as a management tool.

As the case chapter showed, DUTCH did not want to be over-dependent on one vendor. But it created a dilemma in governmentality for itself because at the same time it believed that "the only way to make it successful is when you try to establish a real partnership. That was our goal when we started" (Harry, DUTCH sector manager on IT operations). The intractable dilemma is how to make the two modes of governmentality—contract and relationship—complementary without one undermining the application mode and positive (in managerial terms) performance effects of the other. The dilemma is well described by Harry and would seem to go to the heart of all such outsourcing arrangements:

> *I am not very happy about the fact that we chose three partners … when you make a principal decision about outsourcing it is better to take one partner where you really say "we are partners" and where you also discuss this partnership more thoroughly. … I think that is one of the main issues why this (our present arrangement) is so difficult to make work.*

The disciplinary techniques related to contract, documentation, measurement, and transparency tend to breed different psychological contracts amongst the parties, and perspectives and motivations within individuals, than those techniques related to 'relationship' disciplinarity. From a governmentality and power relations perspective, the instrumentality of 'contract' techniques actually undermines the efficacy of 'relationship' modes when used in the same outsourcing arrangement. Participants cannot commit fully to 'partnering' when techniques that cut across its ethical and operational assumptions and practices are also present. The unease is felt at the point when the individual subject—like Harry—is culturally predisposed to 'partnering' modes, has internalized the psychological contract that relates to 'partnering', and subjectively wants to experience and operate in 'partnering' mode. Foucauldian notions of the subject actively forming the subject, and of care of self, are jarred by living this dissonance. This changes how power circulates at the individual and collective level, with the lack of belief influencing the efficacy of how governmentality is conducted. The internal evidence is that across the three cases, though to a different extent in each, the supplier respondents also had a more pragmatic, commercial view of 'partnering' than a view that could be said to amount to self-identification and personal commitment to the 'relationship' mode of governmentality.

The three DUTCH cases also reveal the effects of internal organization on governmentality effects and power relations. Firstly, within DUTCH itself there were the different attitudes of Interpolis and DUTCH IT. Secondly, there were different customer groupings within DUTCH that had different needs and did not always concur with what had been contracted. Thirdly, as we saw in the case chapter, the internal IT function had definite weaknesses in its retained human/knowledge capabilities, which eroded its ability to manage in a disciplinary/surveillance/transparency mode. This was not helped by weaknesses and complexity in its material capabilities—in particular inherited diverse IT architectures. Foucauldian analysis refers to material artefacts as also having roles in power relations—as can be seen through Foucault's own discussion of panoptic effects through building architecture. These issues rendered DUTCH staff less capable of leveraging disciplinary techniques in the pursuit of their espoused objectives.

But their position was eroded further through how a supplier's internal culture organization, capabilities, and position within the competitive environment played out within the circuit of power relations. For example, respondents talked of a cultural misfit between Supplier B (a history of bureaucracy from being previously government owned, several times described as 'arrogant') and DUTCH's desire to 'partner'—"two cultures which of course eventually collide" (Arnold, DUTCH sector manager for sourcing arrangements). The internal organization of Supplier C was not set up to partner, having many divisions that needed to be related to. Moreover, it seemed to be set up to make the financial numbers rather than provide customer service and responsiveness. Supplier C disciplined its own people's behaviour—through structure, hierarchy, and budgeting modes—in ways that cut across service to and partnering with DUTCH. In the case of Supplier A, DUTCH respondents said Supplier A did try to make it work as a partnership, but some of that came from DUTCH being an important customer and being financially rewarding. Moreover, recent pressure from Supplier A's French holding company was making 'partnering' more uneasy, to the point where DUTCH was considering not giving Supplier A additional business in the next contracting round.

All these issues played through the power relations circuitry pertaining and eroded the strength of DUTCH's position relative to their three suppliers and their ability to leverage partnering modes of governmentality. Across the cases, one can see this pushing them back increasingly into building more 'contract', surveillance, and measurement modes of disciplinarity.

A final comment, looking across all three contracts, is that they show that the Foucauldian totalizing vision that seems to emerge from his studies of disciplinary and bio-power of the 1970s can misrepresent the realities of how governmentality and power relations are conducted and overstate their efficacy in terms of management objectives. It has been commented upon that Foucault's conceptualization has felt like an iron cage being created in which the human role was relatively passive. Of course, Foucault always maintained in his later work that resistance was an inherent part of the circuit of power relations and that the subject also had a conscious role in his/her own creation of him/herself as subject. His 1971 essay on *Nietzsche, Genealogy and History* also stressed the role of chance and contingency in human affairs and in social science theory. However, in looking across these three DUTCH contracts, one is struck by the miscalculations, the accumulation of historical residues that could not be legislated for but had to be lived with, the unpreparedness, the bounded rationality, and the limitations in knowledge operating—such factors that lead to the view not of a perfected disciplining being conducted but instead of the inherent *imperfectibility* of attempts at governmentality. This will emerge in more detail as we discuss each contract.

Supplier A Contract

In the Supplier A case the tensions between contract and relationship modes of governmentality are being played out in distinctive ways. According to the research participants, during the period 2004–2008, DUTCH tended not to make use of formal surveillance mechanisms in the outsourcing arrangement with Supplier A. The two firms had a contract that had been running since 2004 and was amended in 2007 to include the provision of more services to DUTCH. According to the research participants, the contract between DUTCH and Supplier A was lacking precision and was relatively open-ended. Initially this was not seen as problematic.

DUTCH tended culturally to use relationships and people as a means of control rather than surveillance mechanisms based on processes and metrics. It appeared that the wider rationality within DUTCH was that outsourcing relations are in essence 'partnership' relations (which can be also seen in the other two DUTCH cases) and thus not a significant level of detail was needed in the contractual aspect of the arrangement. Edward (DUTCH IT director) explained:

> *We took a bit too large jumps back in 2007 … because we thought that in outsourcing and a partnership relation, you do not have to write every detail down … and that is what we did, we did not write down every detail.*

This 'partnering' rationality for conducting business appeared to work well, and the major cost benefits realized as a result of the outsourcing venture with Supplier A during 2004–2007 worked to encourage DUTCH to continue managing all its outsourcing arrangements on the basis of 'partnerships'. A further reason why DUTCH appeared to be relatively relaxed in the establishment of formal control mechanisms might have to do with its very strong brand name in the Netherlands. The assumption was that DUTCH was one of the most prestigious institutions in the Dutch financial industry and thus an outsourcing supplier should be highly motivated to treat the outsourcing arrangement as a partnership and make it work. Prestige here entered into the calculation of how power relations would proceed. Prestige was a power resource to be utilized in the circuit of power relations.

On this basis, the contract between DUTCH and Supplier A was not precise or detailed. Irene (engagement manager from Supplier A) noted:

> *They did not know how much hardware they had in their datacenters. The contract was signed for 120 million over five years and it turns out to be 200 million. … Storage is the bigger part of the contract and they miscalculated by an enormous percentage. DUTCH IT merged with Interpolis and because they were going to outsource they did not pay attention to the merger. … They thought it is going to happen in the outsourcing and they did not look at the south of Holland. So they did not know their numbers.*

While the contract was lacking precision and detail, and did not establish tight monitoring procedures, it did not appear that this was a problem in the execution of the venture. The ongoing governance was based on informal relationships and the rationale that the outsourcing venture was a partnership. The contract had a secondary role and both parties seemed content with the result of their arrangement. The engagement managers from DUTCH and Supplier A were also very much in favour of a more informal approach to outsourcing governance. From the side of DUTCH, Marco (DUTCH contract manager for Supplier A) noted:

> *The contract is the basis where you can rely on but it must not be part of your work as a vendor manager the whole day. Yes, I know it from the first to the last page and sometimes I have big discussions about it but it is not on a daily basis. … I try to keep as much away from it as possible but what we do is updates. … It is very important that you keep it updated. If we have for example hidden service or things that were not foreseen and sometimes it costs money for DUTCH, I try to attach this change to the contract. … The contract is a living document.*

From Supplier A, Irene (engagement manager from Supplier A) noted that in her view contracts were always limited: "Of course you cannot put everything on paper. We tried that. You first put something in the contract, then in the reality. And also the issue is where does our contract stop?"

She further underlined the importance of relationships in the ongoing management of the outsourcing venture:

> *I do not think that if I have a very good contract, everything will then be okay. You do not get rid of your problems if you only have a good contract; you need very good people. … Once you have to pull the contract off the shelf, it is too late already because then the relationship has not worked.*

What emerges from these comments is the imperfectibility of contract modes of governmentality in these outsourcing arrangements. The respondents actually suggest that the 'contract mode' is inherently not perfectible, for example: "the contract is a living document". This may well act as a corrective to more totalizing applications of Foucauldian notions of disciplinary power.

The attitude by Marco (DUTCH contract manager for Supplier A) and Irene (engagement manager from Supplier A) appeared to be key to maintaining this spirit of 'partnership' between the two firms. They appeared to share the viewpoint that while the contract sets a frame for the outsourcing arrangement, it is the ongoing management by people that makes the progress of the venture smooth and efficient. This 'partnering' notion refers to a greater amount of cognitive and emotional identification with the other party and the outsourcing venture, representing a much more 'bound in' form of governmentality.

This was enhanced by the fact that the management culture of DUTCH and Supplier A appeared to match. Marco (DUTCH contract manager for Supplier A) noted: "Their culture fits the DUTCH culture. … Supplier A seeks to make it a partnership with a goal. … There is a mutual desire to get the best results." On the same issue Gabriel (DUTCH contract manager for Supplier B) emphasized the fit between the DUTCH and the Supplier A culture compared to other suppliers:

> *Supplier A like soft, flexible and more relationship orientated interactions, unlike some other suppliers. … So that suggests that there is a better fit between DUTCH and Supplier A.*

Another factor contributing to the continuation of the spirit of partnership and closeness appears to be related to the close relationship between the DUTCH IT director and his counterpart in Supplier A. Irene (engagement manager from Supplier A) noted:

> *We are lucky there because Edward (DUTCH IT director) is a friend of our managing director in the Netherlands. … They have an emotional bond so they can always speak.*

A further reason might have had to do with the fact that both firms appreciated the prestige of one another. DUTCH regarded Supplier A as an expert supplier in data centres and Supplier A considered DUTCH as one of their top-profile customers in the Netherlands.

While the venture appeared to be progressing well in terms of the cost savings that DUTCH was realizing, it does appear that Supplier A was taking advantage of DUTCH's informal way of conducting business. The relationship mode of control could suboptimize. As an example, it turned out that for some time Supplier A was charging DUTCH higher than the industry standards and this was only corrected with the intervention of a formal benchmarker. From a control perspective, a further signal for DUTCH on the importance of formal surveillance mechanisms had to do with the delay of Supplier A over moving servers to the new data centres. It appeared that DUTCH had no contractual incentives for Supplier A to carry out this task faster. Edward (DUTCH IT director) underlined this issue and noted:

> *If we had contracted it differently and said "this is the date that you are responsible for migrating the services to the FMO and our prices are dropping at that moment", they would get pressured. … Now all the pressure and the issues are with DUTCH, not with our vendors. … They have all the reasons for some time to stay in the PMO or PMO Plus instead of moving with to the Future Mode of Operations. … So basically there is not a natural alignment of incentives. … From a contractual perspective, we did not establish the proper incentive to move to PMO Plus or FMO.*

Interestingly here, the 'partnering' mode of governmentality would also seem not to be perfectible either. Additionally, in the light of further negotiations regarding the investments to the new data centres, Edward (DUTCH IT director) acknowledged the necessity of establishing contractually the original intent of the outsourcing venture between DUTCH and Supplier A:

> *So one of the big reasons why we wanted to outsource was to have a variable cost and a "demand-capacity" type of service. … Consequently it is rather irritating to be confronted with a supplier that basically says "Well, if you want machine X, Y or Z, I want you to guarantee that you will use it for three years otherwise I will not do the investment". … We said to them "What? This is not the way we wanted it". So we are now getting back into contract study and adaptation to the contract because we feel that we further need to clarify what the original intent of the outsourcing was and this should be contractually clear … crystal clear.*

As the outsourcing arrangement proceeded, the need for greater transparency and explicitness emerged. 'Partnering' intent and behaviours could substitute only incompletely for other forms of managerialism. It appears that the formal surveillance mechanisms in place were not initially much used in the governance of the Supplier A arrangement and thus Supplier A was not highly disciplined by formal mechanisms of governmentality. For a long time, the partnering rationality between DUTCH and Supplier A appeared to take over. However, this rationality of governance did not prevent Supplier A from engaging in what TCE would label opportunistic behaviour. Thus DUTCH was turning to the rationality of establishing a stronger contractual framework and executing tighter contractual surveillance.

Supplier B Contract

In this case, we again see the dialectic between two modes of governmentality playing itself out but with different results from the previous case. Similar to the Supplier A outsourcing arrangement, DUTCH embarked on a relationship-based approach with Supplier B. The contract signed between the two firms was lacking important details regarding the products and the level of services. Jacob (DUTCH outsourcing operations for Supplier B) mentioned significant clarity issues:

> *If you ask five people to read the contract … they will come up with five different understandings … that is a major problem we have with the contract.*

Furthermore, the measurement procedures upon which the performance of Supplier B would be examined were not properly defined. Gabriel (DUTCH contract manager for Supplier B) noted:

> *We saw an SLA performance of 50% and Supplier B was saying "it looks like 50%, but there is this … and this … and this" … and they spoke it up to 80%, which is the minimum performance they should achieve.*

On the issue of the disagreements regarding performance assessment, Jacob (DUTCH outsourcing operations for Supplier B) noted: "We said the performance had to be 80%. We show them the rating and it was 70%. … They were always talking to us 70% is not correct … it is actually 85%. … So we are not talking about how we can get the performance to a higher level, but we are talking about the rating."

Another problem was that important processes like planning for disaster recovery were left out of the original contract.

According to the research participants, the contract between DUTCH had neglected significant issues. The prevailing rationale was that outsourcing relations were in essence partnering relations and thus any issues could be worked out in the course of time between the parties. As an example of this expectation by DUTCH, Michiel (engagement manager from Supplier B) noted:

So I know that there are large risks for DUTCH and when a large problem occurs they will say "please help us and we are friends, partnership etc". … So although it is not contracted that way, they will ask us for those measures when it occurs. … So I am setting proactive offers from them right now and we are mitigating these risks … but they still have to establish these processes contractually … not just due to the pressure of (external) regulation, but also because they need to know what they are going to do with their business, the up-time of their internet … or the call centre functionality in case of urgency.

Contrary to the Supplier A case, the relationships and people between DUTCH and Supplier B did not substitute adequately for the absence of strong formal processes and surveillance mechanisms strictly defining the obligations of each party and setting certain disciplines within the ongoing arrangement. The ineffectiveness of the partnership-based approach in the Supplier B venture was attributed to several reasons. Firstly, it seems that Supplier B did not value DUTCH as a customer to the extent that Supplier A did. According to interviewees within DUTCH, the perception was that DUTCH was 'just another' customer for Supplier B and was certainly not treated as a top customer. Jacob (DUTCH outsourcing operations for Supplier B) said: "I believe that they see us as one of their customers. … Just a customer because they have bigger customers. So we are one of their customers. That is how it feels."

He further explained that the relationship between DUTCH and Supplier B did not appear to be a partnership:

DUTCH was looking for a partner … we are partners, we do it like partners. But that is not the case, the practice is that Supplier B sends in the end of a month a bill … it is not really a partnership.

Supplier B's valuation of DUTCH and its lack of partnering desire fed into the circuitry of power relations to undermine the efficacy of DUTCH's (over)dependence on the relationship mode of governmentality.

The research participants within DUTCH opined that Supplier B demonstrated an arrogant attitude. Gabriel (DUTCH contract manager for Supplier B) noted:

Supplier B is the largest network provider in the Netherlands. … Sometimes they behave as if DUTCH should be thankful for the time they spend.

This attitude by Supplier B appeared derived from the monopolistic position Supplier B had in the Netherlands. Arnold (DUTCH sector manager for sourcing arrangements) explained:

> *They had a monopoly position. They were the largest vendor in the Netherlands on networking and voice. So there is a course of arrogance in their culture. And in their culture it is "Either the Supplier B way or the highway". … On the other hand, we as DUTCH, we feel unique … this is also part of the typical customer behavior of course. … We are unique, we are special. … So there you have two cultures which of course eventually collide.*

These attitudes also fed into how power relations were conducted by and through the parties.

Secondly, another reason for the ineffectiveness of the partnership-based approach in the case of Supplier B might have had to do with the lack of significant personal connections and closeness at the executive level. Jacob (DUTCH outsourcing operations for Supplier B) elaborated on this issue:

> *Another problem is that if you want to be a partner the senior management has to have a relationship … you have to go few times and rent a boat, go to the sea and have a nice day and understand each other, talk with each other. Now we are only talking about service levels, about the contract. … There has to be an understanding in a more human way.*

Furthermore, there was an actual clash in preferred modes of governmentality. Contrary to DUTCH, Supplier B appeared to be in favour of a formalistic and standardized way of conducting business. This aspect of Supplier B's way of conducting business might be related to its government background that culturally tended to favour formalistic and bureaucratic approaches. Michiel (engagement manager from Supplier B) explained:

> *DUTCH is possibly more informal and relationship-based … and Supplier B is much more procedurally organized and you know it is very much focused upon standards, the standards have to be kept. This was a problem in the relationship.*

Gabriel (DUTCH contract manager for Supplier B) also commented on the more informal way of conducting business that DUTCH favoured and acknowledged that DUTCH tended to make excessive specialized requirements to Supplier B:

> *DUTCH wants everything as a specialty, really everything has a high priority and it's not standardized. We contracted PDC where all our products are designed, because we wanted to take standard products from Supplier B and Supplier C. The ink wasn't even dry and we had a specialty.*

On the issue of the misfit between the way that DUTCH is conducting business and the Supplier B way of doing work, Michael (DUTCH IT demand manager) also expressed his frustration:

> *It is the culture of the company I guess … not to be stepping aside from the standard process and try to help somebody. They always go back to the standard process. I understand why, but it is horrible to work like this. … And the more you push, the stiffer they get.*

Again this is very revealing language about the clash and tensions between the operations of two different modes of governmentality—and indeed their power relation effects on different parties, for example, frustration for DUTCH and resistance by Supplier B staff.

For a period of about two years there was a significant amount of dissatisfaction on DUTCH's side. In the meantime, however, DUTCH realized the necessity for establishing formal surveillance mechanisms and controls, since it was clear that a relationship-based approach could not be relied upon to produce results. By mid-2010, the two firms had made important progress towards the formalization of their relationship. In this direction, they had stabilized their operational processes and had worked on the establishment of a common measurement system for vendor's performance. Furthermore, they had improved the products' catalogue and they were sticking to the formal governance processes established contractually.

Although there had been an important level of frustration within DUTCH in relation to the performance of Supplier B, it does appear that the two firms stabilized their co-operation and that Supplier B demonstrated significant performance improvements. The improvement in Supplier B performance was attributed to the stabilization of the operational processes, including the measurement systems that produced visibility and self-management. However, the relationship between the two firms remained highly transactional, perhaps further encouraged by this increased formalization and surveillance, and this seemed to be unsatisfactory for DUTCH respondents.

According to the research participants, DUTCH was seeking a proactive attitude from its suppliers, which was highly linked in their view to the existence of a partnership-based model. Arnold (DUTCH sector manager for sourcing arrangements) elaborated on this issue and acknowledged that while Supplier B was an expert in network services, it had not been demonstrating a proactive attitude in line with its capabilities for solving problems:

> *We did some self reflection because you have to be honest. Looking at the infrastructural services, you are talking about commodities. And contracting commodities with vendors is also stating "I apply your best practice". … So I think for infrastructure services it is the Supplier B way. … But then of course talking about behaviour the "Supplier B way" is "leaning on the chair and just waiting for something to happen. … And then, uh, we have a disruption, lets fix it and customer, you have to be very pleased of course if we fix it within the SLA." … But hang on. I thought you had a network operating center with monitoring capabilities in place, didn't you see this coming? That is the right behaviour … being proactive.*

Here Arnold (DUTCH sector manager for sourcing arrangements) expressed the essential dissonance between how a 'relationship' mode of governmentality should work, how the 'contract' mode could undermine this functioning, and how other contingencies, not least the rigidities within Supplier B's organization, capabilities, culture, and attitudes, could throw the 'relationship' mode off its desired managerial course.

Supplier C Contract

Suppler C provides further illustration of the contract/relationship dialectic but where the outsourcing outcomes are indifferent enough for DUTCH to be contemplating contract termination.

There were initial reasons why any mode of governmentality did not start well. Edward (DUTCH IT director) elaborated on the rushed approach of DUTCH when it outsourced its workspace infrastructure to Supplier C:

> *When we outsourced our workspace management systems … we did this too fast and there were a lot of things that we did not know how they worked and we were asking the supplier to explain to us, while it should be the other way around. … This meant that we were actually not in control … and when you are outsourcing, you should know what you need functionally and ask your provider to do it. … And we had a catalogue of services which was really far from complete. … We should have been more accurate because if you outsource garbage, you get garbage back.*

The rationality within DUTCH was that the partnership style of relationship would provide a substitute for the lack of formal contractual processes and surveillance mechanisms and that the two firms would work on the details of their arrangement in the course of time.

However, the partnership-based approach did not appear to be effective at any time in the case of Supplier C. One problem respondents referred to was the general 'attitude' of Supplier C. According to the research participants within DUTCH, there was a lot of finger-pointing by Supplier C and their attitude was negative. It also did not appear that there was any cultural fit between the two firms. According to a number of research participants, the way of conducting business and co-operating within DUTCH was different from Supplier C. Rob (DUTCH contract manager for Supplier C) noted:

> *I also worked together with Supplier A and they have a completely different attitude. … Let's say that Supplier A treats the customer more like a customer and Supplier C does not. … If I would define a KPI on attitude, Supplier A would get seven out of ten, while Supplier C only three. … And we do have the same contract structure, but was you understand, it has to do with ownership. If you do an outsourcing of the workspace, you really want to get a company that takes the contract to solve your problems. Supplier C does not solve problems. What happens is that we ask a question and we get two questions back.*

Furthermore, there were no significant relationships at the executive level in support of the partnership-based approach. Rob (DUTCH contract manager for Supplier C) elaborated on this issue:

> *I know that financially they were actually in a very good position. … I learned that in terms of profit and loss, as long as their customer is green … there is no response. If you ask something, there will be no response. … Internally in Supplier C, above all these client directors there is a man who is vice president, who is responsible for the twenty-five largest accounts. … So as long as his light is green, you do not get any attention. It starts when financially the light becomes red. There is no profit for Supplier C anymore, so they start paying attention.*

Within DUTCH there was a wide dissatisfaction with this attitude of Supplier C. Rob (DUTCH contract manager for Supplier C) very vividly highlighted the instrumental nature of the attitude that Supplier C was demonstrating towards DUTCH:

> *So it is the financials, that is the metric that they are using in the management of the outsourcing … as long as they are getting their profit, they do not really care.*

However, while these reasons are important in explaining why the partnership-based approach did not work, it appears that there were wider issues within Supplier C that created frustration not only to DUTCH but also to a number of other customers of Supplier C. Rob (DUTCH contract manager for Supplier C) explained:

> *It is not just DUTCH … the perception of all their customers is actually the same, they get below what they expect. … I believe that there will become very difficult times for Supplier C. … And I believe also that they will lose a lot of contracts in the next coming two years.*

It appears that Supplier C at some stage in its history decided that it was not cost-efficient enough and that it needed to reduce its cost base, by re-organizing itself with better processes and a way of accounting where money went and who earned what. It thus seems that Supplier C became very internally focused and while trying to re-organize itself it neglected the fact that it was servicing a particular set of customers.

The partnership-based approach with Supplier C progressed in a particularly unsatisfactory way, but there was a lack of effective formal surveillance mechanisms that could provide an alternative means of control of the venture. A problem was that DUTCH and Supplier C had not established a common measurement system and thus there were significant conflicts in relation to the assessment of the performance that Supplier C demonstrated:

> *When we started to work with Supplier C, we measured the time from when a service request enters DUTCH IT until it is sorted out. We measured the total time. Of course, Supplier C said "we did not agree on this total time, we agreed on this part of it, where my work is. … You have to measure me on my performance and this part of the deal."* Harry (DUTCH sector manager on IT operations)

A further problem was that the actual numbers and figures that each company was using were different. Some metrics were very general and thus did not present the real performance problems. Some definitions were differently used by the two firms, creating further miscommunication and disagreements. On this basis, although it was obvious that Supplier C was underperforming, this result was not demonstrated through the use of formal surveillance mechanisms. John (contract manager from Supplier C) explained:

> *The numbers DUTCH uses differs from the numbers Supplier C uses. So we always have these discussions about what the figures represent.*

From the DUTCH side, Rob (DUTCH contract manager for Supplier C) noted:

> *Suppliers however have their own service management tool. … So they have to work with our tooling … and our tooling was going from customer to the Supplier C work-group. … And under Supplier C there were a lot of sub-work groups. … In the end, we could only get reports about the total service that Supplier C provided us. … We have a lot of services … we have workspaces,*

mail etc etc … normally you would expect … that a report addresses all the different service. This was a problem, we only had one general figure. … So it was very difficult to analyze which were the problematic areas. … It took us a lot of time to get into deeper modes of analysis.

He further illustrated the problem of a performance assessment that generates general matrixes that do not reflect the real situation:

With our current reporting we are getting only one figure and no matrix. … Once we are connected to their service management tooling, it is going to be much better in getting reports on detailed figures.

This lack of transparency and differences in measurement left it open for Supplier C to resist the normalizing effects of DUTCH's demands by creating its own discourse and interpretations of events that could not be challenged—due to there being no further evidence. For example, at one point respondents said that DUTCH was unable to terminate the contract with Supplier C without incurring considerable cost, because it could not build enough evidence to claim termination for just cause. This meant that Supplier C could legitimately resist DUTCH's own power plays with its own:

What happens is that we ask a question and we get two questions back … we were always the ones that did not do it well or right … it was never supplier C. (Rob, DUTCH contract manager for Supplier C)

In time, DUTCH and Supplier C established what it saw as the right communication structures and made significant use of formalized surveillance procedures and documentation.

We have sort of adapted the governance to get a smoother form of communication between Supplier C and DUTCH … and it works very well. … but you also have to grow within the governance, not only in making sure that the right people are talking to each other, but also in terms of building quality reports, quality documentation. … We have seen that the quality of the notes that we used to make was not really enough. … So it is not only a matter of having the right people, but also the quality of the content. Rob (DUTCH contract manager for Supplier C)

While the performance of Supplier C improved to some extent, as a result of making the relationship more visible and more disciplined, the relationship between the two firms has been seriously damaged. On this basis, DUTCH has lost confidence in Supplier C having the potential to be the proactive partner it requires. Arnold (DUTCH sector manager for sourcing arrangements) explained that while DUTCH was currently focusing on the value-adding capability of Supplier C, their attitude of not being proactive was an issue to be addressed:

> *When you look at some cultural aspects within Supplier C, for example … taking ownership, being proactive, presenting improvement plans by it self and not because DUTCH asked for it. … There is this cultural aspect that has also been discussed with them. … So meeting the service levels on regular business is not enough for DUTCH. … We are now focusing on their "cultural performance" and we agreed that Supplier C would use the first quarter of 2010 to prove their added value for the DUTCH organization.*

A failing outsourcing arrangement, such as this one, is particularly interesting from a Foucauldian perspective, because Foucault's own histories of disciplinary power, as found in, for example, *The Birth of the Clinic*, *Discipline and Punish*, and *The History of Sexuality (part 1)*, tend to focus on the supremacy and omnicompetence of surveillance/discipline operating in disciplinary societies. Clearly the systems of governmentality applied in these outsourcing arrangements are human creations and are all too often rendered imperfect not just in design and implementation, but they also have unanticipated effects and outcomes. But equally, Foucault through his notion of power relations did move in his 1970s work towards putting the human component back into the motor of events, and this again emerges from these cases, along with the other contingencies impacting on the dynamic of those power relations.

Summary: Applying a Foucauldian Perspective

A Foucauldian perspective on the case studies primarily demonstrated three major themes running through the case studies. Firstly, a major theme that was revealed is related to the dialectical play between contracts and relationships as modes of governance and management. Their use is evolving during the outsourcing arrangement according to the diverse rationalities for governing that emphasize one over the other. In this manner, they appear to emerge as modes of governmentality and utilize different means of surveillance, discipline, and control. Contracts tend to focus on measurements, benchmarks, service levels, and associated formal techniques of control, while relationships emphasized on elements are 'partnering' behaviour.

Secondly, a Foucauldian perspective on power relations illuminated the productive character of power, not only in the production of truth and knowledge but also in terms of practical behaviours seen as positive, legitimate, and useful within the social contexts within which they are enacted.

Thirdly, Foucault's theorization draws attention to the fact that there is a discourse with recurring themes, issues, language, and regularities. This discourse appears to discipline peoples' behaviour, thoughts, and actions and also serves as a political resource that agents within the discourse actively seek as a means of legitimization of their thoughts and beliefs. In this manner, this discourse points to specific correct and incorrect responses and distinguishes between desirable and undesirable types of behaviour.

References

Clegg, S., Pitsis, T., Rura-Polley, T., & Marosszeky, M. (2002). Governmentality Matters: Designing an Alliance Culture of Inter-Organizational Collaboration for Managing Projects. *Organization Studies, 23*(3), 317–337.

Foucault, M. (1972). *Archaeology of Knowledge*. New York: Pantheon.

Foucault, M. (2003). *Society Must Be Defended*. New York: Picador.

Lacity, M., Khan, S., Yan, A., & Willcocks, L. (2010). A Review of the IT Outsourcing Empirical Literature and Future Research Directions. *Journal of Information Technology, 25*(4), 395–433.

Miller, P., & Rose, N. (1990). Governing Economic Life. *Economy and Society, 19*(1), 1–31.

Willcocks, L. P., & Mingers, J. (2004). *Social Theory and Philosophy for Information Systems*. Hoboken, NJ: John Wiley & Sons Ltd.

8

Conclusion: The Global Outsourcing Discourse

Introduction

This final chapter provides an overview of the set-up and research conducted and provides additional commentary on the research findings and contributions.

Our original intention was to contribute methodologically and empirically by analysing several IT outsourcing arrangements using Foucauldian methods and concepts. This was deliberately ambitious and relatively original in information systems studies. We are not aware of anyone else who has applied Foucault's work to IT outsourcing in a research effort as intensive as the present one. The process of actual research led us to see that in the cases investigated, Foucault's work could be very insightful, but it could not be applied in a consistent, rigorous manner. His work, self-confessedly, was provisional and, he always insisted, should inform future research, and methods, rather than be dutifully applied as a set of techniques.

At the same time his notions of discourse, subjugated knowledge, and problematization led us to see an emerging discourse within the interviews, accounts, and documents engaged with that was typical of other

E. Lioliou, L. P. Willcocks, *Global Outsourcing Discourse*, Technology, Work and Globalization, https://doi.org/10.1007/978-3-319-74045-4_8

outsourcing arrangements. Also that many of the themes running through the transaction cost economics (TCE) theorization encountered in the IT outsourcing literature seemed to be particularly relevant to the material being collected and to how respondents talked about their experiences.

It was while actively researching DUTCH that it came to us that a TCE analysis would be relatively easy to accomplish given the rich data accumulated. TCE's popularity is due to its elegant and relatively limited set of concepts pre-organized into a technique that was relatively easy to apply, especially if doing confirmatory research. We resolved to pursue a critique of TCE through empirical research but at the same time wanted to deconstruct its role in establishing an outsourcing discourse that is the way in which academics and practitioners speak of IT outsourcing. We realized at that point that TCE and a Foucauldian-informed perspective could operate as complementary theoretical perspectives but also that Foucault's work could also perhaps act as a critical commentary, even control, on the TCE discourse and on the discourses emerging from the research into the five cases.

In this chapter we look to further critique the role of TCE in the study of IT outsourcing, suggest what may be learned from applying selective Foucauldian concepts in the study of IT outsourcing, and discuss views on the TCE, outsourcing, and Foucauldian discourses that run through this book.

The Role of TCE in IT Outsourcing Studies

An approach to governance that is inspired by the theory of transaction costs focuses primarily on the characteristics of the exchange, namely, asset specificity, frequency, and uncertainty. Based on these dimensions of the exchange, the theory of transaction costs aims to explain the choice of governance, in terms of keeping the activities in-house or outsourcing through a classical, neo-classical, or a relational contract. The theory of transaction costs has received significant critique.

A major criticism on the theory of transaction costs has been developed by Granovetter (1985), who identified as a major limitation of the theory that it ignores that economic exchanges are socially embedded exchanges. More specifically he suggested that economic exchanges depart "from pure economic motives, continuing economic relations often become overlaid with social content that carries strong expectations of trust and abstention from opportunism" (Granovetter 1985). Considering the GIB-PV case, the two organizations had a long-standing history together. The people working in the two organizations were familiar one with another and some of them were co-operating together for 20 years. In other words, due to the history between the two organizations, there were significant 'reputation effects' that influenced the evolution of the relationship and generated partnering behaviour. In the LION-FDL case, there was also a very strong social element involved that had to do with 'reputation effects'. LION is a very important financial institution and thus a prestigious client, which made it attractive for FDL to be flexible and accommodating to its needs. Similarly, in the outsourcing arrangements of DUTCH, there was a significant social element, stemming from its prestige. Furthermore, DUTCH chose Supplier A and Supplier B based very much on their reputations.

The neglect of the social context within which the transactions take place has caused various concerns about the predictive power of transaction cost theory and its ability to provide useful prescriptions for exchange activities. In the field of IT outsourcing, Lacity and Willcocks (1995) found that the context within which outsourcing decisions have been taken matters significantly. The authors further explained that outsourcing decisions can be better understood following an examination in the relevant organization of the senior management view on IT as this has evolved over the years. In line with this thought, our results have indicated that there is a wider outsourcing discourse on keeping strategic IT activities in-house and outsourcing the ones that are considered non-competitive and non-differentiating. As examples, in the GIB case the whole X-RAY project that resulted in major cost savings for GIB was based on the rationale of handing over 'legacy' and 'non-competitive' applications to the vendor. In the case of DUTCH, there was a general view that the data centres, network, and workspace management were not part of the 'core competence' of the firm and thus they should be outsourced. However, DUTCH neglected to take into account in-depth considerations about choice of supplier and how it was going to retain control over the environment being outsourced. The firm did not apply a formal RFP process and, according to a number of interviewees, including the IT director, DUTCH progressed to its outsourcing arrangements too fast. Similar to the observations Lacity and Willcocks (1995) made in their study, it appears that, in this case at least, decision-makers "selected an outcome before the decision process and merely selectively gathered information to justify their preferences". Together, these several points suggest that the reductive economic man rationale central to TCE needs to be heavily qualified and is done insufficiently internally through its attenuated view of human behaviour nestled in the concepts of bounded rationality, vendor opportunism, and information asymmetry.

Another major point of critique of the theory of transaction costs is Williamson's (1979) assumption that the criterion for organizing transactions is strictly an instrumental one and is concerned with the goal of cost economizing. Zazac and Olsen (1993) developed a major critique on this assumption by Williamson. The authors emphasized that the TCE perspective focuses excessively on cost minimization efforts between the exchange partners, to the neglect of their pursuit for mutual value. Along the line of this critique, my results indicated that while the reduction of cost has been a major consideration in all cases under investigation, outsourcing clients tend to have further expectations from their vendors and also in some cases actively pursue 'partnering' arrangements to realize those expectations. These expectations are related to the potential of the vendors for value creation and are manifested partly to the signs of proactive behaviour that the vendors demonstrate. On this basis, it appears that for outsourcing clients the pursuit of cost reduction co-exists with their expectations for value creation. The fact that the theory of transaction costs downplays expectations for value creation, which are hard to quantify and most often not immediately realized, constitutes a major limitation of the theory in understanding outsourcing decisions.

Williamson (1991) further highlighted that economizing is more important than political strategizing, bringing in this way to the foreground the economic rationality of organizations and neglecting the influence of political agendas. In particular, he noted:

> *I furthermore aver that, as between economizing and strategizing, economizing is much the more fundamental. … More importantly, I maintain that a strategizing effort will rarely prevail if a program is burdened by significant cost excesses in production, distribution, or organization. All the clever ploys and positioning, aye, all the king's horses and all the king's men, will rarely save a project that is seriously flawed in first-order economizing respects.* (Williamson 1991)

Lacity and Willcocks (1995, 2009) criticized Williamson's focus on economizing at the expense of strategizing. They argued that the focus of IT outsourcing is shifting from cost considerations to issues of efficiency, innovation, and value. Other research also suggests that IT outsourcing is viewed as a means to improve a firm's overall business performance and achieve its strategic goals (Goles and Chin 2005). In line with these views, our results indicated that the outsourcing clients under investigation put effort into more strategic approaches to outsourcing. While cost has been underlined as a major concern, outsourcing clients tended to be concerned about the value creation capabilities of their suppliers as well as their long-term potential to enhance the strategic positioning of the clients.

Ghoshal and Moran (1996) provided a very strong critique on the theory of transaction costs and suggested that its logic can be particularly dangerous for practitioners. They argued that:

> *the assumption of opportunism can become a self-fulfilling prophecy whereby opportunistic behaviour will increase with sanctions and incentives imposed to curtail it, thus creating the need for even stronger and more elaborate sanctions and incentives. Caught in such a vicious cycle, "hierarchies", as organizations are described by Williamson, would, over time, lose their initial raison d'etre.* (Ghoshal and Moran 1996)

And indeed the assumption of opportunism becoming a self-fulfilling prophecy can be seen across the cases as something that undermined the efficacy of the 'partnering' mode that all client respondents talked of as wanting in each of the five cases—something that was revealed as a result of a more Foucauldian analysis (see Chap. 7).

Another problem with the theory of transaction costs is that it tends to focus on some outsourcing decisions such as keeping the activities in-house, outsourcing using the contract as a tool of governance, or outsourcing using primarily relationships as a tool of governance, ignoring other issues related to the execution of the venture that are equally significant in determining whether the venture will be successful, less successful, or failed. As an example previous research has long demonstrated the choice of the outsourcing venture as a major determinant of the effectiveness of outsourcing arrangements (Currie and Seltsikas 2001). Considering the case of DUTCH and Supplier C, it appears that from a TCE perspective the firm correctly decided to outsource the management of its workspace environment. However, Supplier C lacked the capabilities to deliver. On the same basis, the theory of TCE would prescribe in the LION case to keep the savings and loans activities in-house due to the great levels of uncertainty that surrounded this transaction. However, the delivery and relationship competencies of FDL were particularly significant in making the venture effective.

Furthermore, according to our results, it appears that Williamson (1985) himself relatively downplays the role of uncertainty in the generation of transaction costs. The rationality of the theory of transaction costs appears to be that where transactions are non-specific, there are going to be a lot of alternatives in the market. On this basis, according to TCE, using the markets and more particularly outsourcing using a classical contract should be the preferred choice. This rationality appears to be flawed, however, as the switching costs even in the case of non-specific transactions can be particularly high. As an example, DUTCH was particularly dissatisfied with the performance of Supplier C and yet, it was not taking the decision to terminate the contract because switching costs were prohibitive. From our findings it also appears that an important reason why DUTCH tolerated for so long the underperformance of Supplier B had been the possibility of high switching costs. A TCE proponent might then argue that these cases did not involve non-specific transactions, and we are then back to the problem of TCE's uncalibrated use of terms.

A methodological problem with the theory of transaction costs is that while it appears straightforward in its operationalization, in practice there is some language ambiguity that makes its application often vague. Lacity and Willcocks (1995) also made a similar observation and suggested that part of the anomalies found in their results could be attributed to language ambiguities. While, for example, Williamson (1979) gives a clear definition of the construct of asset specificity and distinguishes different elements to it, he does not give a clear indication of what could be regarded as a 'non-specific', 'mixed', or 'idiosyncratic' transaction. On this basis, it is left to the researcher or the practitioner to make a subjective decision on the level of asset specificity that particular transactions carry. The same issue holds with the classification of the transactions in relation to their frequency as 'occasional' or 'recurrent'. Furthermore, already indicated, Williamson (1975) himself did not provide clear definitions of the construct of uncertainty nor examples of what would constitute high, medium, or low levels of uncertainty. On this basis, as Lacity and Willcocks (1995) argued, proponents of transaction cost theory can make claims on the explanatory power of the theory by appealing to different classifications of the transactions and by operating a sliding scale when it comes to the meaning of important terms, for example how much is 'high' uncertainty? What is a 'highly' idiosyncratic asset? How do you measure degree of information asymmetry?

Consequently, it appears that there are both significant limitations with transaction cost theory regarding its logic (e.g. neglect of the social and historical contexts within which the transactions take place, focus on cost-minimizing efforts from the exchange partners in neglect of their pursuit of mutual value, overemphasis on the possibility of opportunistic behaviour, neglect of multiple-stakeholder perspectives), as well as in respect to its operationalization (e.g. language ambiguity).

It is important to note that David and Han (2004) tried to provide an assessment of the empirical evidence in support of the theory of transaction costs. According to their results, while there is a significant amount of evidence on the association between high levels of asset specificity and keeping the activities in-house, it appears that more research is needed regarding whether this choice is preferable. They also argued that there are relatively low levels of empirical support on the effects of uncertainty (i.e. not a clear association between levels of uncertainty and the decision to outsource) or the effects of uncertainty on the level of transaction costs. The authors found empirical support for TCE prescriptions in only 47% of the studies they assessed, which they found surprising. More specifically they noted: “We expected that a theory of such prominence and disciplinary-spanning power would have clear-cut support”.

Another problem they identified is similar to our own research findings here—there is considerable disagreement on the operationalization of some of TCE’s central constructs and propositions. David and Han (2004) highlighted that there can be social norms and factors that moderate transaction costs and suggested the possibility of a shift from focusing on whether the theory of transaction costs is successful or not to discussing under what circumstances it is successful. My own research suggests that future IT outsourcing studies may well need to use TCE by itself as a theoretical lens for investigation with considerable caution.

Studies from a more ‘social’ perspective have tried to demonstrate that while outsourcing decisions are important, the execution and ongoing management of the venture are also critical. Social exchanges between clients and vendors have been shown to be crucial in the context of outsourcing relations (Kern and Willcocks 2000; Zaheer and Venkatraman 1995). This stream of research has led to an understanding that the relationship between the client and the vendor is critical in the degree of success or failure of the outsourcing arrangement. TCE tends to underplay this critical engagement, relying instead on formal governance structures and transparency and measurement in anything other than what TCE refers to as relational contracts. In practice, we found that in all the cases researched there was a heavy dependence on relational dimensions, the reason being that, as respondents continually told me, formal arrangements, transparency, and measurement could only get outsourcing performance so far. Moreover, all contracts were necessarily incomplete, while governance structures often struggled to keep up with dynamic contexts and challenges in which they were operating. The learning point is that while TCE is a useful analytical tool, it probably greatly underplays the role of people and relationships in delivering outsourcing performance in all contracts and not just the relational ones as labelled by TCE.

Learning from a Foucauldian-Informed Perspective

In using Foucault's work selectively, we have tried to be relatively faithful to the spirit in which we think he operated. His work does not provide a finished tool or easy-to-apply technique that can be utilized unproblematically. Indeed, this may well explain partly the lack of adoption of his work in information systems studies. Learning to use Foucault for intensive research purposes also takes a lot of time.

From a social perspective, the Foucauldian approach demonstrates that there are competing discourses and norms among exchange partners in outsourcing. These discourses are particularly important in shaping the behaviour of clients and suppliers accordingly. A major discourse on outsourcing is that it constitutes a means for the reduction of cost. A cost rationality for governance focuses primarily on cost issues and the quantification of the desired results so that a relatively clear cost-benefit analysis can be undertaken. This approach emphasizes the importance of setting clear goals and targets as well as measuring and benchmarking performance. The contract and the associated service level agreements and key performance indicators serve as key tools in setting down the objectives of the outsourcing venture. We have referred to this at various points as the 'contract' mode of governmentality. Much of this will be familiar to those looking to apply TCE's neo-classical contract prescriptions in IT outsourcing. The research also studied the relevance of, and insights gained from, using Foucauldian-informed concepts such as surveillance, disciplinary power, and transparency when explaining the intended efficacy and power relations producing and produced by these technologies of control.

Considering the GIB case, although it was indicated that personal relationships matter, the firm took a very formalized approach to outsourcing. Clear indicators and guidelines were in place in order to monitor vendor performance. While some of these indicators and matrices worked better than others, GIB tended to adopt more of a cost rationality to its outsourcing arrangement with PV.

At the other extreme, there is a discourse of 'partnering'. This refers, in our own labelling in earlier chapters, to a 'relationship' mode of governmentality. Both clients and suppliers talked about this regularly across the five cases and it appears they did recognize it as an important facilitator in their transactions and communications. This outsourcing discourse in essence conditioned their expectations right at the front, and it constitutes a philosophy whose significance for doing business can hardly be questioned. We found the label 'partnering' signalling a special business relationship, and managers in both clients and suppliers agreed that it was a very desirable element in their interorganizational arrangements. As a business philosophy it seemed to create specific expectations, attitudes, cultures, and belief systems that are relatively common and widely accepted and constituted a way of steering and disciplining behaviour. This kind of disciplining can be seen as an instance of Foucault's disciplinary power (1980a, b) in that power operates in an indirect way through the ethics and good principles of conducting business. This approach to outsourcing governance focused on the significance of the ongoing interactions and communications between people, as well as the generation of trust, commitment, and co-operation between the exchange partners. The five cases are replete with quotes demonstrating this significance across client and supplier managers alike.

Consider the case of DUTCH. Initially the organization tended to adopt a partnering rationality in the governance of its outsourcing arrangement. However, the results were, managerially, rather poor, especially in the case of the Supplier B and Supplier C contracts. For this reason, DUTCH started to abandon the partnering rationality and to engage a more formalized approach to governance, based on matrices, service level agreements, and key performance indicators. On this basis, a Foucauldian perspective demonstrates how competing rationalities around governance co-exist, compete, and take over one from another.

These discourses are reflected in particular rationalities for governing that Foucault named governmentality. Jackson and Carter (1998) suggested governmentality means that:

> *people should voluntarily and willingly delegate their moral autonomy and moral responsibility to obedience to the rules, to being governed in their conduct by a "moral" force … which is external to the "self".*

They also note that this need for obedience is "usually rationalized and justified in terms of a greater collective interest".

On this basis, it appears that a Foucauldian perspective on governance throws light on outsourcing discourses and the way that they create common rationalities for governing. These rationalities for governing, or governmentalities, produce discipline by appealing to the moral autonomy of the individuals. Contrary to the TCE theorization, where discipline is achieved through the contract in light of the assumption of opportunistic behaviour, the Foucauldian perspective focuses on the intertwinement of institutional, collective, and personal goals.

However, our study across the five cases reveals that, if these two modes of governmentality are heavily intertwined in IT outsourcing, then this is in ways that can be both complementary and also, simultaneously, mutually undermining. Too much emphasis on the 'contract' mode creates instrumental forms of psychological contract and economic/instrumental behaviours by all parties, with opportunism, both client and supplier, never far away. This mode erodes the efficacy of any attempts at operating in a 'relationship' mode of governmentality. Where the stress is on the 'relationship' mode, this can leave gaps resulting in suboptimal performance and still may not dissuade parties from opportunistic behaviour or exploiting power dependence and power resources in the dynamic circuitry of power relations. Our case work has found that there are limits to how much the two modes can complement or 'fill in' for the weaknesses of the other in a specific set of circumstances. The interplay emerges as a dynamic dialectic between the two modes that is never comprehensively manageable for any length of time.

What renders governmentality unstable is not just dynamic context but also power relations, into which material objects, designs, people, and knowledge are all brought to circulate and produce effects. The case work demonstrates that the Foucauldian notion of power relations produces rich insights and has greater explanatory power, and applicability, than the notion of power residing in TCE, for example. Power also emerges as inextricably tied to knowledge and its production. In the cases we see client managers meticulously setting down how the supplier should behave and designing detailed measurement systems to ensure conformance and transparency. These are essentially power/knowledge moves. Where power/knowledge is lacking—as in the DUTCH-Suppliers B and C cases—and there is no great possible recourse to the 'relationship' mode, then the client is weaker, the supplier able to be more resistant or opportunistic. The DUTCH cases are interesting in this respect in seeing the clients' flight from a 'relationship' mode that gave them too little power/knowledge to an increasingly 'contract' mode that was set to correct the imbalance.

The case studies are also revealing about client and supplier respondents' roles in creating themselves as subjects with beliefs, ways of talking, and feelings, within larger disciplinary and regulative structures and circuits of power relations. As such, their subjectification is produced by the interplay between those structures, circuits, and their own self-reflectiveness. This produces psychological contracts and guidance for action and actual behaviours, as well as assumptions and beliefs about the conduct of outsourcing and business in specific circumstances.

It also appears that there is a wider discourse in outsourcing, with recurring issues, rhetoric, language, and regularities. This discourse appears to distinguish between desirable and undesirable types of behaviour and correct and incorrect attitudes, and in this way it produces disciplinary effects (see Table 8.1). Along these lines, it serves as a political resource that managers use in order to motivate participants, including themselves, towards particular types of beliefs and behaviours while discouraging other beliefs and behaviours. In this way, a Foucauldian perspective illuminates the productive character of power, not only in terms of the production of truth and knowledge but also in terms of practical behaviours seen, and experienced, as appropriate and useful.

On this basis, a Foucauldian approach to governance illuminates different, wider power issues than TCE theory. While the latter views power as a resource that encourages opportunistic behaviour, the former views power in a more comprehensive way: power is inextricably tied to the production of knowledge, beliefs, and ways of thinking and acting.

While Foucault's theorization constitutes alternative lens in the study of governance, it does not provide a clear-cut and straightforward technique that can be utilized unproblematically for analysis. Although his work is relatively open-ended, which creates methodological challenges, it is worth noting that Foucault himself referred to Nietzsche and suggested

Table 8.1 Three discourses: TCE, outsourcing, and Foucauldian

Discourse		
TCE	Outsourcing	Foucauldian
Cost economizing	Cost economizing Core competencies Competitive advantage	Subjectification processes
Asset specificity	Keep in-house	Power relations
Transaction frequency	Total/selective outsourcing Single/multi-sourcing	Discipline
Uncertainty	Contract Measurement Monitoring	Calculation Standardization Normalization Programming
Information asymmetry	Governance Documentation SLAs/KPIs Retained knowledge	Surveillance
Opportunism	Contractual safeguards Partnering/relationships	Governmentality
Bounded rationality	Co-operation Win-win Synergies	Discourse

that thinkers are shooting arrows in the air, but the key thing for others is to pick them up and shoot them in a different direction (Foucault cited in Willcocks 2006). Along these lines Willcocks (2006) emphasized that Foucault's work, although it is rather open-ended and difficult to use, "also leaves open the possibility of creative applications of his ideas".

The Outsourcing Discourse

Foucault's work focused on one particular discourse, that of the human or social sciences, including such areas as psychology, penology, sociology, and economics. His purpose was to overturn received interpretations about established 'knowledges' and examine the social effects of the knowledges they produced. Given TCE's status as a leading economic theory, it is particularly useful to consider how Foucault's concepts, which themselves form their own discourse, can act as a commentary on the

TCE discourse and the discourse emerging from the present research which we will call here the 'outsourcing discourse'. The founding concepts and terms of these three discourses, the terms as it were under which the discourses are conducted, are shown in Table 8.1.

The ability of TCE to produce 'truth' has been revealed by this and previous studies as problematic in many respects, though some have argued that the problem lies with the misapplication and distortion of TCE when used in a range of empirical studies (see Macher and Richman 2008). The use of Foucauldian analysis here suggests that TCE misses structural, power, and social issues and, as a result, has useful, but limited, predictive power when applied to IT outsourcing. Our own view, based on the present research, is that TCE produces a limited view, with limited predictive capability for IT outsourcing, but nevertheless does pick up in its discursive formation on many concepts that 'feel real' and which, on the evidence from the cases, are adopted in both academic and practitioner discussions and actions with regard to outsourcing. To a noticeable extent the TCE discourse, though using more abstracted labels, does feed into the mix of managerial technical and more 'commonsense' notions that pervade the discourse that emerges from studying clients and respondents in their five outsourcing arrangements.

This 'outsourcing' discourse tends to follow the assumption that outsourcing arrangements are fair, legal collaborative agreements to achieve performance together against more or less specified targets. However, inherent in the discourse are governmentality, power relations, and disciplining issues that saturate the outsourcing terms even when used in seemingly relatively benign ways. The words co-operation, partnership, and win-win, for example, do not really reflect the deep flow of dynamic power relations they ride on the surface of. Outsourcing emerges, from a Foucauldian analysis, as a disciplining exercise in applying modes of governmentality that are often in conflict with one another. This can create variable performance effects that cut across the win-win, strategic relationship and agreed target language of the normative outsourcing discourse that seems to prevail across all five case studies.

And the effect of the normative outsourcing discourse, including its stress on, for example, governance and contract and suppliers doing 'above contract', is also to create subjects that are bound, more or less, into the discourse and, to that extent, are willing to let its power content shape/produce motivation, psychological contracts, and performance.

Of course, Foucault's work and concepts themselves form their own discourse, which represents itself as a deconstructionist 'genealogical' approach to showing how normal discourses operate and create truth and knowledge and how power relations, subjectification processes, and history have essential shaping influences in these processes at work in our institutions, belief systems, and ways of constructing the world. While Foucault's own discourse has been the subject of multiple critiques, nevertheless his work has also been widely applied in the social sciences as a means of problematizing normal explanations/behaviours, identifying the role of disciplining processes, and questioning why things are not otherwise. We have here utilized Foucault's work in a deliberately delimited way, to provide a commentary both on the normative discourse represented by TCE in academic discourse and on the regulating 'commonsense' management discourse adopted by outsourcing practitioners. This is in the belief that outsourcing is a core practice in contemporary work organizations and as such comes under the umbrella of the Foucauldian aspiration to examine how disciplinary power and technologies operate in schools, hospitals, asylums, military barracks, and other work institutions characteristic of modernity, and, by extension for this study, the present.

Conclusion

The primary theoretical contributions of this book are twofold. Firstly, we investigated the predictive power of the theory of transaction costs on the choice of governance structures, in a way that extends the examination carried out by Lacity and Willcocks (1995). Based on the critique by Aubert and Weber (2001), the research examined the construct of asset specificity in terms of specific assets but not specialized assets or assets that are both specific and specialized. Furthermore, we incorporated more detailed types of asset specificity as identified by Williamson (1985), that is, site, physical, human, dedicated, procedural, and temporal asset specificity. We expect that this categorization will both strengthen TCE's predictive power and make the examination of the asset specificity dimension more thorough and thus more appropriate in assessing the usefulness of TCE to explain sourcing decisions.

Against this background, the book investigates the extent to which the findings verify or conflict with the results by Lacity and Willcocks (1995). Furthermore, extending the work by Lacity and Willcocks (1995), we conducted a second level of analysis where we analysed the impact of uncertainty on the choice of governance structures. In investigating the uncertainty construct, we incorporated the impact of "reputation effects" as an indicator of behavioural uncertainty.

Secondly, our research examined how a Foucauldian perspective on what we characterize in its totality as 'power relations' can inform our understanding on governance. To the best of our knowledge, this remains the first comprehensive study that aims to illustrate how the Foucauldian concepts of governmentality, discourse, and power relations can be relevant to the study of outsourcing arrangements.

Methodologically, the main contribution of the study is that it incorporates the perspectives both of client and supplier organizations. Studies that examine the views of both sides in the IT outsourcing relationship appear to be relatively missing in the IT outsourcing literature. Another methodological contribution of the study is that it takes a longitudinal perspective in studying the IT outsourcing relationship from a TCE perspective. Finally, a methodological contribution is demonstrating the usefulness of applying two very different theoretical perspectives to the same data, to see if this enhances explanatory power but also produces a dialectical critique of each theoretical lens brought to bear. Our conclusion is that both explanatory power and dialectical critique proved highly valuable and greatly increased the richness of understanding emerging from our study.

Our findings are also particularly relevant to practitioners. The study provides in-depth illustrations of the evolution of IT outsourcing governance practices and demonstrates how the formal and the relational approaches to governance, which co-exist, compete with but also can complement one another. The study also demonstrates the limitations of the theory of transaction costs, which is a widely used framework, or at least its assumptions are widely used in practice for assessing outsourcing decisions and outcomes. Conversely, we illustrated the importance of people and relationships in delivering outsourcing performance—on which TCE theory tends to provide too narrow a view. Additionally, this research illustrates how clients and suppliers try to produce discipline through the use of rhetoric and language that are related to wider discourses on outsourcing. In this way, we have demonstrated the role of a normative outsourcing discourse in creating ways of thinking and acting and producing motivation, psychological contracts, and performance.

On conservative estimates, by the end of 2018, the global outsourcing contract value for business and IT services was about US $1106.98 billion (BPO US $368.98 billion, ITO US $738.08 billion). ITO compound annual growth rate for the 2016–2020 period was estimated as 2.6%, with BPO at 4% (combined London School of Economics and Political Science (LSE), Everest Group, and HFS Research figures). Horses For Sources (HFS) Research (2018) estimates the combined global market revenues by 2022 as US $1296.7 billion. Clearly the ITO/BPO market will continue to grow, though at a slower rate than in most previous years over the last two decades. Clearly, also, outsourcing has become an almost routine practice for a very large number of organizations in most major economies. Given this phenomenon, the efficacy and relevance of the theories, perspectives, and assumptions brought to shape and inform practices are of critical importance to practitioners.

But this becomes even more critical as the global outsourcing discourse changes yet again with its embrace of the coming automation and digitization. The underlying shift in technologies acts in a dialectical relationship with the normativizing discourse of digital transformation and its subset discourse of automation of knowledge work. Indeed, the discourse has progressed to the extent that the latter has already sometimes been alluded to as 'the new outsourcing' (Oshri et al. 2015). The underlying shift is caught in the statistics presented in Chap. 1. The discursive shift has been inexorably towards 'As-A-Service', 'Digital One Office', 'Digital transformation' and 'Intelligent automation'—to give just some examples of the emerging vocabulary and narrative. This would signal that the application of discourse analysis, as deployed in the present study, to empirically researched detailed longitudinal cases, is ever more relevant and urgent.

References

Aubert, B., & Weber, R. (2001). *Transaction Cost Theory, the Resource Based View, and Information Technology Sourcing Decisions: A Re-Examination of Lacity et al.'s Findings*. Working paper, ISSN 0832-7203.

Foucault, M. (1980a). *Power/Knowledge: Selected Interviews and Other Writings, 1972–1977*. New York: Pantheon.

Foucault, M. (1980b). Two Lectures. In C. Gordon (Ed.), *Power/Knowledge: Selected Interviews*. New York: Pantheon.

Currie, W. L., & Seltsikas, P. (2001). Exploring the Supply-Side of IT Outsourcing: Evaluating the Emerging Role of Application Service Providers. *European Journal of Information Systems, 12*, 123–134.

David, R. J., & Han, S. K. (2004). A Systematic Assessment of the Empirical Support for Transaction Cost Economics. *Strategic Management Journal, 25*(1), 39–58.

Ghoshal, S., & Moran, P. (1996). Bad for Practice: A Critic of the Transaction Cost Theory. *Academy of Management Review, 21*, 13–47.

Goles, T., & Chin, W. (2005). Information Systems Outsourcing Relationship Factors: Detailed Conceptualization and Initial Evidence. *Database for Advances in Information Systems, 36*(4), 47–67.

Granovetter, M. (1985). Economic Action and Social Structure: The Problem of Embeddedness. *American Journal of Sociology, 91*(3), 481–510.

Jackson, N., & Carter, P. (1998). Labour as Dressage. In A. McKinlay & K. Starkey (Eds.), *Foucault, Management and Organization Theory*. London: Sage.

Kern, T., & Willcocks, L. (2000). *The Relationship Advantage*. Oxford: Oxford University Press.

Lacity, M., & Willcocks, L. (1995). Interpreting Information Technology Sourcing Decisions from a Transaction Cost Perspective: Findings and Critique. *Accounting Management and Information Technologies, 5*, 203–244.

Lacity, M., & Willcocks, L. (2009). *Information Systems and Outsourcing: Studies in Theory and Practice*. London: Palgrave.

Macher, J. T., & Richman, B. D. (2008). Transaction Cost Economics: An Assessment of Empirical Research in the Social Sciences. *Business and Politics, 10*, 1–63.

Oshri, I., Kotlarsky, J., & Willcocks, L. (2015). *The Handbook of Global Outsourcing and Offshoring*. London: Palgrave.

Willcocks, L. (2006). Michel Foucault in the Social Study of ICTs: Critique and Reappraisal. *Social Science Computer Review, 24*(3), 274–295.
Williamson, O. E. (1975). *Markets and Hierarchies Analysis and Antitrust Implications: A Study in the Economics of Internal Organization*. London: Collier-Macmillan.
Williamson, O. E. (1979). Transaction-Cost Economics: The Governance of Contractual Relations. *Journal of Law and Economics, 22*(2), 233–261.
Williamson, O. E. (1985). *The Economic Institutions of Capitalism*. New York: Free Press.
Williamson, O. (1991). Strategizing, Economizing, and Economic Organization. *Strategic Management Journal, 12*, 75–94.
Zaheer, A., & Venkatraman, N. (1995). Relational Governance as an Interorganizational Strategy: An Empirical Test of the Role of Trust in Economic Exchange. *Strategic Management Journal, 16*(5), 373–392.
Zazac, E. J., & Olsen, C. P. (1993). From Transactional Cost to Transactional Value Analysis: Implications for the Study of Interorganizational Strategies. *Journal of Management Studies, 30*(1), 131–145.

Appendix A: A Note on Methodology

Research Strategy

The research strategy chosen was the multiple case study research method and we adopted an interpretive stance. A case study "*is an empirical inquiry that investigates a contemporary phenomenon with its real-life context, especially when then boundaries between phenomenon and its context are not clearly defined*" (Yin 2003). The case study research method was considered to be the most suitable because it enables the researcher to study contemporary phenomena over which he/she has little or no control and examine the context within which these phenomena take place (Yin 2003). Other research methods have not been considered to be appropriate in dealing with these issues. For example, experiments deliberately divorce a phenomenon from its context, histories are limited to phenomena of the past, and surveys provide the researcher with a very limited ability to study the context of the phenomena (Yin 2003). Furthermore, the case study research method allows for various interconnected levels of analysis (Pettigrew 1990), a feature which is particularly

E. Lioliou, L. P. Willcocks, *Global Outsourcing Discourse*, Technology, Work and Globalization, https://doi.org/10.1007/978-3-319-74045-4

important for achieving the objective in linking the individual to the organizational level in studying IT outsourcing.

With regard to the suitability of the case study research method in studying information systems (IS), Benbasat et al. (1987) suggested that it is a particularly useful research strategy primarily for two reasons: first of all, the researcher is enabled to study information systems in a natural setting and achieve a better grasp of reality. Second, through the case study method, the researcher is given the ability to answer 'how' and 'why' questions and understand the nature and complexity of the processes taking place (Benbasat et al. 1987). The points made by Benbasat et al. (1987) emphasize the appropriateness of the case study research method not only in IS research but additionally in research within the interpretive paradigm. Along the same lines, Walsham (1995) argued that case studies are the most appropriate method for doing research within the interpretive paradigm because they can link a broader view to continuous processes and their relation to context.

However, the case study research method has its drawbacks. One common (often misconceived) criticism is that case studies do not allow for generalizability of results (Galliers 1992). However, Saunders et al. (1997) emphasized that the aim of interpretive researchers is not to produce a theory that is generalizable but to explain phenomena in their natural setting. On this basis, the difficulty in making generalizations should not necessarily be seen as a handicap of case studies. Furthermore, Creswell (1998) characterized generalizability as a "*term that makes little sense for most qualitative researchers*". On this issue Walsham (1993) noted that the validity of the findings from a case study does not depend on the generalizability of the results but rather on "*the plausibility and cogency of the logical reasoning applied in describing and presenting the results from the cases and in drawing conclusions from them*". Lee and Baskerville (2003) noted that

> *a theory may never be generalized to a setting where it has not yet been empirically tested and confirmed. Along the same lines, neither an increase in the sample size in a statistical study nor an increase in the number of sites in a multisite case study would be an indicator of greater generalizability of a theory to new settings. (…) Whether research is conducted quantitatively or qualitatively, there is only one scientifically acceptable way to establish a theory's generalizability to a new setting: it is for the theory to service an empirical test in that setting.*

Another criticism of the case study research method is related to the subjectivity in the interpretation of the results concerned (Galliers 1992). Nevertheless, Walsham (2006) rightly argues that such subjectivity and bias may be present in all forms of research strategies. As Geertz had suggested, "*what we call our data are really our own constructions of other people's constructions of what they and their compatriots are up to*" (Geertz 1993).

With regard to the choice of conducting a multiple instead of a single case study research method, it has to be highlighted that my aim is by no means to provide any generalizable results. Rather, my intention is to investigate cases that will allow me to generate more profound insights through engaging in a comparative approach. Yin (2003) suggested that multiple case studies are particularly appropriate for generating insights through cross-case case analysis and comparison as well as the investigation of a particular phenomenon in diverse settings.

Data Collection Methods

Semi-structured interviews and participant observation were used as the primary data collection methods. Interviews were used not only because they enable the researcher to obtain rich data which would not be always possible in the case of other data collection methods but also because the immediate interaction enables the researcher to prevent misunderstandings or confusion. Participant observation, on the other hand, is a method that provides the researchers "*with a yardstick against which to measure the completeness of data gathered in other ways*" (Becker and Geer 1957). In other words, participant observation can provide the depth of understanding that comes from directly observing people and listening to what they have to say at the scene (Taylor and Bogdan 1998).

These data collection methods are not without their limitations. With regard to semi-structured interviews, Easterby-Smith et al. (2002) suggested that an important limitation is that alternative researchers might elicit different information from the interviews. Saunders et al. (1997) additionally emphasized that interviewees may not be willing or able to provide the information requested. Nevertheless, Yin (2003) characterized bias, poor recall, and poor or inaccurate articulation as 'common problems' within qualitative research and suggested that interview data should be complemented with data from other sources. For example, documents may be a useful tool in accessing the match between what people say and how they perceive their actions and what is written on paper, as well as a source of valuable data for assessment.

With regard to participant observations, Adler and Adler (1994) recognized two limitations: firstly, the subjectivity in the perceptions and interpretations made by the researcher and secondly, the fact that observations do not allow for generalizations. However, these are the same criticisms made of the case study research strategy in general and the same defence can be applied. Bias and subjectivity may be present in all forms of data collection methods and the generalizability of the results does not account for the validity of the research.

Fieldwork

For the research we conducted three case studies, from the perspective of both the clients and the suppliers. While details of the organizations and the outsourcing contracts under investigation will be provided in the chapter of the case studies, it is worth mentioning that all three outsourcing clients are major players in the financial service sector. The names of the firms and the interviewees will not be revealed, as requested by the firms that participated in the study.

The first case study is a major insurance company based in the Netherlands. The firm will be named LION. Our investigation was focused on a contract with a major American supplier that had a branch in the Netherlands that will be named FDL. The contract included the development, support, and maintenance of software applications. Part of the outsourced work was performed in India. In total, I gathered 11 interviews during the period of January 2010. As indicated in Table A.1, the roles of the research participants included:

The second case study is a major bank based in the UK. Our study was focused on a contract with a major Indian supplier. The contract included the support and maintenance of applications that were of relatively low

Table A.1 Research participants from LION and FDL

LION case study	
Research participants from LION	Role
Ron	Director
Boris	Lawyer
Bamse	Business manager
Liam	Demand manager
Sandro	Contract manger
Daniel	Contract manager
Mari	Senior manager
Martin	Service manager
Research participants from FDL	**Role**
Jeremy	Contract manager
Haresh	Account manager
Rajesh	Consultant
Manoj	Programme manager

Table A.2 Research participants from GIB and PV

GIB case study	
Research participants from GIB	Role
Andrea	Vendor decisions/Relationship management
Bart	Director of risk
Mark	Lawyer
Carsten	IBIT Sourcing and Vendor Management of IT portfolio
Daryn	Lawyer
Andrea	Consultant
Eric	Global technology outsourcing vendor management
Simon	Senior manager in operations
Sunu	X-RAY product manager
David	Client solutions partner
Research participants from PV	**Role**
Rao	Head of integrated services delivery
Mani	Global account manager
Rajesh	X-RAY Global transformation manager
Philip	X-RAY European programme manager

Table A.3 Research participants from DUTCH and Suppliers A, B, and C

DUTCH case study	
Research participants from DUTCH	Role
Edward	IT director
Arnold	Sector manager for sourcing arrangements
Harry	Sector manager on IT operations
Michael	IT demand manager
Liam	Consultant
Marco	Contract manager for Supplier A
Gabriel	Contract manager for Supplier B
Rob	Contract manager for Supplier C
Jacob	Outsourcing operations for Supplier B
Research participants from Supplier A	**Role**
Irene	Engagement manager
Research participants from Supplier B	**Role**
Michiel	Engagement manager
Research participants from Supplier C	**Role**
John	Client director
John	Contract manager

strategic importance to the bank. The banks will be named GIB and its supplier PV. The two organizations had a long-standing history that will be further illustrated in the chapter containing the case studies. In total we gathered 20 interviewees during the period of October 2009–March 2010. The roles of the research participants included:

The third case study is a prestigious insurance company based in the Netherlands. The firm will be named DUTCH in this thesis. My investigation was focused on three contracts. The first contract was on data centre services and was signed with a French firm that had a branch in the Netherlands. The second contract was on network applications and was signed with a prestigious Dutch internet provider. The third contract was on workspace management and was signed with a Dutch firm. The three suppliers will be named Supplier A, Supplier B, and Supplier C respectively. The roles of the research participants are included in Table A.3.

All interviews were transcribed, coded, and analysed using the Atlas software. The codes used were determined by the structure of the interviews in conjunction with the pattern of the given responses.

Appendix B: Skills and Capabilities

A capability is a distinctive set of skills, practices, techniques, behaviours, and attitudes that when applied can transform resources into specific business activities. The existence and combination of capabilities create strategic competencies that are fundamental for the strategic positioning and competitiveness of the firm. Willcocks and Craig (2008) identified nine such capabilities and this categorization will be utilized for the presentation of the client capabilities in the GIB and DUTCH case studies.

1. *Leadership*: This capability is related to the challenge of integrating IT efforts with business goals and practices.
2. *Business systems thinking*: This capability is related to the challenge of envisioning the business process in terms of its functions, efficacy, and utility as a result of technology.
3. *Relationship building*: This capability is related to the challenge of getting the business engaged in IT issues in a constructive way.

E. Lioliou, L. P. Willcocks, *Global Outsourcing Discourse*, Technology, Work and Globalization, https://doi.org/10.1007/978-3-319-74045-4

4. *Architectural planning and design*: This capability is related to the challenge of creating a coherent design of a technical platform that will be able to support current and future business needs.
5. *Making technology work*: This capability is associated with the challenge of rapidly achieving technical progress.
6. *Informed buying*: This capability is related to the challenge of managing the IT outsourcing strategy in a way that meets the interests, priorities, and goals of the business.
7. *Contract facilitation*: This capability is associated with the necessity of managing and governing the relationship between suppliers and business users.
8. *Contract monitoring*: This capability is concerned with protecting the current and future contractual position of the firm. It involves the contributions to the development and maintenance of a robust contract as a fundamental element of efficient governance.
9. *Vendor development*: This capability is linked to identifying the potential of IT service suppliers to provide added value.

Table B.1 illustrates these nine capabilities, as well as the way that their combination contributes to the delivery of the four fundamental tasks of the IT function. These include:

1. *Governance*: This task is referred to the dynamic alignment of the IT function's activities with those of the overall organization.
2. *Business and function vision*: This is a demand-driven task which is associated with defining the systems, information, and processes needed and exploiting them to generate business efficiency.
3. *Architecture planning and design*: This task is supply driven and is associated with defining the architecture of the evolving technical platform and dealing with risks of non-routine technical issues.
4. *Delivery of service*: This task is concerned with managing the sourcing strategy. It seeks to investigate and understand the external market and the ability to select, engage, and manage third-party IT resources and service delivery.

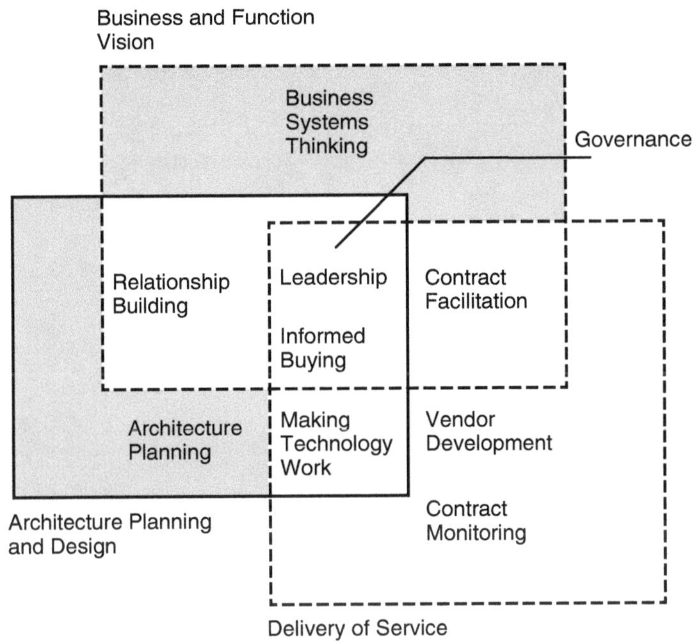

Table B.1 Nine core IS capabilities (Willcocks and Craig 2008)

Appendix C: Supplier Capabilities

Willcocks et al. (2011) identified 12 key supplier capabilities that clients should take into account when looking for a vendor:

1. *Leadership*: Leadership is referred to the capability of delivering the desired result throughout the deal.
2. *Business management*: This is the capability to deliver products and services according to the agreement and the business plans of both parties.
3. *Domain expertise*: This is the capability to retain and apply professional knowledge. The key issue here is not only the supplier's technical expertise or know-how but also the ability to understand and manage the business needs of the customer.
4. *Behaviour management*: Behaviour management refers to the ability to motivate and inspire people to deliver services of high value.
5. *Sourcing*: It is the ability to access the needed resources. This ability may take the form of the generation of economies of scale, the utili-

E. Lioliou, L. P. Willcocks, *Global Outsourcing Discourse*, Technology, Work and Globalization, https://doi.org/10.1007/978-3-319-74045-4

zation of superior infrastructure, and the exploitation of efficient procurement practices.

6. *Process improvement*: This is the capability to change processes in a way that generates a dramatic improvement.
7. *Technology exploitation*: This is referred to the capability of rapidly deploying new technology. This capability requires careful evaluation from the customer's perspective and should go beyond the pure technical skills of the supplier.
8. *Programme management*: Programme management does not refer only to project-level capabilities but to the capability of delivering a set of interrelated projects. More specifically, it involves the processes of prioritizing, coordinating, and mobilizing the organization and promoting a series of tasks that aim towards change and improvement.
9. *Customer development*: This is the capability to enable clients to become customers who can make informed choices about their business needs, service levels, and costs.
10. *Planning and contracting*: In essence, it is the capability to produce beneficial results for both sides. The planning component involves the creation and communication of a vision of the potential reward for both parties and how this could be achieved.
11. *Organizational design*: It is the capability of designing and implementing successful organizational arrangements.
12. *Governance*: This referred to the ability to monitor and measure performance. Although the responsibility for governance arrangements concerns the client, every supplier will have some type of service review committee that tracks and measures performance over time. Key areas for consideration include: What kind of reporting mechanisms will be in place? What procedures will be initiated for dealing with escalating problems? What powers and authorities will be constituted through the governance structure?

These 12 core capabilities of the supplier can be leveraged into three key competences. These competencies are illustrated in Table A.2 and were used for the discussion of the supplier capabilities in the GIB and the DUTCH case studies. They include:

1. *Delivery competency*: It is based on the supplier's ability to respond to the customer's ongoing needs. As it is illustrated in Table A.3, this competency primarily involves the supplier's leadership, business management, domain expertise, behaviour management, sourcing, programme management, and governance capabilities.
2. *Transformation competency*: It is based on the supplier's ability to deliver radically improved service in terms of both quality and cost. As it is shown in Table C.1, this competency primarily involves the supplier's leadership, behaviour management, sourcing, process improvement, technology exploitation, programme management, and customer development capabilities.
3. *Relationship competency*: It is based on the supplier's willingness and ability to align its business model to the values, goals, and needs of the customer. As it is illustrated in Table C.1, the key capabilities that this competency includes are leadership, customer development, planning and contracting, organizational design, governance, and programme management. Among these, the planning and contracting capability presents the major challenges as it is not easy to align the goals and incentives of the two sides.

Table C.1 Twelve supplier capabilities (Willcocks et al. 2011)

References

Adler, P., & Adler, P. (1994). Observational Techniques. In N. Denzin & Y. Lincoln (Eds.), *Handbook of Qualitative Research*. London: Sage.

Becker, H. S., & Geer, B. (1957). Participant Observation and Interviewing: A Comparison. *Human Organization, 16*(3), 28–32.

Benbasat, I., Goldstein, D., & Mead, M. (1987). The Case Research Strategy in Studies of Information Systems. *MIS Quarterly, 11*(3), 368–387.

Creswell, J. W. (1998). *Qualitative Inquiry and Research Design: Choosing Among Five Traditions*. London: Sage.

Easterby-Smith, M. R., Thorpe, R., & Lowe, A. (2002). *Management Research: An Introduction*. London: Sage.

Galliers, R. D. (1992). Choosing Information Systems Research Approaches. In *Information Systems Research: Issues, Methods and Practical Guidelines*. London: Alfred Waller.

Geertz, C. (1993). *The Interpretation of Cultures: Selected Essays*. London: Fontana Press.

Lee, A., & Baskerville, R. (2003). Generalizing Generalizability in Information Systems Research. *Information Systems Research, 14*(3), 221–243.

Pettigrew, A. M. (1990). Longitudinal Field Research on Change: Theory and Practice. *Organization Science, 1*(3), 267–292.

Saunders, C., Gebelt, M., & Hu, Q. (1997). Achieving Success in Information Systems Outsourcing. *California Management Review, 39*(2), 63–79.

Taylor, S. J., & Bogdan, R. (1998). *Introduction to Qualitative Research Methods*. Chichester: John Wiley.

Walsham, G. (1993). *Interpreting Information Systems in Organizations*. Chichester: Wiley.

Walsham, G. (1995). Interpretive Case Studies in IS Research: Nature and Method. *European Journal of Information Systems, 4*(2), 74–81.

Walsham, G. (2006). Doing Interpretive Research. *European Journal of Information Systems, 15*(3), 320–330.

Willcocks, L., Cullen, S., & Craig, A. (2011). *The Outsourcing Enterprise: From Cost Management to Collaborative Innovation*. London: Palgrave.

Yin, R. (2003). *Case Study Research: Design and Methods*. London: Sage.

Kolibri 360 GmbH
Ferdinand-Jühlke-Straße 7
99095 Erfurt, Deutschland
produktsicherheit@kolibri360.de